WINNING MARKET SYSTEMS

WINDSOR BOOKS
Brightwaters, New York

Published by Windsor Books
P.O. Box 280
Brightwaters, N.Y., 11718

Manufactured in the United States of America

ISBN 0-930233-33-6

CAVEAT: It should be noted that all commodity trades, patterns, charts, systems, etc., discussed in this book are for illustrative purposes only and are not to be construed as specific advisory recommendations. Further note that no method of trading or investing is foolproof or without difficulty, and past performance is no guarantee of future performance. All ideas and material presented are entirely those of the author and do not necessarily reflect those of the publisher or bookseller.

CONTENTS

ART DIRECTOR: CARL HERRMAN

ILLUSTRATIONS: NORM DOHERTY

To Judy,
My best investment,
and
Marvin and Marion,
My best returns.

ORIGINAL INTRODUCTION FROM FIRST EDITION

This is a "how to" book, plain and simple. And the how is how to beat the market, one really challenging, frustrating, difficult, and, yet, potentially gratifying endeavor.

The stock market is a quagmire. It is a crap game. It is America in action. It is exciting, crooked, cutthroat, intriguing, irrational, and for most people better left alone. Once it gets you though, it gets you. It will not go away and after you're hooked, it will not be ignored. Generations of flyers fly and crash, bear markets inexorably follow bull and investors get clobbered, cycle in and cycle out. But the market goes on and on, and sooner or later the patsies come back for more—and they get it.

And why are most patsies patsies? Largely, for one reason. A poker game may be gambling for me, maybe for you, but not for a pro. And not because he cheats either—a professional rarely has to. The professional card player is a master of applied mathematics. The percentages—the odds in the pot as opposed to the odds of filling an inside straight—are always with him, and he plays only when the percentages are on his side. Most unsuccessful stock traders do not. Emotions dictate their play—greed, fear, shame, the need for a good ego trip, stubbornness and refusal to face a mistake. The odds are disregarded and fleeced again the patsies are—by the pros who play it right.

The market can be beaten. Not on every hand, to be sure and nothing can be guaranteed. But, year by year, good market or bad, you can come up smelling like roses, 20-30% ahead, maybe more. The prerequisites? Work. It takes time, study, interest and an attitude that you're in the game to make money, that it's your own hard saved cash to increase, keep or lose and that only if you stay objective can you make out. If you can't handle your feelings, if even a small loss is more than you can take, if you rattle easily and can't stick to a decision, if a mistake will throw you into a depression—bury this book right now, stay out, put your money in the bank and relax. Come back after your psychoanalysis or something.

Still here? Fine. This book is about systems—systems of trading, of moving long and short with the market, systems of deciding not only what to buy and sell, but more important, when. Largely, this is a book dealing with technical analysis—the art of using the action of the stock market itself to forecast future price action. Our paraphenalia includes charts, indicators, a good ruler and slide rule, and some luck. As a contrast, fundamental analysis is the technique of predicting future market and stock price movement by way of investigating the economy, corporate growth, balance sheets, financial structure, money supply and so forth. These approaches are not contradictory. Indeed, for the complete investor, they are supplementary. It is possible, however, for the do-it-yourself investor to chart market action at home with a relatively small investment of time. Fundamental analysis requires intricate familiarity with each corporation and its industry, not to mention interrelated international and national developments. Fundamentally based decisions, in any case, are frequently, guess-work, estimate, hope and dream. Even corporate insiders err in the estimates of their company futures—witness the Edsel. In theory, the composite man's expectations, knowledge and evaluation regarding securities and the total economy will be reflected in those securities'market action and in the action of the stock market as a whole. Technical analysis attempts to track the flow of smart money into and out of the market and to move with it. We will discuss ways you can do this. It will be up to you to do the work.

Is the work worth it? I think so. The Dow Jones Industrial Average ended 1971 at about 890, up approximately fifty points for the year. However, major moves during the year totalled about 550 points, three hundred up and two hundred and fifty down. Some stocks could have been bought and held all year—Levitz Furniture for one—but most vacillated within trading ranges, ending the year near where they started. Yet, fantastic profits could have been made by moving in and out, long and short with the intermediate swings. Is this kind of trading for you? Do you prefer even shorter term action? Or do you have neither the time, inclination nor interest in trading, but do want to keep abreast of long term movement?

Whichever way you want to swing, there are useful systems to achieve your goal. I prefer moving with the intermediate trends; you may not. However, whatever your investment outlook, select a trading or investment system or two from this book, or better yet, a combination of several, and use them. It will take work. Some systems require frequent attention and some charting labor. Sufficient instruction is given with each system for the reader to set up the necessary work. The original source is cited for those who wish to investigate further. Stay with your systems. Familiarize yourself, get their feel—your confidence will increase, and with it your profits. Let your systems make your decisions. Stay objective, act on your signals and total the results at the end of the year. As I said, you will have losers—plenty of them. However, if you play it right your losses will be small and should be more than compensated by big winners.

I would like to extend my appreciation to the many market technicians and advisory services who so generously shared with me the results of their original studies, and to the charting services which made their work available for this publication. And most of all, my appreciation to my wife, Judy, for her labors—computing data, charting, typing, handling correspondence and, at the same time, filling for the kids the spaces left by me during the preparation of this book.

From here on in, it's up to you. Good luck.

Gerald Appel

PREFACE TO THE THIRD EDITION

It has been many years now since the first edition of WINNING MARKET SYSTEMS saw the light of day, nearly seventeen years as a matter of fact.

Many things have changed in the interim. My children, to whom the book was dedicated, have grown—Marvin now well along at medical school, Marion now out of college and embarked on her own career. Whether from age or from seventeen years of playing against the stock market, I've turned gray. (My wife, though doesn't seem to age.)

More things have changed in the stock market. Introduced since the first years of the 1970's—listed options on stocks, stock index futures contracts, telephone switch mutual funds, volume exceeding 200 million shares with great regularity, a 500 point decline within a single day (October 19, 1987), Ivan Boesky, at least one new generation of stock market advisory services, probably two, the institutionalization of the stock market, The Financial News Network, the home computer as an investment tool, stock quotation machines for the home trader, the great 1974 - 1987 (?) bull market and the rise of Japan as an economic power in many ways surpassing ourselves.

And yet...the more things change, the more they seem to remain the same.

Is the recent takeover fervor really different from the growth of the great conglomerates during the late 1960's? A fine advisor by the name of Robert Prechter achieved fame by borrowing from the old ideas of Elliott. Larry Williams, who has always been generous in sharing his work, continues to thrive in the advisory field along with Joe Granville, Bob Gross, James Dines and many others. Dr. Martin E. Zweig, probably the foremost investment advisor of our time, first achieved widespread popularity at just about the time I started to write WINNING MARKET SYSTEMS. Marty has proven to be one of the few advisors to remain durably in the forefront of the industry. I, myself, initiated my own stock market newsletter, Systems and Forecasts, in 1973; it is still in publication.

More to the immediate point was my reaction when I first set about to review WINNING MARKET SYSTEMS for corrections and updates for this reprinting. Given the age of the book, and given the many projects and the amount of research I have conducted since, I expected to find many, many areas which required revision. In fact, I found virtually none.

Yes, trading volume is higher than it was during 1971. But patterns and volume signals remain the same. Momentum divergences remain similar. Timing cycles have not changed. Trendlines are still trendlines. The McClellan Oscillator still becomes overbought at + 100 and still becomes oversold at − 100. The bond market still dominates the stock market in the end. And the Dow is still expensive when dividend yields fall to below 3%.

One area has seemed to change over the years. The individual trader occupies a much lesser role in the stock market than he did in the past—individuals turning more to mutual funds, which themselves have become a part of the institutionalization of the stock market. As a result, indicators centering around odd-lot short sales, specialist short sales and perhaps the entire short interest ratio on the NYSE have been considerably reduced in significance. Whereas the specialists used to account for short selling in parameters of between 45% (bullish) and 65% (bearish), their activity now ranges between 30% of total short sales on the NYSE (bullish) and about 50% (bearish). Short selling now is more often the result of arbitrage relationships between stocks and stock market derivatives such as futures contracts than the result of outright bearishness on the part of members of the NYSE.

I have conducted much research over the years, the results of which have appeared in many publications. WINNING MARKET SYSTEMS stands on its own as a basic technical text but I did want to include some tools that I have found to be particularly helpful over the years. These tools appear in Chapter 12 at the end of this book.

In the meantime, let's just conclude with the observation tha the basic laws of supply and demand, of momentum, of time and of mass psychology appear timeless. The concepts presented in this book are as valid today as they were seventeen years ago, and I expect that they will remain equally valid seventeen years from now. It's still up to you to learn and to apply what you have learned and will learn over the years to come.

Gerald Appel
December 1988

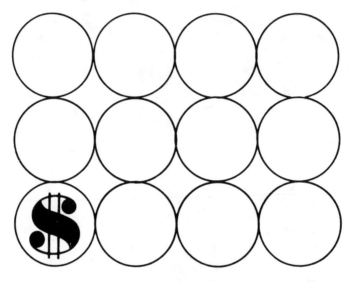

chapter one

CHARTS AND TRENDLINES:
IF YOU CAN DRAW A STRAIGHT LINE
YOU CAN MAKE MONEY

The movement of the stock market has been compared to the movement of tides. Tides are comprised of waves and ripples, in cumulative action creating major ebbs and flows. The movement of stock prices likewise may be viewed as a series of major ebbs and flows interrupted by reverse waves and ripples. The major flow or ebb is referred to as the primary trend. It may last several months to several years. The primary movement consists of intermediate movements—in the primary direction and in reaction—lasting several weeks to several months. The intermediate trend is comprised of minor moves—in the intermediate direction and in reaction—each lasting several days to several weeks.

Each phase of the market has its own cycle of accumulation, price mark up, distribution, price decline and re-accumulation.

Accumulation is the process during which bullish investors, traders, big money and small, acquire stock in anticipation of price mark-up. The process may take months or even years for major moves, weeks or months for intermediate, perhaps days for minor moves.

Distribution is the reverse process—the process during which the smart money prepares and disposes of stock in anticipation of a subsequent decline in stock prices. The longer the periods of accumulation and distribution, by and large, the further the subsequent moves will carry. I will be discussing techniques of measuring the strength of accumulation and distribution in following chapters.

The phases and action of the market may be depicted graphically by means of charts. A linear chart of the movement of stock prices would appear as follows:

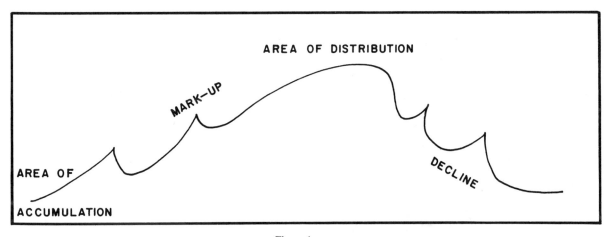

Figure 1

Uptrends—periods of rising prices—are marked by a succession of price rallies, each carrying further than the one previous. These are interrupted by reactions, periods of decline, which are each reversed at successively higher levels for a resumption of the up-move. Downtrends—periods of declining prices—are marked by a series of rallies, each successively stopped below the previous rally high, and declines, each carrying below the preceding dip.

The long term investor seeks to enter the market as soon as he determines the presence of a major bullish or primary uptrend and remains invested until the primary trend is reversed. Intermediate and short term traders attempt to move in and out of stocks with shorter term reversals, hoping to scalp profits on each move, since the composite sum of the segments or legs of the primary move is greater than the total primary move itself. Generally, the intermediate trader will refer more frequently to charts and act upon more signals than the long-term investor. Both, however, require charts to achieve perspective regarding the current state of the market and to time their purchases and sales. The linear chart, Figure 1, is such a chart but provides, in itself, frequently insufficient information for interpretive purposes.

Cumulative Line Charts

There is one form of line chart widely employed—the cumulative line chart. Data is plotted within such charts by connecting lines between entries of the last data. The last plotting figure in a cumulative line chart results from an addition or subtraction of the most recent data from the sum of past data. For example, the advance-decline line is charted in this manner. The most recent sum of advances minus declines is added (if more advances) or subtracted (if more declines) from the total of the advance-decline line to that point. The result is a perpetual cumulative line.

Other line charts in wide use are moving average lines or plots of various overbought-oversold indices. The methodologies of entry will be discussed within sections relating to these techniques.

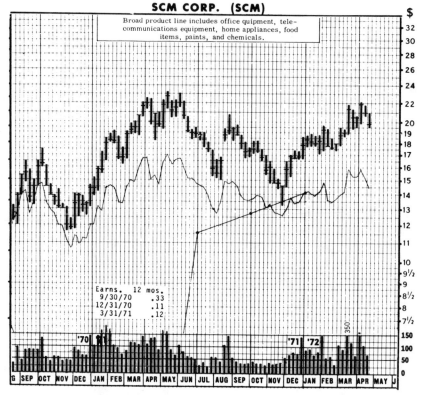

Figure 2

A typical weekly bar chart. Price scale is on the right, above. Volume scale on the right below.
Source: Securities Research Co., 208 Newbury Street, Boston, Mass. 02116

Bar Charts

Figure 2 is a bar chart, one of the most frequently employed representations of market action. Bar charts are simple to construct and to read. They may be plotted for any period of time, usually daily, weekly or monthly. Each line represents the spread (trading range) for the period plotted. The cross line represents the closing price at the end of the trading period. Generally, bar charts include volume readings, plotted below price action. This is important since volume carries its own significance (Chapter 2). Point and figure charting and its uses will be discussed in Chapter 4.

Trendlines

Trendlines are lines connecting two or more price reversal points. During uptrends, the trendline will connect bottom reversal points; during downtrends, the trendline will be drawn to connect top reversal points. Breaking or violation of the trendline indicates the termination of the existing trend, and at the least, a strong possibility of a market reversal. The greater the number of reversal points comprising the trendline, the more significant is the associated trendline and the more significant will be its violation.

Trendline System #1
The Basic System

The basic trendline system consists simply of initiating purchases (in bull markets) upon violations of reactive downtrends, preferably near primary uptrendlines, and holding positions long until the trend reverses. During bear markets, the basic system calls for shorting near the primary downtrendline and holding your short positions (or if you're cautious, cash) until the primary downtrend is broken. Refinements to follow. First, let's examine your results if this method had been followed over recent years.

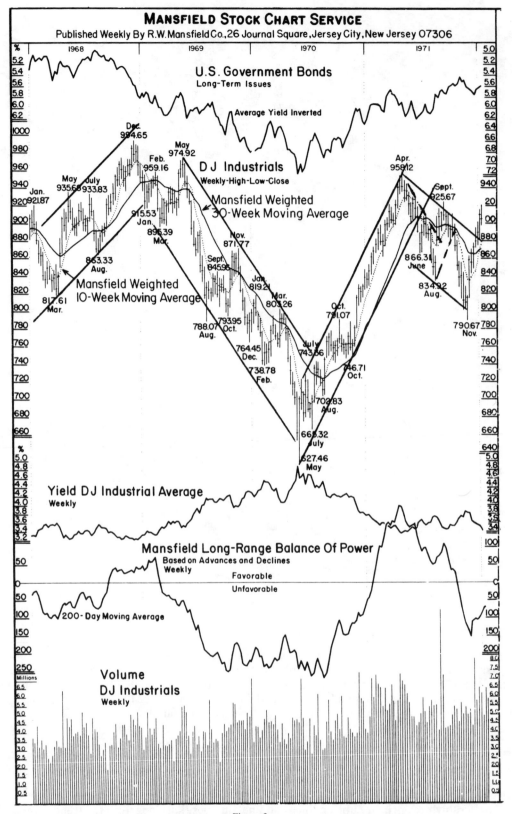

Figure 3

Source: Mansfield Stock Chart Service, 26 Journal Square, Jersey City, N.J. 07306
[Trendlines by author]

Figure 3 is a weekly chart of the Dow Jones Industrials Averages with primary uptrend and downtrendlines drawn in. During the period shown, a primary sell signal was given at D.J. 940 (February, 1969), a buy at D.J. 730 (August, 1970), and a sell at D.J. 890 (May, 1971). Total gain, long and short—370 D.J. points. Losses— none. During this total period, the market lost 50 points! Secondary purchases on reactions to the trendline would have been made in November 1970 and August 1971, at the dashed trendline. Positions taken in August 1971 would have been stopped out quickly as the trendline was violated, possibly for small losses. Short sales would have been initiated in May 1969, November 1969, March 1970, and June 1971.

Trendline System #2
Channels

Further study of Figure 3 will show that during uptrends, a line drawn across the peaks of upthrusts, parallel to the supporting uptrendlines, will generally contain rallies. A channel is created encompassing price movements by drawing this line, prices oscillating between the upper and lower boundaries until the trend is terminated. Likewise, during downtrends, a channel line may be drawn parallel to the downtrendline, across the lowest downthrust points. This line will usually contain declines. Rallies or declines surpassing the boundaries of the channel are generally climactic and signify the near termination of the move. The 1969-1970 bear market ended in May 1970 with a climactic downthrust below channel boundaries. (See Figure 3). By combining the use of intermediate channeling and trendlines with the use of a primary trendline, traders can achieve excellent timing results. The strategy here is to sell (if long) or to put tight stop loss orders on stocks as the channel extremity is reached and to seek to re-invest at the lower end of the primary or intermediate channels. Weekly or monthly charts should be employed for the determination of significant primary and intermediate market and stock channels, daily charts for the determination of short term trends. As the primary channel boundary is reached, use the daily chart to determine the short term trendline violation which will provide your signal.

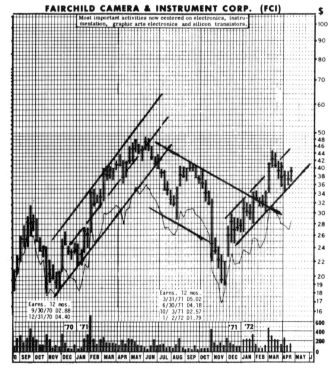

Figure 4

Source: Securities Research Co., 208 Newbury Street, Boston, Mass. 02116
[Trendlines by author]

Figure 4 is a weekly chart of Fairchild Camera and Instrument Corporation. Note how the channel boundaries contained the 1970-1971 rise and how the decline in November 1971 ended with a climactic penetration of the channel boundaries.

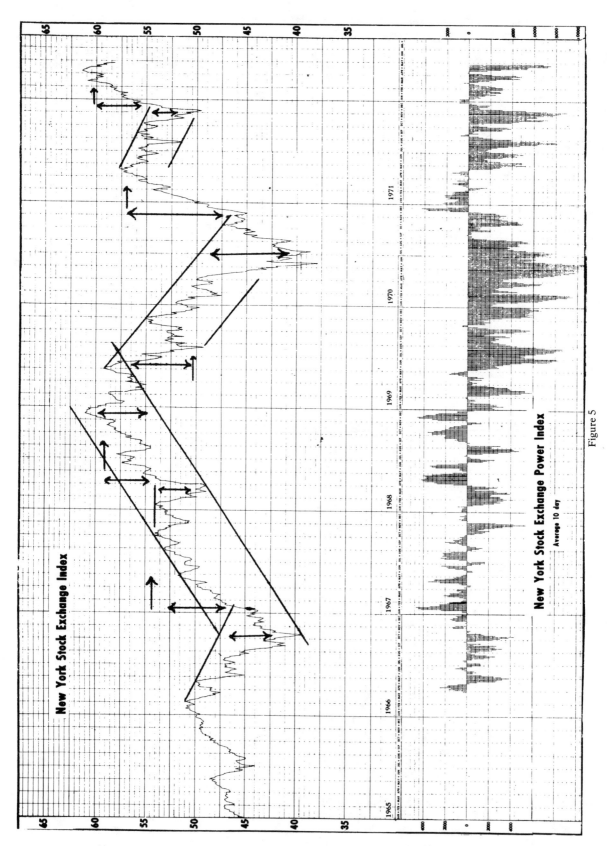

Figure 5

The Trendline Measuring Method. For example, the distance between the November, 1971 lows and the April-November, 1971 downtrendline was approximately $6.00. The downtrendline was violated in December, 1971 at $55.00. Adding 6 to 55 yielded an upside objective of approximately 61.

Source: Worden's Chart Folio, 1915 Florenada Road, Fort Lauderdale, Florida 33308

[Trendlines by author]

The Mid-Channel Support And Resistance Line

Stocks and the overall market do not usually move freely from channel extremity to channel extremity. Prices often pause at mid-channel. Frequently, a line drawn through the center of a primary channel will serve before its penetration on the upside as a resistance to further advance and after its penetration as support. Should this line act as support for any period of time, its violation implies a strong possibility that the underlying primary trend is in danger. Fairchild Camera's major uptrend was destroyed in June 1971, but this was presaged by the violation of its mid-channel line a month earlier. In any case, a crossing of the mid-channel line generally indicates that the move will carry at least to the channel boundary. In fact, the most rapid price moves, up and down, often follow the breakthrough of mid-channel lines.

Trendline System #3
Using Trendline Breaks To Measure The Probable Extent Of Moves

Study of charts and trendline breaks will demonstrate that the placement of the trendline itself may be employed to determine with surprising accuracy the extent of moves following trendline violations. To put it more simply, the trendline tends to bisect market moves. The distance the market will travel following the break will be roughly equivalent to the distance between the trendline and the extremity of the formation that preceded the trendline break.

The following methodology may be employed to determine price objectives following trendline breaks. Upon a clear trendline violation, refer to the formation preceding the violation. In the event of a downside violation, measure from the trendline itself the maximum distance between the trendline and the formation peak directly above. In the case of an upside penetration, measure from the trendline to the low of the preceding formation. Measure an equivalent distance from the point of penetration vertically in the direction of the penetration. The result is the price objective for the move signified by the trendline violation. A significant reaction will almost invariably follow upon the attainment of the objective so determined.

Example: Refer to Figure 5. Note the downtrendline that connected the April and August 1971 peaks. The distance between the lows in November 1971 and that trendline was approximately 6.00 on the N.Y.S.E. Index. The April-August downtrendline was penetrated in December 1971 at N.Y.S.E. Index, 55.00. We add the 6.00 to 55.00 for an upside objective of 61.00. Actual high, May 1972, 61.38!

Results

Figure 5 illustrates the application of this method, which works most effectively with the broad market averages, such as the New York Stock Exchange or the Standard and Poor's 500 Indices. Some of the major operating trendlines from 1965-1972 and the associated measuring distances are drawn in. Horizontal arrows indicate the theoretical objectives of the associated moves. Not visible on this chart is the long term primary trendline connecting the 1962, 1966 and 1968 lows. The maximum height of the bull formation above this trendline was approximately 270 Dow points, measured from the trendline to the February, 1966 peak. This 1962-1968 trendline was penetrated in June, 1969 at Dow Jones 890. Major downside objective: 620 (890 minus 270). Actual Dow Jones low, May 1970, 627.5!

With this system you could have predicted almost exactly the extent of the 1967 bull market, the 1968 bull market, the April 1971 market peak, the November 1971 low and the end of the 1970 bear market.

Trendline System #4
A Second Method For Estimating The Extent Of Decline Following A Trendline Break

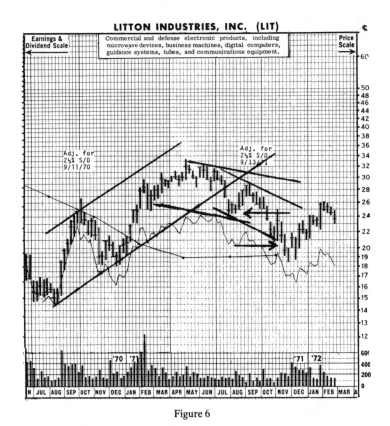

Figure 6

Sources: Securities Research Co., 208 Newbury Street, Boston, Mass. 02116
[Trendlines by author]

This method does not yield an ultimate price objective as does System #3 but is very useful nonetheless. The methodology is relatively simple. Following a downside trendline break, draw a line connecting the two previous tops. Draw a second line, parallel to the first, using as a starting point, the low point of the previous decline. The decline signalled by the trendline break will frequently stop at the lower line so constructed. Following a subsequent rally (assuming a new uptrend is not signalled), again connect the high points and draw a line parallel from the most recent low. This line frequently will contain the next subsequent decline. By this process, you are actually constructing a curving channel marking the roll-over of prices during the distribution phase. On Figure 6, the arrows mark theoretical objectives.

Trendline System #5
Using Trendlines To Predict The Limit Of The Next Moves, Following A Market Reversal And Then A Resumption Of The Original Trend

This is less complicated than it sounds. Presume first, a stock or the market is moving in an uptrend. The uptrend is broken, and a down-move starts. A rally then develops. Almost always, the rally will halt at or below the uptrendline that existed prior to the trendline violation. The trendline that formerly represented support now represents resistance. The move may subsequently continue but not before a probable reaction at that point, or else, will continue at an angle that does not penetrate that line from below. See Figure 7, on which I

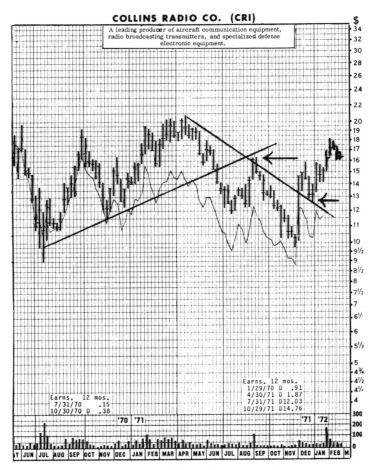

Figure 7

Collins Radio violated its uptrendline in June, 1971. Subsequent rallies in
August,1971 and February, 1972 were halted by the reverse side of the
uptrendline that had previously served as support.
Source: Securities Research Co., 208 Newbury Street, Boston, Mass. 02116
[*Trendlines by author*]

have drawn in trendlines indicating this action. The arrows mark the points where the trendline acted as
resistance. Conversely, assume a stock breaks its downtrend. It rallies through its downtrendline, signalling an
uptrend. Frequently, the stock (or the market) will react to the downtrendline from above. The decline may
resume, but is unlikely to penetrate the downtrendline previously crossed, or a trend reversal may occur
following a return to this line. Figure 7 also illustrates this action during December, 1971.

Results

This system signalled the May 1969 top, the July 1969 bottom and even the May 1970 bottom. The long term
downtrendline, which initiated the 1969-1970 bear market, was penetrated on the upside in February 1971.
The upper edge of this line served to stop the August and November 1971 declines nearly three years after its
formation, and served as the starting point for major bull legs.

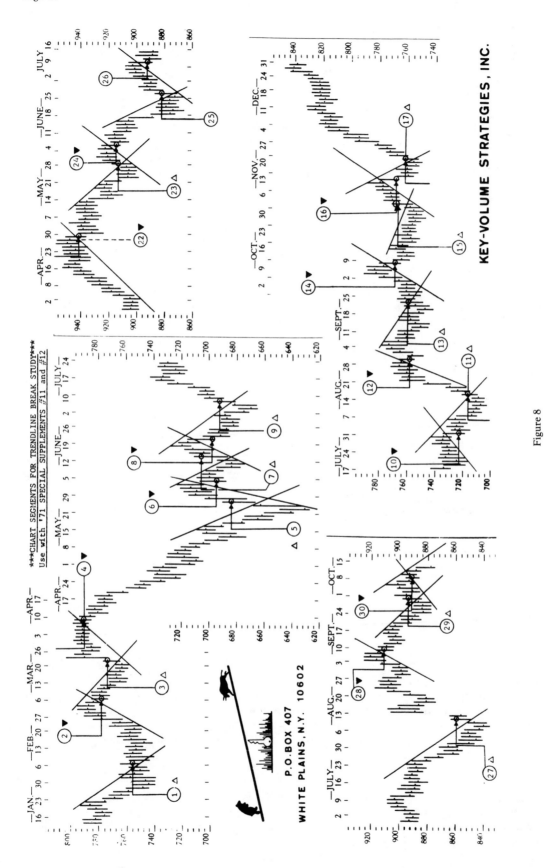

Figure 8

Source: Key-Volume Strategies, P.O. Box 407, White Plains, N.Y. 10602

Trendline System #6
Using Chart Segments And Trendlines To Predict Moves Of At Least 40 Dow-Jones Points

Key-Volume Strategies, a weekly short term trading service, has pioneered a number of interesting and useful trading systems. A further description of the service will appear in Chapter 10; other *Key-Volume Strategies* systems will be scattered throughout this book. Publisher Conrad has devised the following system for using trendline breaks to predict moves of at least 40 Dow Jones points, for participating in longer moves, and for reversing positions on false signals. The system appears a bit complicated at first look, but a little study should suffice to clarify the procedures and will be worth the effort for short term traders.

A chart segment is a clearly distinguishable small portion of a chart, encompassing a minor market move and the beginning of its reversal. These occur at intervals of approximately fourteen trading days, on average. Daily charts are employed in this system, preferably large format charts such as appear in *The Wall Street Journal*. Requirements for the chart segment include, (1) a definite short term trendline broken on a *closing* basis and, (2) that the price close the day the market breaks the trendline exceeds (if upside break) or is below (if downside break) *four or more* or *five out of six* of the immediately preceding pre-break closes. If the market has been in an uptrend, the signalling close will be below the previous closes; reverse this if the market has been in a downtrend. The segments in Figure 8, comprising segments of the 1970-1971 market, will illustrate the placements of trendlines and the signal points.

This system employs the steepest trendlines that can be drawn across intraday tops and bottoms. For accelerating trends, steeper trendlines are drawn in to modify original trendlines. However, if a trendline break occurs that does not meet the "closings exceeded" criteria, the trendline is moved down to the low point or up to the high point of the trendline break day.

According to *Key-Volume Strategies*, profit maximization is achieved if the following procedures are employed:

(1) Act on every trendline break that exceeds either four previous closings or five out of the previous six.

(2) Forty Dow Jones points is the initial objective. Within two trading days after each trendline break, take action (there is frequently a pullback towards the trendline after breaks—see Trendline system #5). The forty Dow Jones points should be achieved within 2 x CE days after the trendline break. (CE = the number of previous closes exceeded, upside or downside, by the closing price the day the trendline break signal was given.) For instance, if the closing price on the signal day exceeded five previous days' closings, the forty point gain should be achieved within ten trading days. However, approximately half the time, a forty Dow point move will occur within CE trading days.

(3) There is a procedure for benefitting from longer than forty point moves. After taking a minimum of 20 points profits, wait for CE trading days for a reverse signal. If you profitted long, you are looking for a sell and vice versa. If a valid reverse signal does not occur within CE trading days, re-enter the market with a target of a total of 100 points profit, including profits previously taken. Do this immediately on the CEth trading day or one day later. Do not re-enter if your profit on the preceding move was less than 20 points. From February 1970-March 1972, eight of eleven completed re-entries reached the one hundred point goal. The longest re-entry stay permissible, however, is through the fourth segment following the re-entry—at the conclusion of this fourth segment, close out positions.

(4) Protective action, immediate liquidation, should be taken if a reverse trendline break follows the one you acted on within CE trading days. In most situations, despite gains of less than forty points, some profit will accrue. If, within 2 x CE trading days after the signal, a forty point move has not materialized, close out positions. Occasionally, these slower moves will have to be re-entered for longer profits. This will occur if no reverse signal takes place within CE trading days after you have closed out positions. The market has remained within a minor trading range. A move will be suspect if, after the trendline break, some reversal back towards the trendline did not immediately follow the penetration, or if the segment started while a try for 100 points in the other direction was still in effect.

(5) In any event, place protective stops under any purchases in accordance with suggestions appearing throughout this book.

Results

Key-Volume Strategies totalled results from signals during the period from February 1970-March 1972. Results were impressive. Forty-four of forty-five signals were winners, totalling nearly 1501 points, against one sixteen point loser. However, this system shares the disadvantages inherent in any short term signalling system—extra commissions and missed rides on the really good movers. And, of course, no long term gains. Offsetting this are the protective features. With such systems you can play the market long and short. The protective systems prevent serious loss. Possibly, a compromise strategy is a hedge—selling some positions on short term trading signals—holding others for the longer pull.

Trendline System #7
Speed Resistance Lines

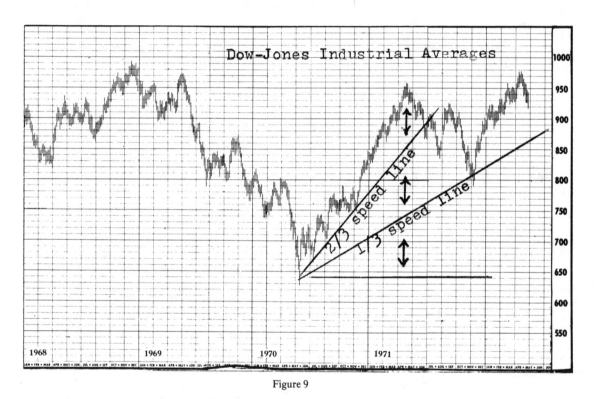

Figure 9

Source: Worden's Chart Folio, 1915 Florenada Rd., Ft. Lauderdale, Florida 33308
[Trendlines by author]

This concept was developed by Edson Gould of *Findings And Forecasts*, and is used extensively as well by Ike Hasson of *The Consultant*. It is not, in actuality, a trendline system, but because of similarities, is grouped within this chapter.

Speed resistance lines are constructed in the following manner. Using a bar chart, construct a right triangle from the base of an up-move or top of a downmove, using the distance between the start of the move and the highest or lowest point of the move itself as the long diagonal of the triangle. A line drawn from the last high or low of the move to the baseline (calendar time line) comprises one side of the triangle. See Figure 9 for an example. The length of this line and the angle of the diagonal from the base indicate the rate of rise or decline of the market. Using either two-thirds of the angle cited above, or measuring two-thirds of the distance vertically from the peak of the move to the base, draw a line indicating two-thirds the rate of rise (or drop). Do the same to create a line indicating one-third the rate of rise (or drop). The lines so drawn are two-thirds and one-third speed resistance lines. *These lines must be redrawn whenever the market or a stock makes a new high or a new low*. For example, every time a new high is made, the ascending speed resistance lines are recalculated. The new line may or may not rise at the same angle as the previously computed lines. A strong up-market will stay above its two-thirds speed resistance line; a weak declining market below its two-thirds speed resistance line. These lines will usually offer resistance or support to the market. Should the two-thirds speed resistance line be penetrated, the reaction is likely to carry to the one-third speed resistance line. In bull markets, attempts to rally are likely to take place from ascending speed resistance lines. In bear markets, declines are likely to resume from areas where rallies approach descending speed resistance lines. Penetration of the one-third speed resistance line implies a basic and rapid change in the primary trend of the market. Thus, if in a declining market, the one-third speed resistance line is penetrated, the downtrend is likely over and a strong rise is to be expected.

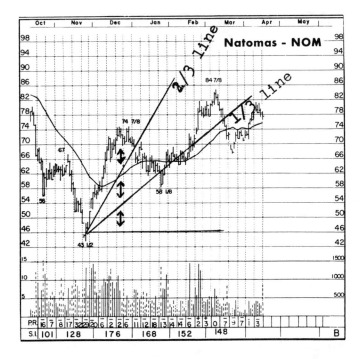

Figure 10

Speed Resistance Lines: Natomas rallied almost exactly from the 1/3 speed resistance line formed from the November, 1971 low to the December, 1971 high. Other speed resistance lines would have been drawn as the stock made new highs in March. Not shown on the chart are the new lines which would have been so created. The rally in March, 1972 occurred at the 2/3 speed resistance line from the November, 1971 low to the March, 1972 high. Construct this line yourself. Note how the old 1/3 speed resistance line, violated in early March, served as resistance to the March-April rally.
Source: R.W.Mansfield Co., 26 Journal Square, Jersey City, N.J. 07306
[*Trendlines by author*]

Results

This system offers investors a way to predict *in advance* where declines during a bull and rallies during a bear market are likely to end. The one-third speed resistance line halted all rallies during the 1969-1970 bear market. In 1971, the two-thirds speed resistance line provided a rally point in June. Following its penetration in July, the market declined until August, then rallied back to the underside of the line (System #5 again), and finally declined to the one-third speed resistance line in November, from almost exactly which point the major year-end rally began. The downside one-third April-November speed resistance line was penetrated on the upside in December, 1971, signalling the powerful bull thrust that followed. This same system may be applied to individual stocks as well as to the market, frequently with excellent results. (Figure 10). Long term speed resistance lines may be established for major trends by beginning calculations at the start of primary moves. Within that context, each shorter term move will show speed resistance characteristics, measurements for each segment taken at the start of that segment. Secure some charts and experiment with long, intermediate and short term lines. You will be amazed at how frequently speed resistance lines call the turns. I consider this system an extremely powerful tool for the home technician.

Trendline System #8
Predicting Trendline Violations

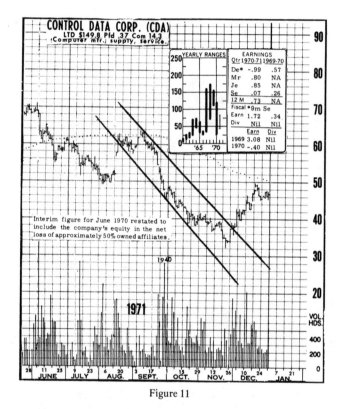

Figure 11

Source: Trendline Daily Basis Stock Charts, 345 Hudson Street,
New York, N.Y. 10014
[Trendlines by author]

It is frequently possible to predict trendline violations in advance of their occurance. The benefits of this are clear. You can take long positions at lower prices and sell or short at higher prices than are available at the signal point. Subsequent chapters will provide many tools to accomplish this. However, based upon the content so far discussed, the most straightforward method involves the use of channeling and the counting of the number of times the trendline has been touched in the past.

Generally speaking, a strong move will carry to its channel extremity or near to it. Major or significant down-moves, for instance, tend to end in either of two ways. Either the stock (or market) climaxes with a downthrust through channel extremities, accompanied by climactic volume (1970 low), or drift lower with decelerating force, usually but not always on low volume, and not reaching the channel extremity (Figure 11). The March 1968 market bottom was formed in this manner. The climactic bottom provides little chance to act, since the price rebounds involved are emotional, sharp and initially difficult to distinguish from bear market rallies. The rounding or wedge bottom, however, provides ample opportunity to establish positions at low prices, its major characteristic *involving the failure of the decline to reach the lower channel extremity.* Should heavy volume accompany this down to sidewise drift away from the channel extremity, the upside price action that follows the subsequent upside trendline break is frequently sharp and very profitable. Figure 11 illustrates this action of Control Data during November 1971. The downside action here was fairly typical as the influence of the downtrendline forced CDA temporarily lower just prior to the breakout. Note, however, the low volume on the last dip and the sharp increase in volume as the stock returned to and penetrated the trendline. Occasionally, a terminal decline or shakeout will follow the trendline break (System #5). If this stops you out, reinstate long positions quickly as the stock penetrates its overhead supply. Reverse the above principles for predicting downside breakouts.

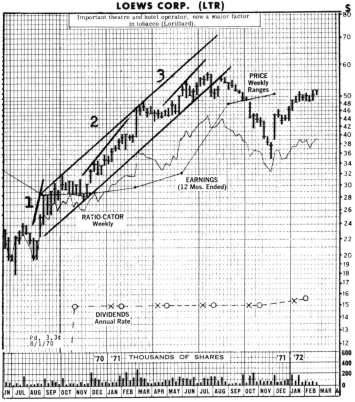

Figure 12

Source: Securities Research Co., 208 Newbury Street, Boston, Mass. 02116
[Trendlines by author]

Stock market movements frequently occur in three waves following the breakout from a base. That is, major movements will consist of three waves in the primary direction, interrupted by two corrective waves. Therefore, the third reaction to the trendline is frequently penetrative. This may be anticipated if two corrective reactions to the trendline have already occured. Selling, therefore, may be indicated, in the event that the primary move has been up, initiated near the upper channel boundary following the third upthrust following an upside breakout. In reverse, the 1970 market bottom followed the third major downwave in the bear cycle. Use weekly charts to determine wave sequence in most instances, unless you are a very short term trader. Major intermediate moves consist of shorter waves, also frequently divided into five segments (three primary, two corrective). Daily charts demonstrate the segmentation of the shorter waves, but perspective may be lost and overtrading result. The Elliott Wave Theory which describes this phenomenon will be discussed more fully in Chapter 6. On Figure 12, the three legs of the movement of Loew's Corporation during 1970-1971 have been marked off. Note the trendline break that followed. Note also, how the failure of LTR to reach its upper channel boundary presaged its major intermediate trend reversal in August 1971.

Trendline System #9
The Most Bullish Trendline Formation

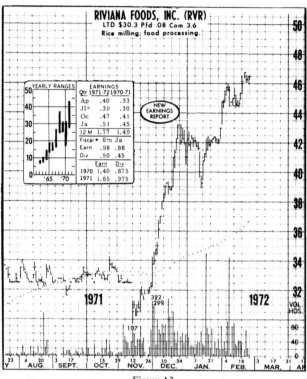

Figure 13

Note the upside reversal in November through the overhanging trading range. The accompanying surge in volume confirmed the significance of the move.

Source: Trendline Daily Basis Stock Charts, 345 Hudson Street, New York, N.Y. 10014

The most bullish trendline formation involves the following:

(1) A long decline (optional), usually ending in climactic volume (See Chapter 2).

(2) Following the automatic post-climax rally, a slightly downward to sideways meandering for a period of time, marked by frequent short term trend reversals within a trading range.

(3) A downside break below the trading range, which may or may not be accompanied by heavy volume— frequently triggered by bearish news.

(4) Here is the key! A sharp upside reversal through the trading range from which the stock has just dipped.

Buy as soon as the last downtrend is reversed or immediately upon the first price reaction following action #4.

Straight Answers To Tricky Trendline Questions:

1. What do you do about stocks that move up at an accelerating rate?

Trendlines are not necessarily straight. They may be drawn in as a series of lines as moves accelerate or decelerate, or as curved lines, encompassing moves, in which case the associated channel may similarly curve. Treat signals from this curvilinear trendline as a straight trendline.

2. How do you find a sell point for stocks that are blowing off and rising almost perpendicularly?

If you find a really good way, tell me. Trendlines aren't too much help here although channeling may provide some clues. Wave counting helps (Is it the third upwave?). So does volume study. The chapter on formations will offer some suggestions as will the construction of a stock oscillator, described in Chapter 5. Terminal blowoffs frequently carry further than any logical system can predict.

3. What about stocks that penetrate their trendlines, move sideways and then continue in the original direction?

This *is* another sticky problem. Very strong stocks, following a powerful intermediate move frequently consolidate without giving any significant ground, moving either upwards but at a lesser rate (be careful; see wedges in Chapter 3) or sideways, before resuming their uptrend. You can invoke a rule—do not sell on a trendline violation unless it is a downwards violation with a close at least one point (or two for high priced stocks) below the trendline. In the case of lateral penetrations, establish the trading range and place a protective stop one or two points below the formation. If in doubt, *get out*. Cash never hurts. Reverse the procedure if short, for stocks moving sidewise out of a downtrend. Trendlines at greater than a forty-five degree angle are suspect. These are usually short term trendlines, destined to be broken. If technical evidence exists for a strong intermediate to primary move, you may defer selling on the violation of very steep trendlines and await the development of a more gradual trendline formation. However, if the trendline accelerates its angle as the move progresses, sell on the violation. This is often blow-off action.

4. It all sounds easy. I have dutifully subscribed to daily and weekly chart services which I receive on Mondays. But after receiving the charts I notice that many breakouts have occurred during the week of stocks which have risen too far by Monday for me to buy. Any suggestions?

Professional traders, of course, stay at their local brokerage offices, charts in hand, updated sometimes hourly or transaction by transaction. Short of doing the same, hounding your broker to death or ignoring wife, family, business or profession, there is one suggestion. Mark the trendline of the stocks in which you have interest, determine the breakout points and place daily buy or sell stop orders with your broker, which will be executed at the market as soon as your stop is touched. Keep your broker on his toes; alert him to your intentions and have him call you on breakouts. If he knows you mean business he will usually be glad to keep you posted. The recommendation for do-it-yourself traders is to avoid the big institutional brokers. They will be too busy to worry about your hundred share lot. Otherwise, await the first reaction. Use speed resistance lines to predict likely stopping points for pullbacks.

5. I have been studying charts and notice short term, intermediate and long term trends, with many reaction points. How do I know which reversal points to use in the consideration of my trendline?

That depends upon the type of trading you wish to do. Very short term traders may wish to employ reversal points spaced eight to ten days apart. However, this will usually result in over-trading, with commissions wiping out a good piece of your profits. The following procedure should help. By combining trend analysis with time cycle analysis (Chapter 6), you will have a pretty good notion as to when an intermediate trend reversal is due. Let us assume the intermediate trend has been down. As the expected period of downtrend termination approaches, begin to draw in daily downtrendlines, as closely following the most recent segment of the decline as possible. Initiate purchases upon the first violation of this line, but preferably not investing all your capital.

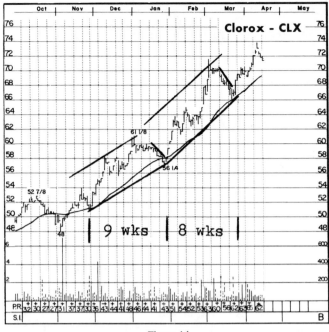

Figure 14

Source: R.W. Mansfield Co., 26 Journal Squre, Jersey City, N.J. 07306
[Trendlines by author]

Place a stop-loss order about a point beneath the lows of the most recent decline. You will have initiated purchases near these lows. Following the first downside reversal after your purchase, and a renewal of the rally, connect a trendline between the intermediate low and this first reaction low. If you want to be certain of protecting profits, you may move your stop-loss point to just below the first reaction point following your purchase. However, trendlines formed from closely spaced reaction points are not reliable and are readily violated during base building processes. Approximately six to eight weeks after an intermediate bottom, stocks and the market frequently undergo a more meaningful reaction. Upon the violation of the immediately preceding short term downtrendline and the initiation of a rally from the eight week reaction point, stop-loss points should be placed just below the reaction lows and remaining funds committed. A trendline may be established between the intermediate lows and the first six to eight week reaction point following. This will frequently hold as a significant intermediate and often as a significant long term trendline as well. The up-trendline that encompassed the whole market move from May 1970 into 1972 was established within six weeks by joining the May 1970 and July 1970 lows. Should the stock or market accelerate its rise, the trendline may be accelerated by joining eight week low points. Stop-loss points should be progressively raised as the stock advances. Intermediate channels may be based upon these eight-week trendlines, with sales prior to actual violation initiated as per System #8, or by the employment of a short term trendline as the stock reaches its channel extremity. Reverse the whole procedure if short selling.

To sum up: Intermediate traders should employ channels and trendlines based upon reaction points spaced approximately six to eight weeks apart. Long term traders should employ trendlines based upon reaction points spaced approximately thirteen weeks to six months apart. And primary term traders should employ reaction points spaced approximately six months apart.

Definition

A loss-cut or stop-loss order is an order placed with your broker to execute a sell (if long) or buy (if short) order at the earliest possible transaction following a stock's touching a certain price level. For example, should you wish to sell a long position if your stock falls below 39, you would place a sell-stop at 38-7/8. This would become a market sell order to be executed as soon as possible after the stock touched that price. You may or may not get 38-7/8. You could conceivably get more, usually a little less since you may have to wait on line until previously placed stop orders at that level are executed and you have to take the bid price. Round lot stop orders are not accepted on the American Exchange. Buy stops, placed either if you are short or to pick up a breakout, are the reverse, a market order to buy at the market should a stock penetrate above a certain level.

Limit Orders

Limit orders are orders to buy and/or sell at a specified price. Limit orders can be employed in lieu of stop orders, placed to go into effect when a stock reaches a certain price, up or down. The order then becomes an execution order *at that price*. The advantage is that you aren't clipped by having to take the next bid. The disadvantage is that the price may skip right by your limit and you are stuck with your position, until you change your order.

Trailing Stops

This is a highly recommended strategy. It involves moving your stop orders to follow the movement of your stock. For instance, you can raise your stops just below each successive reaction point as your stock advances or, if short, just above each upthrust point, as your stock declines. This ensures automatic profit protection and automatically sets your decisions. Using trendlines, you can move your order up or down with the trendline.

Mental vs. Actually Placed Orders

Many traders who stay close to the tape prefer not to employ open stop orders. Chartists tend to place stops at similar points, many stops becoming triggered at the same time, prices driven down quickly. Following such action, some rally frequently occurs which provides a better opportunity for favorable liquidation. Therefore, mental stops are sometimes more advantageous; you place your order at the crucial moment. This requires your availability and an alert broker. Another advantage of mental stops is that they preclude your being shaken out by some sudden news, e.g. the Israeli war of 1967.

In any event, take your loss-cut points seriously. Every so often you will be caught in a false shakeout, but they guarantee against serious loss, and that's the way to stay healthy in the market.

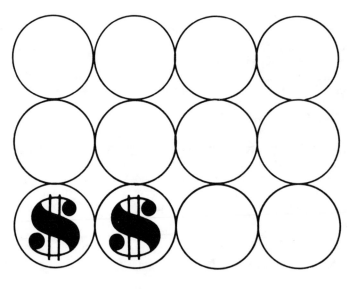

chapter two

VOLUME: WHEN TO JOIN THE CROWD AND WHEN TO BE YOUR OWN MAN

Volume is to the stock market what gasoline is to an automobile. Only one thing makes a stock rise—fuel, buyers, the more the better. The amount and type of interest in stocks, reflected in the particular combination of trading activity (volume) and price action, provide significant clues as to future developments. The market requires volume to eat through and digest overhead supply, to continue rallies through periods of profit taking and to generate the sort of public interest in and excitement regarding stocks that lead to big moves.

Conversely, bearish inferences may be drawn from certain combinations of price and volume configuration. In this chapter we will examine bullish and bearish implications derived from volume action, and appropriate trading strategy in the various contingencies.

First, let us consider the typical formation of a significant market (or stock) bottom. These occur usually in one of three ways. The market may decline precipitously, with mounting volume as the fall accelerates, the down-move culminating in a selling climax. A selling climax is marked by a one or two day price reversal, accompanied by a surge of heavy volume. The market may open the climax period sharply down—volume increasing as the public dumps in panic. Suddenly, amidst a flurry of active trading, the decline stops and the stocks close the climax day or two-day period near their intra-day highs. What has happened is that in a burst of pessimism and panic, a mammoth shakeout has taken place—the public has handed its stock over to the smart money. The 1966 and 1970 bear markets ended in this manner. A sharp immediate rally almost always follows upon a selling climax, and a subsequent retest of the lows is likewise almost inevitable. In fact, the selling climax lows may be violated, but if this occurs as a low volume side to downward drift, the back of the bear has been broken. A major reversal is imminent. Figure 1 illustrates the climactic bottom made by Eckard Corp. in May 1970. Note the heavy volume as the stock completed a two day reversal, the drying up of volume as the stock based into August, and the pickup in volume as the stock broke upside at the end of August.

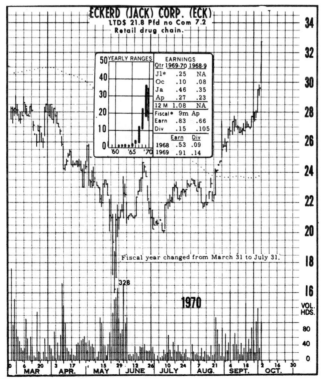

Figure 1

A selling climax: Note the volume surge as Eckard Corp. hit bottom in May 1970.
Source: Trendline Daily Basis Stock Charts, 345 Hudson Street, New York, N.Y. 10014

A second type bottoming action takes longer. The sellers do not panic. Rather they are worn out by slow attrition. Stocks drift downwards, perhaps with a climax but usually without; however, buyers do not step in rapidly. Instead, the market (or a stock) drifts on low volume into a base, a trading range in which it may meander for weeks, months or even years. During this time, stock is being quietly accumulated, taken by patient operators from impatient holders. Eventually cheap supply becomes exhausted and the professionals accumulating have to reach higher for positions. At this juncture, the public begins to become aware that the stock is beginning to rise and starts to join the operators. Volume begins to increase and the mark-up is under way. Figure 2 demonstrates this action. Note the low volume during accumulation, the gradual rise as the stock moves out of its base.

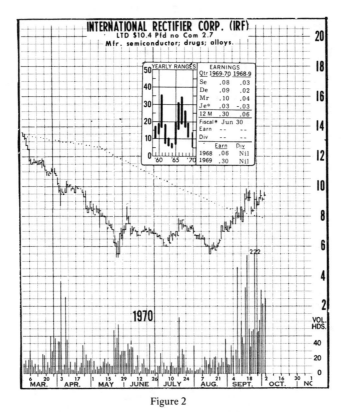

Figure 2

Source: Trendline Daily Basis Stock Charts, 345 Hudson Street, New York, N.Y. 10014

In a third action, stocks wander quietly within an accumulation base, suddenly exploding out in a huge surge of volume. There is no gradual pick up of volume within the base prior to the breakout. The March 1968 market decline ended in this manner. See Figure 3 for an example.

The key to these bullish conclusions is the volume action in each case. The evidence that a mark-up is imminent lies with the increasing volume as the stock breaks from its lows. Careful study of areas of stock accumulation generally reveals periodic volume spikes within base formations, usually at low points within the trading range, an indication that good demand exists within this range, smart money not yet ready to force the stock up, but ready to support the current price range. Figure 4 demonstrates such a trading range, with significant accumulation volume peaks noted. I have found that, say a thirty-dollar stock, accumulated for several weeks in this manner often produces a move of ten points or more.

Appropriate action is clear. Buy into the selling climax. Some rally is inevitable. Should you observe the sort of trading range noted in Figure 4, you may buy into the low area before the stock breaks out or else take

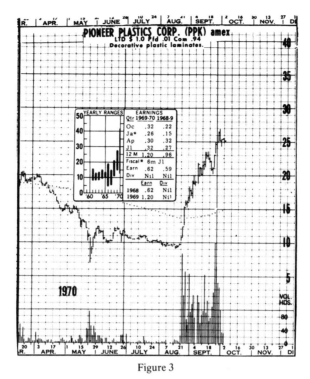

Figure 3

Source: Trendline Daily Basis Stock Charts, 345 Hudson Street
New York, N.Y. 10014

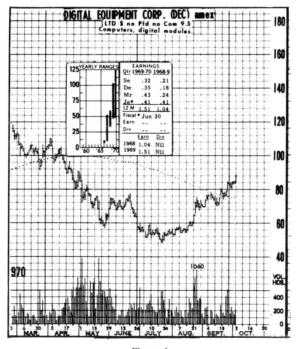

Figure 4

The volume spikes in June, July and finally at the breakout in August
indicated the strong accumulation taking place in Digital Equipment.
Source: Trendline Daily Basis Stock Charts, 345 Hudson Street,
New York, N.Y. 10014

positions as the stock emerges *on good volume* from the base. The former action involves less risk since stop points are placed just below the base formation in either case but may require time to work out. You will pay more for the stock after the breakout but will enjoy a more immediate rise if your strategy is correct. Keep in mind, however, two things. Following the "automatic" selling climax rally, a testing decline will take place. Usually, the lows will hold. Sometimes not. You may or may not want to try to scalp a few quick points in the hope that you can come back in a little cheaper. This requires fast action—the whole process may take no more than one to three trading days. If climactic volume has existed for several trading days prior to the actual low and the stock has given up relatively little ground during this time, *do not scalp*. The odds favor a really good upmove.

The second thing to keep in mind is that volume is relative. Depending upon a stock's capitalization, the floating supply, and public interest, it will develop normal volume, low volume and climactic volume patterns of its own. You will need to consult your charts to determine what constitutes low, normal and climactic volume for a particular stock. Usually, volume three to four times a stock's average volume can be considered climactic volume. The total market seems to be changing its volume characteristics over the years due largely to institutional big block, rapid turnover activity and increasing public participation. In 1966, ten million shares represented climactic activity; by 1971 this had risen to twenty-five million shares.

To Sum Up

Volume System #1

Take one of the two following actions:

(A) If, after a decline, or within a base, a stock (or the market) develops heavy volume while resisting further decline—buy.

(B) If a stock breaks upwards out of a trading range on heavy volume—buy, either on the breakout or on the first pullback.

In either case, place a stop one or two points below the base trading range. Occasionally, before a stock's price is marked up, operators allow or create a last shakeout to trigger stops and to clean stock from the last weak hands. If (1) every other technical evidence points to higher prices (2) the stock is fundamentally dirt cheap and (3) you have nerves of steel, you may elect to ride out the shakeout. A safer procedure is to act chicken and buy in again if the stock reverses upside.

Strong stocks follow fairly typical courses following a move out of a base. The stronger and more protracted the initial price-volume surge the further are subsequent moves likely to carry.

Rule: *Increasing volume, increasing spread on the upside—higher prices to follow.*

Following the initial surge, the stock is likely to pause, move sideways or decline slightly. Volume should diminish during this consolidation. Bidders will initially try to come in under the market but sellers will be scarce and volume will quickly dry up until the buyers are ready to come to the sellers. Suddenly, volume will increase as the stock moves out of the consolidation range. This process will repeat as the stock advances to a top.

The topping process is similar to the bottoming process—in reverse. As the public was pessimistic at the bottom, dumping unceremoniously, so it is now euphoric. The stock's rise has attracted a public following, weak hands, eager to get in on the joyride. Time for the operators to give the public what it wants—stock at high prices. Volume increases to climactic proportions, *this time following a long upmove.* This is the signal that distribution is taking place, particularly if heavy volume churning is evident, the stock trading heavily but going nowhere. There are occasions when this action may be misleading, usually early in a bull rise just under previous supply. In these cases, other technical considerations often offer clues that the advance has been stopped not by distribution, but simply because time is required to digest overhead supply. Usually, however, high volume churning indicates the end of the move is at hand, sharp up and down movements during the

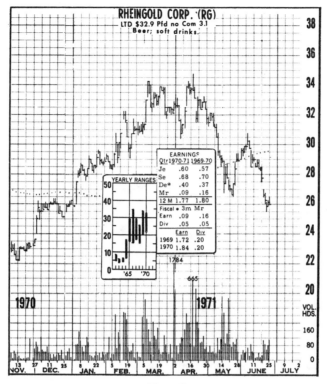

Figure 5

The high volume churning during March and April presaged the
decline in Rheingold that followed.
Source: Trendline Daily Basis Stock Charts, 345 Hudson Street,
New York, N.Y. 10014

topping formation notwithstanding. See Figure 5. You can observe the high volume trading in Rheingold
during March and April 1971, with no price appreciation; the decline that followed was almost inevitable.

Rule: *Increasing volume, decreasing spread—price reversal is imminent.*

Volume System #2

If your stock, following a protracted upmove, develops climactic volume—sell. This is particularly true if a
downside reversal has occurred.

Stocks may continue to rise prior to or without a buying climax or continue to fall prior to or without a selling
climax on diminishing volume. Continued rise on diminishing volume carries bearish implications; volume
should expand as the stock advances. However, reversal is not imminent as in the case of buying climaxes;
caution, though, is in order. Declines on low volume, contrary to general opinion, *are not bullish*. At best, they
are neutral. A stock usually requires volume to rise; it can fall under its own weight. Low volume declines are
bullish only when they represent pauses during upmoves, in which cases volume dries rapidly, or during basing
operations, in which cases the downward slopes are very gradual and the volume continues low for long periods
of time. Most declines do not end until volume increases, the only evidence that big money is ready to step in.
Witness the 1966 and 1970 bear markets. Declines on large volume, however, are very bearish when the volume
is heavy at the beginning of the decline.

Rule: *Initial downthrust, wide spread, heavy volume—lower prices to come.*

Volume System #3

If your stock suddenly drops through its trendline or from a trading area on heavy volume—sell, either instantly or upon the first rally thereafter. Do not play games.

False bear market rallies can be identified by the lack of volume follow through. Short covering during bear markets propels the prices of trading stocks quickly as the shorts scramble to cover. However, there is no follow through buying; upside volume dries up and the stock quickly reverses downside. Valid rallies are marked by the refusal of stocks to give ground and strong secondary surges of buying power. During false bear market rallies, the highest prices occur often during the opening hour the second day of the rally. Churning quickly sets in. During the "Nixon rally", August 1971, the highest recovery prices were seen in many instances near the opening the *first* day of the rally. The key lies in the presence or absence of a good secondary surge, following the initial pullback. If the previous lows, however, were hit on climactic volume, near channel extremities, again do not play games—cover shorts and buy.

To Sum Up The Basic Volume Rules

(1) Heavy volume following a protracted decline indicates that the decline is nearly complete—particularly if the stock gives ground grudgingly as the volume increases. Big money is stepping in.

(2) Climactic volume following a long upmove indicates a near termination of the move, particularly if the heavy volume is not accompanied by further price progress. The big money is feeding stock to the public.

(3) A breakout from a trading range in either direction accompanied by heavy volume and wide spread indicates the validity of the breakout. Further movement is likely to take place in the direction of the breakout.

(4) An increase in volume during base building implies that an upside breakout is approaching, particularly if volume peaks develop while the stock is in the lower portion of the trading range.

We will investigate volume further in Chapter 3 during our consideration of formations. Many attempts have been made to pursue volume study with the goal of determining whether the activity within trading ranges or during a stock's progress represents the process of accumulation or distribution. At the same time, many technicians have devised different systems of charting, designed to combine more directly than the classical bar chart, the elements of price and volume.

Volume System #4

Joseph E. Granville's *On-Balance Volume System* (from *Granville's New Key To Stock Market Profits*, by Joseph E. Granville, Prentice-Hall, Englewood Cliffs, N.J., 1963). Joseph Granville is a widely followed and respected market technician. The following is, of necessity, a brief condensation of his on-balance study; I suggest that those interested in this system secure the above book.

Essentially, the system works best in discerning potential price breakouts during a stock's price oscillations within base trading ranges. It rests upon the premise that price action will follow upon volume action and that the latter will presage the former.

The system itself is relatively simple. Volume is not plotted beneath price changes in the usual manner, that is, by vertical lines denoting daily volume. Rather, volume is plotted in a linear manner, as a cumulative line. The total daily volume for any stock (or the market) is entered as a plus if the stock is up for the day, as a minus if the stock is down for the day. Each day's total is added (if plus) or subtracted (if minus) from the cumulative total recorded up to that day. A line, charting the cumulative total, is maintained beneath the price chart, plotting points of the line matched under the appropriate day's price activity.

The OBV (on balance volume) line is interpreted in much the same manner as are price charts. A series of higher highs and higher lows is bullish. Descending lows in the line are bearish. Climactic peaks or troughs

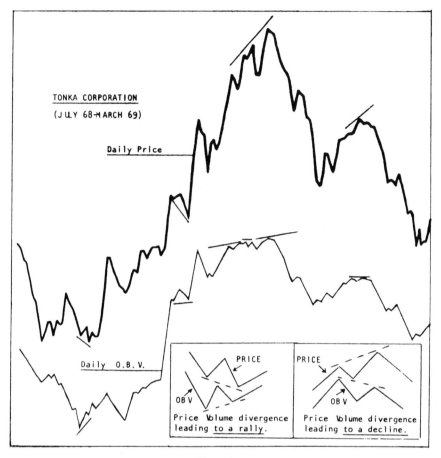

Figure 6

Figure 6 illustrates the relationship between the OBV line and subsequent
price action. Notice the flattening of the OBV line as Tonka peaked.
Source: Williams Reports, Box 1552, Carmel, California 93921

indicate a reversal of trend. Support and resistance levels operate with the OBV line as with price and its action
is subject to trendline and other study. *Divergences between the action of the OBV line and price are
significant.* Should the OBV line break upside, the price of the stock is likely to follow. Conversely, should a
stock's price rise while its OBV line falls or remains flat, a downside reversal is imminent. New highs in a stock
should be accompanied by new highs in its OBV line. At any point, for instance during consolidations, the
stock's OBV level should be compared to its OBV level during prior periods of trading within that range, for an
assessment of its current accumulation-distribution activity.

Results

Application of this system freqently provides an early action signal, prior to price action signals. Granville
suggests daily plotting. However, this is liable to discourage application of his system, which may work well with
weekly entries.

Volume System #5
The Williams Accumulation/Distribution Formula

Larry Williams, former publisher of *The Williams Reports*, is always an interesting and original technician

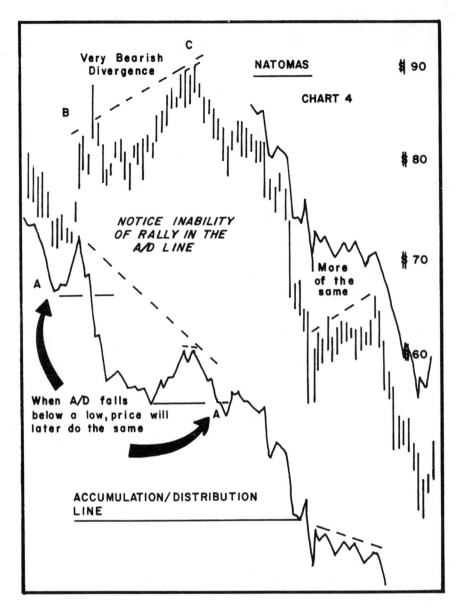

Figure 7

Figure 7 illustrates the operation of the accumulation-distribution line and
its relationship to stock price forecasting.
Source: Williams Reports, Box 1552, Carmel, California 93921

and his market letter has been known both for his clear position statements (no hedging) and for its technical
innovations. Williams' formula is similar in concept and use to Granville's OBV, but with a significant
difference. Granville allots the total volume for a given day in one direction only, depending upon whether the
stock closed up for the day or down. This, however, does not take into account whether most of the volume went
into upside or downside action on that day. Buying climaxes, for instance, high volume reversal days, frequently
end with the stock up for the day, but well off its highs. The Williams A/D formula attempts to reflect intra-day
activity more precisely.

The system operates under the same premises as Granville's OBV system and is charted in the same manner.
(Figure 7).

Rules

New highs in price must be matched by new highs in the accumulation-distribution line; converse for new price lows. Divergence indicates forthcoming price reversal.

Williams' formula to arrive at the per cent of buying volume for a given day is as follows:

(High price for day minus opening price) plus (closing price minus low price) divided by twice the daily range equals the per cent of buying, or:

$$\text{H-O} + \text{C-L} \div 2 \text{ times daily range} = \% \text{ of buying}$$

The day's total volume is then multiplied by the per cent of buying to provide total buying volume. Selling volume is derived by subtracting buying volume from total volume. The difference between buying and selling volume is added (if buying volume is greater) or subtracted (if selling volume is greater), from the cumulative total, line plotted.

Results

Quite good. The use of this formula will improve stock selection and help you prepare early for selling and short selling. In many instances, this method will signal ahead of Granville's OBV technique.

Volume System #6
Martel's Short Term Supply-Demand Charting System

This system has been devised by Dr. R. F. Martel, and presented in a brief book, *Charting Supply and Demand For Stock Analysis*, Martel and Company, Reading, Pa., 1972. Dr. Martel has founded an advisory service based upon this technique. The system is similar in many respects to standard point and figure charting. Dr. Martel recommends a system in which columns marking price rises employ X's as entries; columns representing declines employ O's for entries. Those readers not familiar with point and figure charting might turn to the beginning sections of Chapter 4, in which this charting system is discussed.

The supply-demand charting system charts volume action, based again on the theory that strong volume during advances and weak volume during declines represent bullish activity. Erratic price behavior during heavy volume periods is bearish. Before charts are drawn, "a volume divisor" has to be established for the stock. This is achieved by study of the average daily volume of transactions for that stock over a significant period of time. A divisor is derived such that it represents one half to one third the average daily volume of the stock. For example, should a stock average a volume of 50,000 shares per day, a divisor of 20,000 might be employed. This divisor may have to be altered periodically should the character of the stock's activity change. Only whole numbers should be employed for charting, so results are rounded to the nearest whole number.

The charting itself is relatively simple. Charts are entered daily on point and figure paper, entries within the squares. A column is employed for each day's trading. The X and O entries are computed by comparing the stock's spread for the day against the previous day's closing price. For instance, should a stock trade for the day up to one point higher and as low as one-half point lower than the previous day's close, all the volume for that

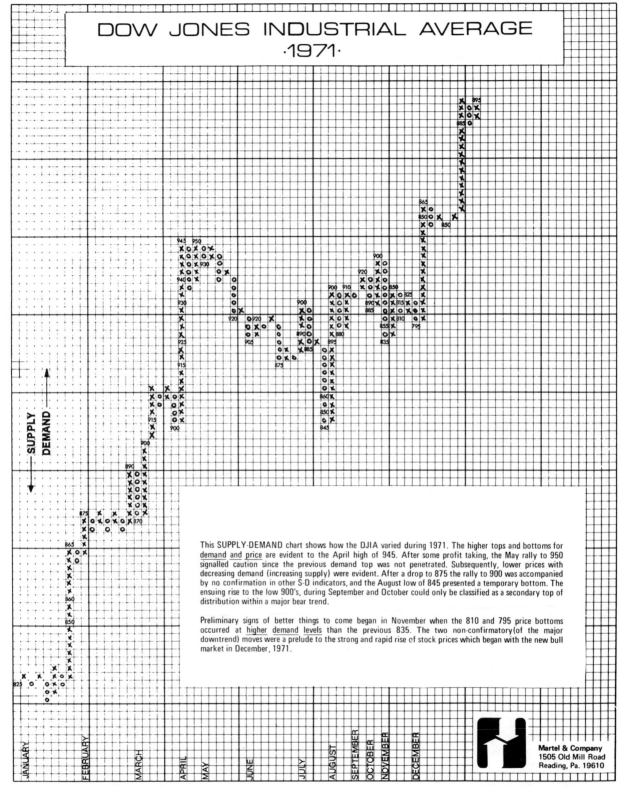

DOW JONES INDUSTRIAL AVERAGE ·1971·

This SUPPLY-DEMAND chart shows how the DJIA varied during 1971. The higher tops and bottoms for demand and price are evident to the April high of 945. After some profit taking, the May rally to 950 signalled caution since the previous demand top was not penetrated. Subsequently, lower prices with decreasing demand (increasing supply) were evident. After a drop to 875 the rally to 900 was accompanied by no confirmation in other S-D indicators, and the August low of 845 presented a temporary bottom. The ensuing rise to the low 900's, during September and October could only be classified as a secondary top of distribution within a major bear trend.

Preliminary signs of better things to come began in November when the 810 and 795 price bottoms occurred at higher demand levels than the previous 835. The two non-confirmatory (of the major downtrend) moves were a prelude to the strong and rapid rise of stock prices which began with the new bull market in December, 1971.

Martel & Company
1505 Old Mill Road
Reading, Pa. 19610

Figure 8

Source: Martel and Co., 1505 Old Mill Rd., Reading, Pa. 19610

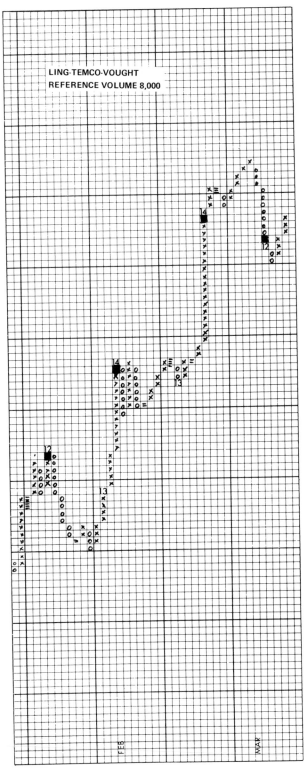

Figure 9

A typical supply-demand chart.
Source: Martel and Co., 1505 Old Mill Rd., Reading, Pa. 19610

day would be assigned upwards in a row of X's. The amount of X squares entered would be determined by dividing the volume for that day by the divisor. Should most of the spread have been below the previous day's close, the volume for that day would be considered as down volume, entered in that day's column as a series of O's, downwards. On days in which the daily spread straddles the previous close evenly, lateral dashes are entered into that day's column. The number of dashes entered into a single box for that day's column is equivalent to the daily volume divided by the divisor. The high or low price (in whole numbers) is recorded at the conclusion of either a series of up days or a series of down days. Should a stock reach its series high during a down (reversal) day, the high price for that day is noted on the chart, connected by an arrow to the previous up column. The above is the methodology for short term supply-demand charts. Longer term charts may be constructed by restricting reversal entries to three or five point changes in direction. Unlike usual point and figure charts, supply-demand charts may have only a single entry mark within a column. Figures 8 and 9 are samples of supply-demand charts.

Interpretation

The principles underlying interpretation are similar to the OBV and A/D systems. Higher prices should be confirmed by higher demand levels, and higher demand levels should be accompanied by higher prices, particularly following a long advance. Prior to a major advance, however, higher demand implies higher price action to come. Other divergences suggest reversal possibilities. Similar to the above systems, these charts are subject to the usual forms of technical analysis.

General Conclusions

The system's concept appears viable, is readily maintained and like any system must be lived with for a time before one gets a real feel for it. Note: climactic volume periods are represented by sudden spurts, several squares in length. Although the stock may be moving up or down during these periods in phase with the supply-demand movement, the implications of climactic action remain (Review Volume Systems 1, 2).

Volume System #7
Don Worden's Tick Volume System

This system is included with some reservation, not because it is of doubtful concept (it is an excellent system) but because there is no feasible way for the home chartist to secure his own data. Use of this system would require subscription to Don Worden's service, an excellent though fairly expensive advisory. Worden's $100,000 indices are widely quoted as a major indicator of primary trend. Should this system interest you, direct your inquiry to Worden and Worden, 1915 Florenada Road, Ft. Lauderdale, Florida 33308. Trial subscriptions have been available.

Briefly stated, Worden's concept differs from those above in that his measures of accumulation and distribution operate completely independently of price action. The entries in the Granville, Martel and Williams systems are all related to the price action of the stock or market. Worden measures the number of shares traded on upticks as opposed to the number of shares traded on downticks. The differential is plotted, daily and as ten-day, thirty-day and sixty-day moving totals. A stock showing consistent buying pressures (uptick transactions) is a candidate for purchase. Conversely, selling pressures (preponderance of downtick transactions) indicates weakness.

The $100,000 indices are measures of uptick-downtick action for transactions involving $100,000 or more—the really big money operations. These have had excellent success in signalling the onset of primary bull moves.

Figure 10 is a chart demonstrating a relationship between Worden's DAV's, (differential activity value), stock price and Granville's on-balance volume study in one situation. Notice that in this case, at least, Worden's method predicted the move to follow far in advance of the OBV technique.

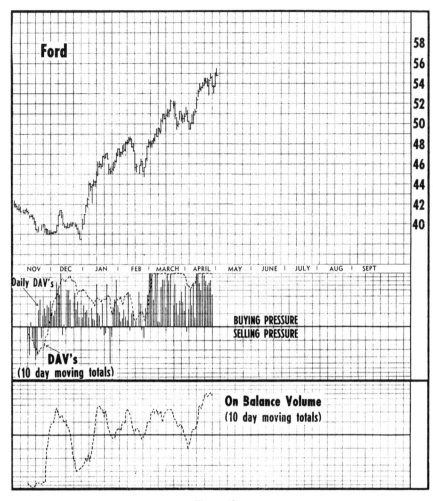

Figure 10

Source: Worden and Worden, Inc., 1915 Florenada Road,
Fort Lauderdale, Florida 33308

Volume System #8
Volume-Price Trend Charting

This system was introduced by David L. Markstein in his book, *How To Chart Your Way To Stock Market Profits*, Parker Publishing Company, West Nyack, N.Y., 1966. It is a simple, effective system. In concept, volume-price trend (VPT) charting combines the elements of price change and volume into a single entry, which measures the flow and impact of big money. The system has two advantages which invite its use. First, entries are posted weekly, not daily, from readily available information. Second, interpretation is straightforward. I strongly advise you, based upon my own experience, to act upon your VPT signals. The major disadvantage to the VPT system lies in the fact that it is a weekly system. This renders it somewhat less sensitive than daily systems. However, this system is readily used because of its simplicity; a sensitive but ignored system is of no use to anyone.

VPT charts are plotted as cumulative line charts, that is, each new week's entry is added to or subtracted form the previous week's total. The new figure is entered on the chart and a line drawn from the previous week's plot to the newest entry point. Result is a line, somewhat approximating the weekly closing prices of the stock.

The plotting figures are derived in the following manner:

1. Compute the percentage of price change for the week. A ten dollar stock that has risen to twelve has increased by twenty per cent. A twelve dollar stock that has declined to nine has lost twenty-five per cent. If the price has risen, the VPT entry is added to the previous total; if the price has declined the percentage is treated as a minus.

2. Multiply the per cent of price change by the stock's weekly volume. I have found that volume expressed in thousands or tens of thousands of shares simplifies calculations. Thus, if a stock traded 856,000 shares within the week, multiple by 85.6 or 856. Add to or subtract from the previous week's total.

3. Draw lines connecting each week's entries, plotted on square graph paper. Some experimentation will be required to devise a workable scale for each stock.

Action Signals

There are two action signals within this system.

1. Buy or sell upon trendline breaks. This involves the use of the most recent, steep trendline available. The steeper the trendline, the closer to the end of the move will be its violation and the more profitable will be your transaction. Do not attempt to separate major, minor or intermediate trendlines. A trendline in this system is a line connecting the two most recent reaction points. However, the trendline violation must be in a reverse direction. Line charts readily break trendlines while still moving in their pre-violation direction.

2. Buy and sell upon penetrations of support and resistance areas. Any rise above a previous high is a buy signal; any decline below a previous low is a sell signal.

Use VPT charts in conjunction with bar and point and figure charts. Within congestion areas, VPT charts tend to whipsaw so avoid action so long as the stock price remains locked within a trading range. As usual, do not fight the overall trend of the market or the major trend of the stock. Do not employ this system with thin stocks.

Results

My own experience with this system has been favorable. The action signals are clear; weekly posting is not an onerous task. False signals are occasionally received, of course, but then again, nothing is perfect. Also, some practice is required for accurate trendline construction. Strongly recommended: that you secure some back issues of *Barron's*, plot a VPT chart on some of your stocks and experiment for yourself.

Volume System #9
Equivolume Charting

This system and systems #10 and #11 below, are described more fully by their originator, Richard W. Arms, Jr., in *Profits In Volume*, published by Investors Intelligence, Inc., Larchmont, N.Y. 1971.

In concept, this system of charting attempts to more graphically represent the interplay of price movement and volume than do bar charts. Closing prices are held as having little significance. Spread and volume are significant.

The Equivolume chart is constructed with a combination horizontal and vertical scale. The vertical scale will be representative of the stock's usual trading pattern and will be similar to that stock's bar chart. The horizontal scale is constructed over columns (squared graph paper is used). Each column will represent approximately 67 per cent of the stock's average daily trading volume, rounded to an easily used round number. The plot for each day will be a rectangle, consisting of two vertical sides the length of the trading range for that

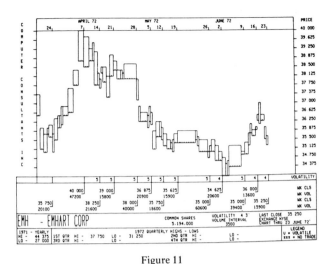

Figure 11

Source: Computer Consultants Inc., 1613 University Boulevard,
Albuqueque, N.M. 87106

day and two horizontal sides, the width in columns of the volume plot. Therefore an Equivolume Chart is two dimensional, rather than simply linear. A date scale may be placed above the chart.

Interpretation of this chart is similar to bar charting. Support and resistance levels are studied and trendlines are pertinent. A major difference lies in the ease of perceiving price-volume relationships. A small price spread on heavy volume will appear as either a square or flat rectangle (wide horizontal volume side, narrow vertical side). A large spread on light volume will appear as a long thin rectangle. Square or flat rectangles indicate the imminence of price reversals (Volume Systems #1, #2 again).

Results

The concept certainly appears valid although I would opt for some inclusion of closing price which I consider significant, particularly since reversal days do frequently occur with a wide spread. Some system of incorporating closing price into the chart could be readily improvised.

Volume System #10
The Short Term Trading Index

This device has become increasingly popular with traders in recent years, particularly since many brokerage houses have secured machines which have been programmed to carry the current calculation. The Short Term Index measures the relative strength of volume entering advancing stocks against the strength of volume entering declining stocks. Bullish readings imply further upside action; bearish readings the reverse. This is a quite sensitive indicator and frequently changes direction moments in advance of market turnarounds on an intra-day basis. It is useful in trading operations but its extreme sensitivity does result in false signals and fosters emotional activity. However, used with some care, the Short Term Index can pinpoint the decisive moments for action.

The calculations of the index are achieved through the following formula:

$$\frac{\text{Number of Stocks Advancing}}{\text{Number of Stocks Declining}} \div \frac{\text{Advancing Volume}}{\text{Declining Volume}} = \text{Short Term Trading Index}$$

Presume that 800 stocks are advancing; 400 declining; that upside volume is 5,000,000 shares; downside 2,000,000. The results would be as follows:

$$\frac{800}{400} \div \frac{5,000,000}{2,000,000} = \frac{2}{1} \div \frac{5}{2} = .80$$

Readings below 1.0 are bullish; readings above 1.0 are bearish. Extreme readings are in the areas of 1.50 to 2.00 and below .50 (I once found briefly a reading of .07). Climactic readings are above 2.00 and below .30, at which points the market is likely to have seen its lows and highs for the day. Buying action may be instituted if the market has been down five to six points and the index suddenly rises to below 1.00. Selling (strictly short term) is indicated if the market has been up six points and the index drops to 1.20. Generally, speculative trading issues will move first with the index; the slower stocks follow a bit later.

Except for the most nimble of traders, I do not recommend short term in and out trading in accordance with index signals. However, the fluctuations of the index can enhance profits by helping you to pinpoint the moments for pre-planned action, saving you eighths, quarters and even full points on action days. For instance, should you be short and want to cover on weakness, look to a 175 to 200 reading and act. Should your broker not have a pre-programmed machine, you can readily calculate the Short Term Index by the above formula while he waits on the phone.

Short term trading signals sufficiently sensitive for trading purposes but not so extremely sensitive as to foster overtrading can be secured by plotting a five-day moving average of the Short Term Trading Index, based on total daily activity. The data necessary for the plotting is available in *Barron's*. A sell signal is generated when the five day moving average of the Short Term Trading Index rises above 1.00; a buy when it falls below 1.00.

Volume System #11
Application Of The Short Term Trading Index To Intermediate And Long Term Trading

The ten-day moving average of the Short Term Index has predictive value as an overbought-oversold index. If you do not know how to compute moving averages, turn ahead to Chapter 6, where the methodology is described.

Overbought-oversold indices operate in a manner similar to climactic volume. Historically, certain levels reached usually represent maximum rally points (extreme bullish readings) and lowest decline points (extreme bearish readings). The market will generally decline or rally from these points.

The ten-day moving average of the Short Term Index is plotted on a line graph. Such graphs are subject to trendline, support and resistance study. In Chapter 6, the interpretation and treatment of overbought-oversold indices is discussed in considerably more detail. Suffice to say at this point that a ten-day moving average of from .70 to .80 of the Short Term Index represents an overbought condition, and from 115 to 130 represents an oversold condition. During bear markets .80 will represent the overbought side; 1.30 oversold. During bull markets, the extremes will shift to .70 and 1.15. Plot the ten-day moving average beneath a daily price scale, using the Standard and Poor's 500 or The New York Stock Exchange Composite. Look for divergences, e.g., the averages making new highs while the index drops. Implication: rally soon to end. This is a good intermediate indicator, well worth the trouble to plot.

This indicator may also be employed as a timing indicator by plotting 10-day and 25-day moving averages and acting upon moving average crossings (suggested by *Trendway*). See Chapter 6 for an explanation of this technique.

Volume System #12
Predicting Market Moves By Big Block Activity

From *Key-Volume Strategies*. Price objectives for the Dow Jones Industrials can be secured by a simple computation involving big block transactions. For any series of consecutive up days on more than twelve million shares volume, with at least 100 big blocks traded, add the total number of big blocks traded in the series. Drop the rightmost digit. Add the remainder to the Dow Jones Industrial Averages low of the day the series started. Result: price objective for the move. Example: Big block series for six consecutive up days, 120 + 105 + 125 + 140 + 130 + 110. Total 720. Drop the right digit; result 72. Add to low the first day of rally. Presume Dow 825 is the low. Price Objective Dow 897 (825 + 72). For downside objectives, reverse process for consecutive down day series.

Big blocks are trades of 10,000 shares or more. Data can be found daily in *The Wall Street Journal*. This system yields surprisingly good results.

Volume System #13
The Option Activity Ratio

This system appeared first in *Barron's*, November 1970, originated by Dr. Martin E. Zweig. It has since come into wide use, particularly since Dr. Zweig discovered an application of the system to intermediate stock moves. His system's call for a severe decline in May 1971 was right on target.

In concept, the Option Activity Ratio (O.A.R.) system measures the relative amount of speculative market activity, as reflected in the ratio between option volume and New York Stock Exchange volume. Since option activity rises with speculative fever, it follows that the higher the degree of option activity, the more speculative the market, the further progressed the market is towards its major bull tops.

The Option Activity Ratio is computed by dividing the weekly volume of the New York Stock Exchange into the weekly option volume. A ten-week moving average is then computed, which has historically ranged from approximately 0.70% at bear market bottoms to 1.30% at primary tops. Bull market top signals occur when both the weekly reading and the ten-week moving average of the O.A.R. rise above 1.25. Bear market bottom signals occur when both the last weekly reading and the ten-week moving average of the O.A.R. fall below 0.75, at which point speculative activity is very low. The last bull market signal was flashed in July 1970, the Dow at 700. At that time, the weekly O.A.R. stood at 0.48 and the ten-week moving average at 0.73. A bear market signal developed in December 1968, with the weekly O.A.R. at 1.45 and the ten-week moving average at 1.25. Previous buy signals occured in October 1966 and June 1962. The February 1966 top was not signalled by this method; the ten week moving average of the O.A.R. peaked at 1.13. Despite one failure, the indicator has an excellent record as a primary trend barometer and is simple to maintain (only weekly postings required).

The intermediate applications further enhance the usefulness of the O.A.R. system. Intermediate top signals are given when the ten-week moving average of the O.A.R. rises .20 above a previous intermediate low point. Such a signal developed in April 1971, just two weeks prior to a drop that eventually took the Dow Jones Industrial Averages down some 160 points. These signals have preceeded declines averaging 37 Dow points in scope and six weeks in time.

Related to the O.A.R. is the Puts/Calls Ratio (P/C). This is a four-week moving average of weekly put option volume divided by weekly call option volume. A rise in the P/C ratio indicates mounting bearishness since put buyers are betting on a decline. A very low reading indicates excessive bullishness. Changes in the P/C ratio of a magnitude of .20 are rare and carry stong significance. A drop of .20 from a previous peak implies a serious decline of at least intermediate proportion. Peak P/C ratios were reached in October 1962, September 1966 and August 1970, all near ultimate bear market lows. Sell signals were given in May 1965, October 1968 and April 1971. All were followed by serious decline.

The data necessary to compute the O.A.R. and P/C ratios is available in *Barron's* each week, in the Market Laboratory.

Volume System #14
Ratio Of American Stock Exchange Volume To New York Stock Exchange Volume

RATIO OF ASE VOLUME TO NYSE VOLUME - MONTHLY

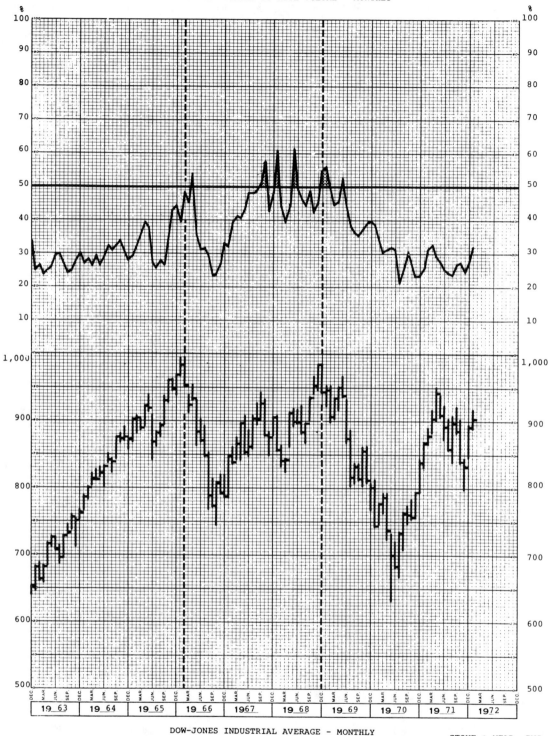

DOW-JONES INDUSTRIAL AVERAGE - MONTHLY

STONE & MEAD, INC.

Figure 12

Source: Stone and Mead, Inc., Long-Term Technical Trends,
15 Broad Street, Boston, Mass. 02109

The concept of this system is similar to the concept underlying the O.A.R. system, that is, that the more speculative the market, the more dangerous. One certain sign of mounting speculation is renewed interest in Amex cats and dogs, particularly relative to N.Y.S.E. activity.

Historically, important market declines have followed periods during which Amex volume has exceeded fifty per cent of N.Y.S.E. volume. Bullish action follows periods during which Amex volume dips to approximately twenty per cent of N.Y.S.E. volume. Figure 12 demonstrates the relationships involved. The data is computed monthly, and is widely available.

This system and system #13 are primary indicator systems. They do not provide signals for in and out moves, but should be maintained to provide a broad perspective of the market. Professional trading requires playing with the percentages. That means avoiding "that last trade" in a hot market. Someone is going to be the last on the buyer's line. It should not be you.

Volume System #15
An Early Warning System

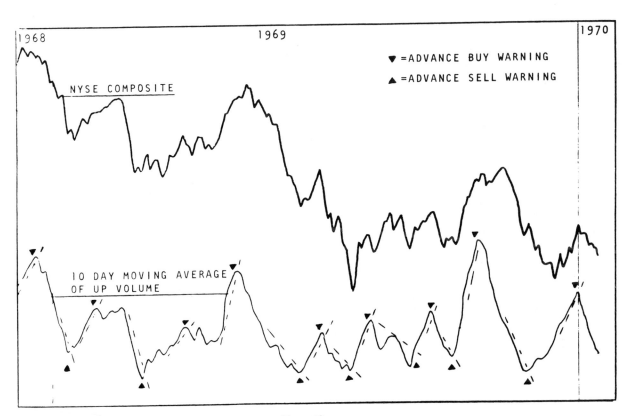

Figure 13

Source: Williams Reports, Box 1552, Carmel, California 93921

From *Williams Reports*. Charts of the ten-day moving averages of up and down volume are available from several sources (e.g. *Trendline*) or can be drawn by hand from data available in *Barron's*. Up volume is the volume going into advancing stocks; down volume is the volume going into declining stocks.

A tight trendline drawn to the up volume line will provide advance warning of market reversals. Should an uptrendline be violated on the downside, a decline is indicated. The reverse holds true for an upwards violation of a downtrendline.

These signals may or may not carry strong significance beyond a minor correction, but for short to intermediate term movements are quite effective. Figure 13 illustrates the actions involved.

Volume System #16
Observing Extreme Levels Of Up And Down Volume

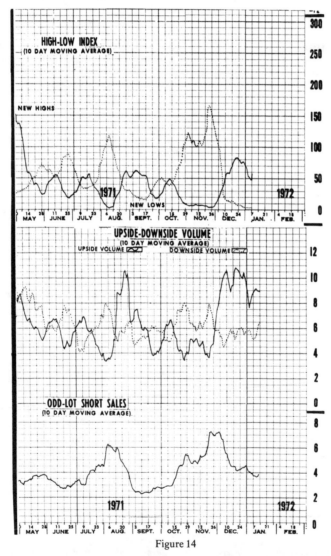

Figure 14

Figure 14 demonstrates the relationship between upside-downside volume and other indicators. Note that the new lows peak as the upside volume reaches its lowest level and how the market tends to reach as extreme readings of the volume indicator occur.

Source: Trendline Daily Basis Stock Charts, 345 Hudson Street, New York, N.Y. 10014

Plots of ten-day moving averages of up volume and down volume may serve as overbought-oversold indices for short to intermediate term trading. Empirically, certain levels of optimism and pessimism tend to signal the end of market moves. Charts such as Figure 14 from *Trendline*, mentioned above, demonstrate that when the up and down volume ten-day moving averages reach certain peaks and troughs a market reversal is in the offing. These peaks do not necessarily result in an instant reversal. During strong bull and bear moves, the market can stay overbought or oversold for considerable periods of time. However, strongly overbought or oversold readings cannot be ignored and must be seriously considered as part of the overall technical picture.

Market buy and sell signals are often generated by a crossing of the up and down volume lines. In other words, when the ten-day moving average of down volume exceeds the ten-day moving average of up volume, a sell signal is generated. So long as the up volume line remains above the down volume line a bullish condition continues to exist.

Volume System #17
Trendway's Negative Volume Index

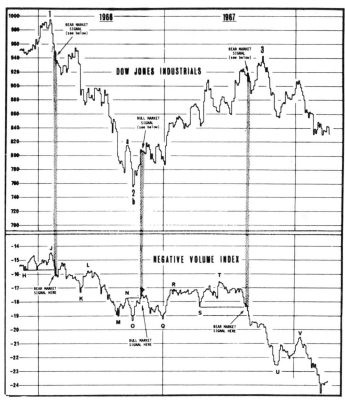

Figure 15

Source: Trendway Advisory Service, P.O.Box 7184, St. Matthews Station,
Louisville, Kentucky 40207

This system was devised by Paul Dysart who founded the *Trendway Advisory Service* in 1933. The service is now administered by Richard Dysart, the son of the founder. The NVI is considered by *Trendway* to be its most important indicator.

In concept, the Negative Volume Index measures smart money accumulation, which frequently develops quietly during periods of market quiescence. Good buying is rarely hurried; it takes place apart from the crowd.

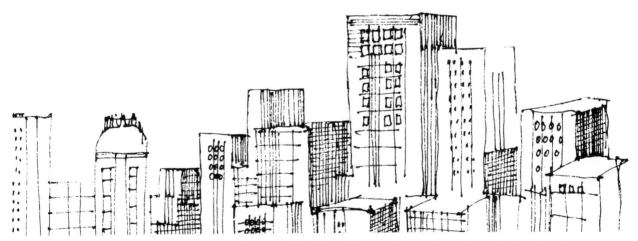

Professionals prefer not to compete with the public. Therefore on low volume days, buying is often better informed than during high volume activity.

The NVI itself is a cumulative plot of advances minus declines on the New York Stock Exchange, charted only on days in which that day's volume is *lower* than the volume of the day previous. There has been a downward bias to the NVI over recent years. However, at significant bull market bottoms, it has rendered a buy signal by recording a peak above a previous peak. Bear markets are signalled when previous low points are violated. Theoretically, for a signal to be valid, the NVI should drop steadily, rally at least 1200 units, drop again at least 1200 units, and then rally through the old highs. The end of the 1966 bull market was indicated early by this system. However, the 1970 bull turn was not indicated because the required secondary decline of 1200 units did not take place, the secondary decline lasting only approximately 900 units. Following this decline, the NVI did surpass its previous high during mid-1970. Except for the requirement of a 1200 unit secondary dip, this would have called the turn quite well—so, perhaps, some discretion may be useful in interpreting the Index. Figure 15 illustrates the NVI.

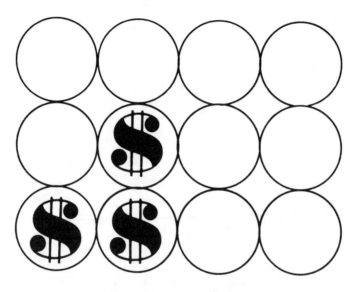

chapter three

CHART FORMATIONS: HOW TO DRAW PROFITABLE PICTURES

Stock prices do not move in straight lines. Even strongly trended stocks must at some point pause before resuming their movement (consolidation), or will at some other point change their primary direction (reversal) altogether. The movements involved, when charted, frequently reveal characteristic patterns. These patterns provide clues regarding the future direction of price movement and also some assessment of the probable extent of the move to follow the pattern resolution.

Is pattern or formation study profitable? On balance, yes. While false breakouts, sad to say, do occur from time to time, the implications of formations cannot be ignored. Similar to any technical tool, formation study should not be employed in isolation. In conjunction, however, with other techniques, formation study should improve your winning percentages.

For intermediate traders, the use of weekly bar charts for formation identification is suggested. Although daily charts may be employed, weekly charts better demonstrate the larger, significant formations which are more useful for intermediate trading. One word of caution—it is easy to create in your imagination, from charts, formations which will *appear* to be *what you want to see*. Make certain that the volume characteristics which will be described are present in the chart and prepare yourself for the worst contingencies.

Support And Resistance Levels

Before we consider chart formations, let us examine the concepts of support and resistance levels, which are operative within any chart formation.

A *support level* is a price level at which demand for a stock is likely to develop sufficiently to impede or to completely reverse a down-move.

A *resistance level* is a price level at which supply is likely to appear sufficient to impede or to completely halt further price advance. A support level represents a congestion of demand; a resistance level represents a congestion of supply.

Support and resistance levels represent areas in which a considerable amount of the stock has changed hands. Psychologically, it works in this manner. Presume Stock A has traded down from 60 to 50, at which point the decline halts amidst a selling climax. The stock rallies to 57. Many traders, observing this action, regret the day they didn't hop in at 50. However, the stock dips down to 52. (Remember, retest after selling climax.) These same traders, recalling that 50 halted the last decline, step in—the stock rallies again, this time to 60. There is another dip to the low 50's. Twice, purchases here have produced profits; traders step in again, creating another price surge. The low 50's represent a support area. Perhaps, the stock moves up, eventually to 70, and then begins a serious decline. As it nears 50, traders, recalling that in the past, 50 was the "magic number", try for another joyride. The stock stops declining, perhaps rallies a bit, but no follow through develops and the price collapses—down to 45. Here a rally attempt begins; the stock reaches 49.

What happens then? The stock has many disenchanted holders now, all the traders over the years who bought in at 50 and never sold out—most itching to get out even. Seeing their chance, they offer stock for sale. The old support area has become a resistance area. *Rule*: A support area, once penetrated becomes a resistance area. A resistance area, once penetrated becomes a support area.

It is more precise to speak of support and resistance zones or areas rather than specific price level supports. For instance, consider the stock that bounced upwards from 50. As it retraces towards 50, impatient traders will begin to edge in for positions sooner, say at 52 or 51. The whole area, from 50-53, will act as support, maybe even a little higher at 54. The support characteristics of a support zone intensify as the lower limits of the area are approached. However, once the zone is penetrated, any support falls away rapidly and price declines accelerate. Place stops about one point below support areas and raise stops as new support areas develop. Resistance areas, of course, operate in reverse. Resistance builds up as the stock begins to penetrate into the resistance area. However, a penetration through the area frequently results in good upside action, with the old resistance now supporting against further decline. That is why many traders prefer to "buy high". Stocks breaking into all time high ground have no overhanging supply from poor souls just waiting to get their money back.

From the preceeding, it should be apparent that the heavier the volume traded within a given area in the past, the stronger will be the support and resistance qualities of that area and the more the work that will be required to penetrate that zone. The ability of a stock to penetrate overhead supply is a definite sign of strength. Conversely, the inability to firm at support levels is a definite sign of weakness.

Other Supports And Resistances

As noted in Chapter 1, trendlines provide support and resistance to stocks' movements, even in the absence of major congestion areas at the trendline. So do moving average lines, which will be described in Chapter 6. Perhaps, this is because there are so many technicians around. In strong bull markets, support zones will tend to operate near upper limits. In bear markets, resistance zones will operate powerfully even at their lower limits.

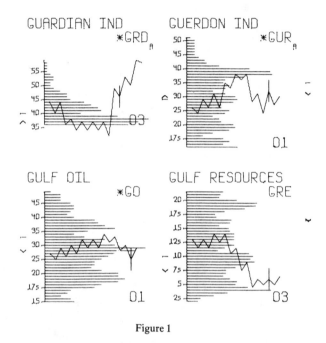

Figure 1

Support and resistance charts.
Source: Chart Service Institute, Winter Park, Florida 32789

At least one charting service has attempted to create a charting system designed to delineate support and resistance levels. Resistance and support charts are issued by *The Chart Service Institute*, examples of which appear in Figure 1. The wider areas represent heavy congestion zones. Price scale is on the left. The zig-zag lines moving up and down represent the smoothed price action of the stocks. Notice how Guerdon stopped moving up when it hit the resistance level near $40 and how readily Guardian moved once it penetrated the congestion near 35. *Trading tip*: Rallying stocks tend to penetrate the first overhanging resistance area quite readily. However, the second overhang becomes much more difficult to penetrate. Declining stocks frequently penetrate the first support level but will rally off the second.

Consolidation And Reversal Formations

A consolidation formation is a congestion area in which stocks pause before a further move in the direction of the price trend that preceded the formation. Consolidation refers to the processes of profit taking and re-accumulation or re-distribution following extensive market moves.

Reversal formations are formations that imply a basic change in direction of price movement.

Formation System #1
Recognizing Consolidation Formations And Selecting The Proper Time To Act

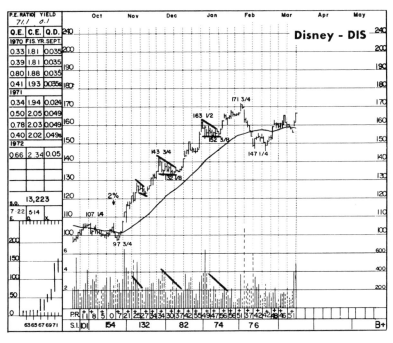

Figure 2

The advance in Disney was interrupted by a series of short pennants. Note
the drying of volume and the downslope of the pennant formations.
Source: R.W.Mansfield Co., 26 Journal Square, Jersey City, N.J. 07306
[*Trendlines by author*]

Flags And Pennants

Figure 2 illustrates the flag. A bull flag is a narrowly channelled, usually down-sloping consolidation on *steadily diminishing volume*, developing after a strong upmove. In the classic flag (or pennant, if the channel converges), volume must continue to diminish as the consolidation proceeds. When the sellers have become exhausted, a burst of buying pressure propels the stock out of its flag channel. The likely extent of the post-breakout move will be equal to the length of move that preceded the formation. Flags usually develop over a period of two to four weeks. Should the consolidation extend beyond three to four weeks, the bullish implication becomes suspect. Flags usually have a downward slope; however, they occasionally form sideways or, more occasionally, with a slight upwards bias. In the last case, they may be difficult to distinguish from wedges which carry an altogether different implication.

Bearish flags, interrupting declines, usually slant upwards but have the same volume characteristics as bullish flags and the same implication for a continuation of the pre-flag direction, in this case down.

Review

Pennants and flags favor a continuation of the pre-formation move. Volume must dry up as the formation develops. The formation should last no longer than four weeks. Buy immediately upon upside breakouts, particularly if it is accompanied by heavy volume. This is a rather reliable formation, but if the stock stalls on heavy volume following the breakout, be prepared to sell. Reverse for selling or short selling during intermediate or primary declines.

Flags and pennants are characteristic of rapid moves and occur most frequently during later phases of bull markets. However, this is not always the situation and, as usual, the total technical picture must be evaluated.

Triangles

Fairly frequently, we encounter chart formations which form nearly perfect triangles. These may develop as symmetrical triangles—both upper and lower boundaries converging, or as right triangles, ascending and descending. Ascending triangles are characterized by an upward sloping hypotenuse; descending triangles by a downward sloping hypotenuse.

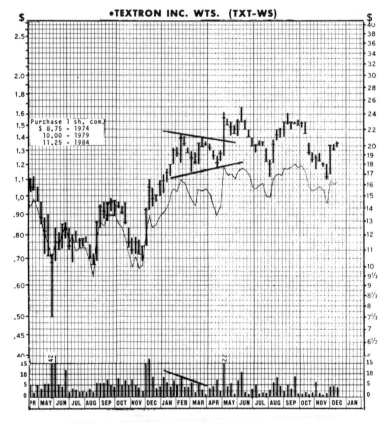

Figure 3

A symmetrical triangle: Note the converging lines and diminishing volume between January and March, and the volume increase on the breakout.
Source: Securities Research Co., 208 Newbury Street, Boston, Mass. 02116
[Trendlines by author]

Figures 3, 4 and 5 illustrate symmetrical, ascending and descending triangles respectively.

Triangles result from the battle between bullish and bearish operators. Following a market move, presume upwards, profit taking ensues driving stock prices down, to a point where bargain hunting sets in. Prices then rally, only to meet supply. These oscillations continue as the buyers and sellers come closer together, until the one side or the other becomes exhausted and a breakout from the formation takes place. According to Edwards and Magee (*Technical Analysis of Stock Trends*), three out of four triangles, and rectangles (described below) resolve as consolidation rather than reversal formations.

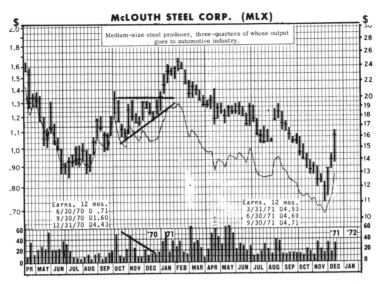

Figure 4

An ascending triangle, formed from October through December, 1970.
Source: Securities Research Co., 208 Newbury Street, Boston, Mass. 02116
[Trendlines by author]

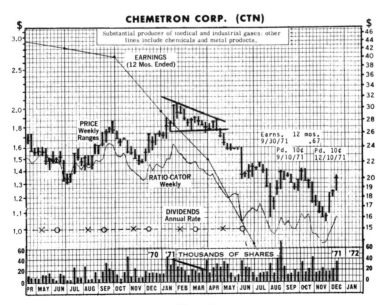

Figure 5

A descending triangle, January through March.
Source: Securities Research Co., 208 Newbury Street, Boston, Mass. 02116
[Trendlines by author]

Volume in any consolidation formation should diminish as the formation develops. Triangles are no exception to this rule. However, again, the breakout should be accompanied by a volume surge. It is difficult to predict in which direction the breakout will occur, although again the percentages favor the triangle's development as a consolidation pattern. Other indications can be taken from the action of other stocks within the same industry group and the market as a whole. One favorable indication arises from the action within the triangle itself. Since accumulation tends to occur at the lower end of trading ranges, it is more bullish if most activity has taken place near the lower area of the triangle.

Price Action Following Breakout

A breakout from a triangle usually carries a price objective equal to the length of the first rally which initiated the formation, measured from the breakout point. Figure 6 illustrates the measurement.

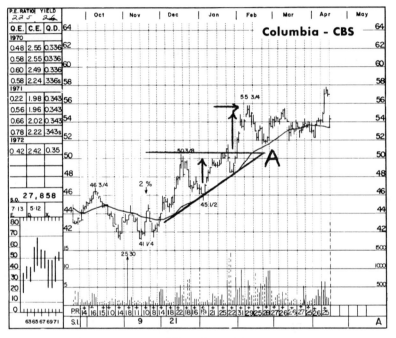

Figure 6

The arrows mark the count arising from the breakout. Note the volume surge on the breakout and the return to the apex at point A.
Source: R.W.Mansfield Co., 26 Journal Square, Jersey City, N.J. 07306
[Trendlines by author]

This objective will be likely of realization if the breakout occurs not too near the apex of the triangle. Moves that occur at or near the apex appear usually to have little force behind them. Following the breakout, usually before the price objective is reached, the stock will frequently retrace to or near the apex point of the triangle. This reaction provides an excellent secondary buying opportunity (reverse for downside breakout). The angle of the subsequent move will frequently be similar to the angle of the move that preceded the triangle formation.

Interestingly, while upside breakouts should be accompanied by heavy volume as a test of validity, downside breakouts on heavy volume are apt to be false, particularly if near the apex. Valid downside breakouts usually begin on more moderate volume, volume not increasing until a support level has been violated. From time to time, price objectives will not achieve realization and the triangle will develop into a rectangle. *C'est la vie.*

Rectangles

Figure 7

A classic rectangle.
Source: Securities Research Co., 208 Newbury Street, Boston, Mass. 02116
[*Trendlines by author*]

A rectangle consists of a series of alternating up and down price movements, the boundaries of which comprise a trading range which can be encompassed by parallel horizontal lines drawn across the tops and the bottoms. See Figure 7 for an illustration.

This action represents an even battle between buyers and sellers, continuing until the issue becomes finally resolved. Volume pattern is similar to triangle activity; and should diminish as the consolidation proceeds. However, examine whether peak volume spurts occur near the bottom areas of the rectangle (bullish) or near the top (bearish).

Rectangles are reliable formations and a breakout *on strong volume* carries high significance. A minimum price objective would be a distance from the breakout point equivalent to the depth of the rectangle. Broad rectangles can carry even greater price objectives. Price objectives may be determined by use of point and figure counting techniques (Chapter 4). A rough price and time objective can be obtained by measuring the width of the rectangle, projecting this distance vertically and placing the high point at a 45-degree angle from the base. (Figure 8.)

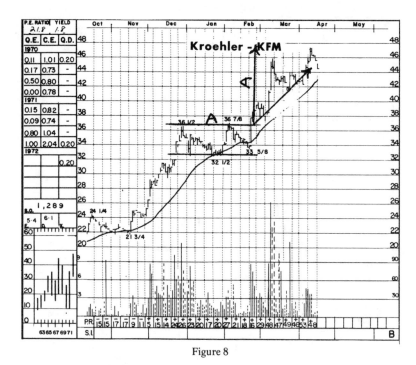

Figure 8

To set a price-time objective, measure the width of the rectangle (A).
Project it vertically (A). A 45 degree line drawn to the vertical height
indicates the approximate time required to reach the objective.
Source: R.W.Mansfield Co., 26 Journal Square, Jersey City, N.J. 07306
[*Trendlines by author*]

Trading Tactics

The disadvantage of initiating positions while a stock is trading within a rectangle lies in the uncertainty as to just when a breakout will occur. Rectangle formations can last for considerable periods of time. In contrast, triangles, by their converging lines, provide advance indications regarding potential breakout periods.

The breakout, to be valid, must occur on increasing spread and increasing volume. Initiate your positions either immediately or upon the first pullback. Some traders attempt to play the trading range, that is, to buy at the lower boundary of the rectangle and sell at the higher. This can be profitable if the depth of the rectangle is sufficient to cover commissions and provides sufficient profit potential to offset those occasions when you will be stopped out.

Formation System #2
Recognizing Reversal Patterns And Selecting The Proper Time To Act

We have defined reversal formations as chart formations that imply a basic reversal of the direction of price movement. We will limit this to reversals of at least intermediate magnitude, although reversal formations do appear with short term significance. In general, bottoms are more readily defined than tops which frequently round off rather than rebound sharply. The bottoms of the 1966 and 1970 bear markets were marked by climactic action and sharp upthrusts. By contrast, the 1966 and 1968 tops were several weeks in the making, and not nearly so dramatic in their formation.

The Head And Shoulders Top

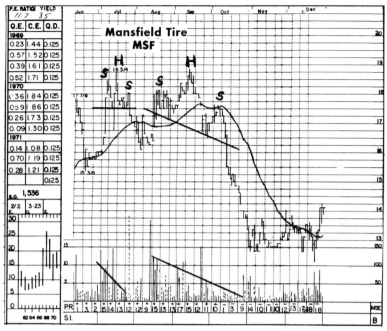

Figure 9

Mansfield Tire topped with two head and shoulders formations. Note how
the volume dried from the left to the right shoulder on both occasions.
Source: R.W.Mansfield Co., 26 Journal Square, Jersey City, N.J. 07306
[Trendlines by author]

The grand-daddy of all reversal formations is the head and shoulders top, a formation that is readily discerned, reliable and very significant. The 1966-1968 bull market ended with a head and shoulders formation. The rise from May 1970-April 1971 ended similarly.

The head and shoulders formation (Figure 9) is characterized by the following processes:

(1) There is a strong rally on heavy volume, followed by a dip on diminished volume. The peak of this rally comprises the left shoulder.

(2) There follows a subsequent rally, to a point above the first (the head), but on *lesser volume*, indicating that although a new high has been made, there is less buying pressure behind the move. This is followed by a dip roughly to the level of the preceding decline but in any case below the level of the left shoulder peak.

(3) There is a third rise on *still lesser volume*, which fails to make a new high. This comprises the right shoulder.

(4) Finally, a decline sets in which breaks below the support line created by connecting the two previous bottoms (neckline). This penetration may or may not occur on heavy volume.

(5) Following the penetration, there occurs usually a rally back to the neckline which should be used for liquidation or short selling.

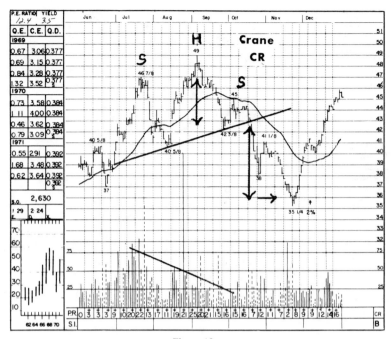

Figure 10

The arrows show the measurement from the neckline to the peak of the
head, carried almost precisely down from the penetration of the neckline.
Source: R.W.Mansfield Co., 26 Journal Square, Jersey City, N.J. 07306
[*Trendlines by author*]

A *minimum* downside price objective can be secured by measuring the distance from the neckline to the head, and then measuring this distance vertically from the neckline down from the point at which the neckline is penetrated (Figure 10). This is a rather reliable counting technique.

Review

The head and shoulders formation consists of three peaks, the middle peak being the highest. Volume confirmation occurs when volume diminishes with the formation respectively of each peak. *Volume confirmation is essential.* The formation is completed as prices penetrate the neckline.

Head and shoulders formations generally consist of three peaks and give a somewhat symmetrical appearance. However, we frequently encounter multiple head and shoulders formations including, for instance, two left and two right shoulders or multiple heads. The implications are similar except that the broader the formation, the more significant will be its completion. Although this is a highly reliable formation, false breakdowns do occur from time to time and the formation in effect becomes one of consolidation rather than reversal. Again, be certain that volume confirmation exists. Should the penetration of the neckline following the third decline not materialize, consider the threat itself as a preliminary sign of weakness; the stock in any case is probably near the termination of its bull move. Finally, since the head and shoulders is a reversal formation, it must have something to reverse. Valid head and shoulders formations follow strong upmoves or occur during major bear phases following intermediate rallies. Head and shoulders formations following extensive decline are not nearly so frequently valid.

The neckline within the formation may lie flat, or slant upwards or downwards. A downsloping neckline represents an added evidence of weakness, since the downside price objective is measured from the point of neckline penetration.

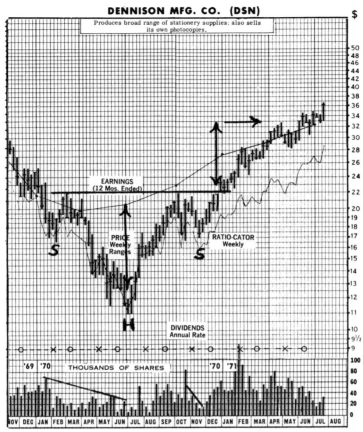

Figure 11

Dennison Mfg. Co. completed a nearly perfect, symmetrical inverse head and shoulders formation between January and November. Note how the eleven point measuring count was quickly achieved.
Source: Securities Research Co., 208 Newbury Street, Boston, Mass. 02116
[Trendlines by author]

Trading Tactics

The head and shoulders is such a significant formation that chartists are constantly alert to its presence. Some traders will sell upon their estimate that a head is forming. Others will anticipate the formation and sell as soon as the right shoulder begins to hunch down, particularly if its formation developed on light volume. Upon a penetration of the neckline, if long, liquidate either immediately or upon the first return to the neckline. Do not play games. Shorting can be instituted on the right shoulder with careful stops or upon the return to the neckline. In strong bull markets, you can look to acquire long positions following intermediate declines by placing buy orders at the downside price objective. Stocks, during bull markets frequently rebound sharply once their objectives have been met.

Head And Shoulders Bottoms

The head and shoulders bottom, or inverse head and shoulders, resembles the head and shoulders top, in reverse. Following a decline with heavy volume, the stock rallies, dips to a *lower low on lower volume*, rallies to a neckline, dips again on still lower volume. Following this action, on the next rise, *volume should increase noticeably* as the stock penetrates the neckline. (The head and shoulders top does not require heavy volume at the neckline penetration.) A minimum upside count is secured in the same manner, by measurement from the head to the neckline and projecting from the penetration point. Other methods of developing price objectives for head and shoulders formations are described in Chapter 4.

The head and shoulders bottom is likewise a highly reliable chart formation. The 1966 and 1969-1970 bear markets both ended in classical head and shoulders bottoms and the upside price objective derived from the related inverse head and shoulders formations proved very significant and quite exact.

Double Tops And Bottoms

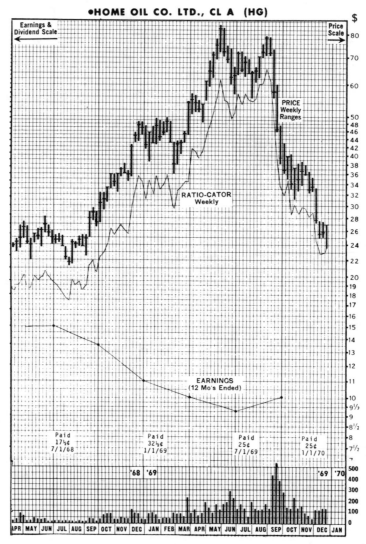

Figure 12

Source: Securities Research Co., 208 Newbury Street, Boston, Mass. 02116

A double top develops when a stock rallies to a level, declines into a valley, then rallies on lesser volume to a similar peak and finally declines below the support level created by the valley. The time between peaks is usually some months and the whole formation has major significance. Double bottoms consist of the same process in reverse. Triple tops and triple bottoms consist of three peaks and three low points. Validation occurs at the breakout. Double bottoms are worth gambling on, particularly if the stock begins to move up from the second bottom on increasing volume. Figure 12, a chart of Home Oil Ltd., shows a classic double top, formed between May and August.

The Broadening Formation

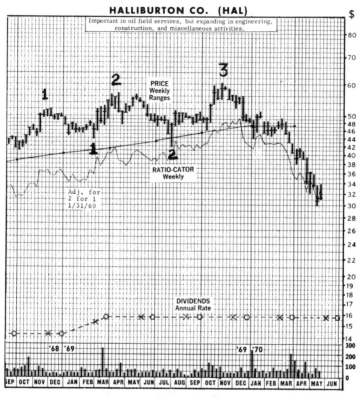

Figure 13

Source: Securities Research Co., 208 Newbury Street, Boston, Mass. 02116
[Numbered peaks and troughs by author]

This is a top formation, associated with the tail end of speculative moves, during which phase price movements are subject to wide fluctuation. The formation is characterized by a sequence in which a stock shows three peaks at successively higher levels, interrupted by two bottoms, the second lower than the first. The formation is complete when the stock price penetrates the level of the second bottom.

This is a less frequently encountered formation than the head and shoulders, but carries roughly the same measuring implications. However, the volume activity is different. Whereas volume dries up as a head and shoulders formation progresses, the broadening top forms amidst increasing speculation and volume increases during the formation's creation. Figure 13, Halliburton Co., illustrates the broadening formation. The three peaks are numbered, as are the two bottoms. Note the ascending peaks, the descending bottoms and the gradual increase in volume.

Wedge Formations

The wedge is not a primary formation but can carry strong intermediate or lesser minor significance. The rising wedge consists of two upwards slanting but converging lines, a sort of triangle, but one in which the upper boundary is uptrended. Volume *diminishes* as the move progresses. The wedge indicates that although the

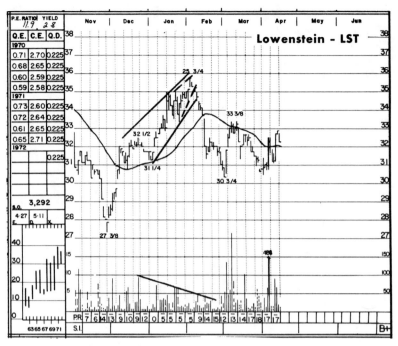

Figure 14

Source: R.W. Mansfield Co., 26 Journal Square, Jersey City, N.J. 07306
[Trendlines by author]

stock is making new highs, its days of glory are numbered. Many intermediate advances end in wedge formations. Occasionally, prices break upwards from a wedge in one last burst and then decline. Most often, prices decline rapidly from a wedge possibly with one last return rally to the wedge point. The downside objective after the breakout is at least to the price level at which the volume began to decline, possibly further. Wedges or weak rallies (no volume follow through) are common in bear markets. The wedge formation itself is likely to be composed of five segments, three up and two down, the whole formation comprising the last leg of an intermediate move.

As rising wedges are bearish, so falling wedges are frequently quite bullish. These are characterized by decreasing volume as the stock converges to new lows. The March 1968 decline ended in a falling wedge, but most often prices do not shoot as directly upwards from a falling wedge. Figure 14 illustrates the wedge. Note the large wedge formation and the smaller wedge within as Lowenstein topped out, the diminishing volume on the rise, and the rapid breakdown in price.

Trading Tactics

Sell instantly upon your stock's breakdown from a wedge. It is not advisable to sell upon the mere suspicion of a wedge; prices often carry further than one might think. However, the threat of a breakdown should alert you to be particularly careful regarding trendlines or for possible short sale operations. A top wedge is sometimes difficult to tell on a chart from the action of a stock when it is digesting overhead supply, and actually consolidating. Should the stock be early in a move, suspect the latter, particularly during early bull moves. Late in an intermediate move, suspect a true wedge top.

The breakdown from wedge formations is sharp; however, a sharp rally following the breakdown back to the trendline often follows. This provides a second chance to get out or an opportunity to feed out shorts. Act quickly.

Saucer Bottoms And Tops

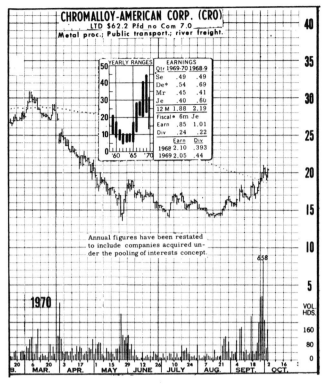

Figure 15

A saucer bottom: The volume pattern conforms to the saucer shape of
the formation and begins to expand early in the move.
Source: Trendline Daily Basis Stock Charts, 345 Hudson Street,
New York, N.Y. 10014

Saucer bottoms are encountered fairly frequently; my own estimate is that saucer tops appear somewhat less frequently.

The saucer bottom is the end result of a decline that loses its force gradually. Volume, near the conclusion of the decline slackens and the stock gradually drifts downwards to sidewise on diminishing volumd. This is a slow formation. The subsequent rise begins very slowly, gradually accelerating both in upward price movement and in parallel volume increase as the move progresses. The bull move that follows may result finally in a very strong and protracted advance or in a truncated rally carrying no further upwards on the right than the left rim of the saucer (for bottom saucers).

Trading Tactics

The initial strong upthrust on good volume may be only the first leg of a major move. Positions may be taken on the first pullback into the saucer center. This is a good formation in which to assume low risk positions, if one is patient. These can be taken often very close to the bottom of the formation. If you suspect a saucer, be alert to any volume increase which often slightly precedes price mark-up and initiate positions *in advance* of price breakout. If the volume increase is noticeable, initiate positions quickly. Frequently, price increase will follow shortly. The On-Balance Volume techniques described in Chapter 2 work very well with saucer formations.

Saucer formations may also appear as consolidations, following an upmove—the stock correcting in a saucer. Trading tactics are similar to the above, but the total formation may take less time in its development.

The volume characteristics of rounding tops are not similar to the saucer bottom. The volume pattern of the true saucer bottom has a characteristic saucer shape in itself, usually matching the price action quite precisely. The volume action in rounding tops is irregular, with spurts here and there. The pattern is therefore more difficult to identify and may resemble a head and shoulders.

Rectangles And Triangles

These have already been described as consolidation formations. However, although this is usually the case for these formations, a number of rectangles and triangles do resolve as reversal formations. Bearish implications may be drawn if the volume does not gradually diminish during the development of the formation, but rather remains high or irregular.

One And Two Day Reversals

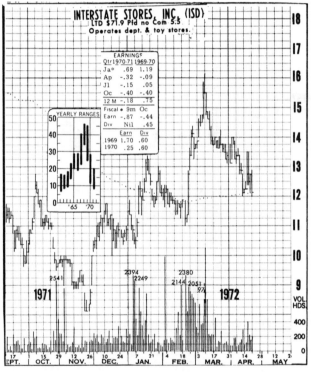

Figure 16

A two day reversal: Interstate Stores, Inc., topped in only two days, between March 9 and 10. Note the price and volume spikes, the stock closing the second day at its daily lows.
Source: Trendline Daily Basis Stock Charts, 345 Hudson Street, New York, N.Y. 10014

These actions were described in Chapter 2 during the discussion of buying and selling climaxes. Essentially the action consists of one or two days of climactic price-volume activity, with the price trend sharply reversing on heavy volume. The formation appears as a spike. The highs or lows may be subsequently tested but the reversal day itself implies a forthcoming change in direction.

Similar action sometimes follows a breakout, for instance, the stock following an upside breakout, backing and filling on heavy volume. This is *not* always a reversal but rather a high volume test of the breakout. The issue becomes resolved when the stock again reverses to the upside. This process usually takes no longer than a few days. If you missed the original breakout, get in on the subsequent move.

Gaps

A gap appears on bar charts as a space between the high of one day and the low of the day following (if upside) or the low of one day and the high of the following (if downside). It represents an area, the prices within which no trading took place. For instance, if a stock trades Thursday between 32 and 33, opens Friday at 33½ and goes no lower, the space between 33 and 33½ will appear as a gap in the chart. Occasionally, gaps appear in the market averages (the April 1968 and the August 1971 rallies), but with much less frequency than in individual stock charts.

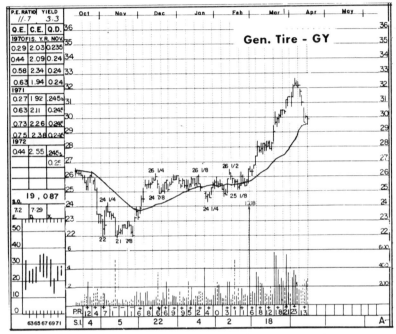

Figure 17

Source: R.W. Mansfield Co., 26 Journal Square, Jersey City, N.J. 07306

Area Gaps

These occur within trading ranges and usually have no particular significance. Area gaps are marked by moderate volume, occur within congestion areas, are generally shortly filled on the chart. Area gaps are quite common. Examine Figure 17. Note the number of gaps within the consolidation from November through February and how rapidly there were filled.

Breakaway Gaps

These have much greater significance. Breakaway gaps, as the name implies, develop as a stock breaks out of a consolidation area. The breakout may be from a triangle, a rectangle, a head and shoulders neckline. Sometimes these gaps are closed in subsequent trading; sometimes, they are not. If the breakaway gap develops, with heavy volume on the far side of the congestion area from which the stock emerged, the gap is less likely to be filled than if the gap occurred on light volume. In the latter case, the gap is likely to be filled. Questor broke away from its congestion area on heavy volume in February, leaving two gaps along the way. Only the second was subsequently filled.

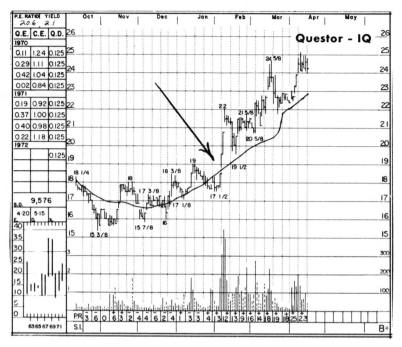

Figure 18

Source: R.W. Mansfield Co., 26 Journal Square, Jersey City, N.J. 07306
[Arrow by author]

Continuation Gaps

Occasionally, during the course of a strong move, a gap will develop within the movement of a stock. These do not occur at the point that the stock breaks from a consolidation, but rather right at the *mid-point* of an advance or decline, not near any congestion area. These gaps are also referred to as measuring gaps because they can be used to estimate the probable extent of the subsequent moves to follow. These gaps are not necessarily closed for some time. The arrow (Figure 19) points to the continuation gap in the chart of Weyerhaeuser which almost perfectly bisected the move from 44-52.

Exhaustion Gaps

Exhaustion gaps signify the completion of a move. As contrasted to continuation gaps, exhaustion gaps occur on high volume days, prices slow to advance. The prime danger signal takes place the day after the gap, if prices fail to advance or, more significantly, decline. This is all the more likely if measurements by previous measuring gaps, point and figure techniques or channel study, indicate that price objectives have been met. Exhaustion gaps close rapidly. Channel study indicated that the third gap in Figure 20 was an exhaustion gap. This indication was confirmed by subsequent price action.

Trading Tactics

To a large degree, trading tactics are implicit in the descriptions of the gaps above. Quick traders can hop onto continuation gaps since the moves that follow are generally sharp and quite profitable. It has to be kept in mind, however, that measuring gaps present little support during declines and little resistance to advance. False shakeouts often involve light volume, downside gap action. These gaps are readily filled as the market turns.

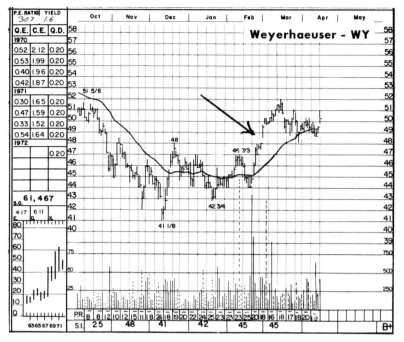

Figure 19

Source: R.W. Mansfield Co., 26 Journal Square, Jersey City, N.J. 07306
[Arrow by author]

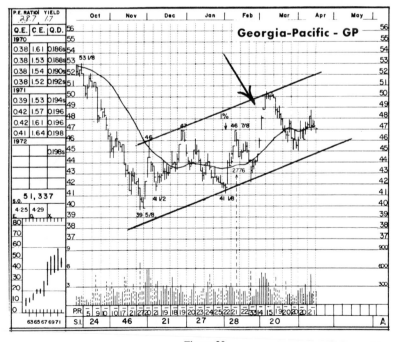

Figure 20

The arrow points to the exhaustion gap near the upper channel boundary.
Source: R.W. Mansfield Co., 26 Journal Square, Jersey City, N.J. 07306
[Trendlines by author]

I place most of my trading orders at the market opening, if I really want the stock, sometimes at the market and sometimes with a limit one-quarter point above the previous day's close. This allows for some gap from the last day's price, but not so large a gap that some fill during the day will be unlikely. On most occasions, a gap on the opening will be filled during the day, at least partially. So, if short, and the market opens on a gap, try to cover somewhere between the opening price and the previous day's close. Do not play for the fill of the complete gap; you can get annihilated while trying to save twenty-five dollars. If you *really* like a stock, just put in a market order and forget about gaps. I remember that, in 1968, International Industries had just completed an inverse head and shoulders and looked great on the chart. It closed one day at 39. I put in an order at 39-1/4 to buy. The stock opened at 39-5/8, backed down only to 39-1/2 and took off promptly to 56. I waited some 16 odd points for that half point gap to fill. Needless to say, by the time it did fill I wanted no more of International Industries.

chapter four

POINT AND FIGURE SYSTEMS:
X MARKS THE SPOT

Up to now, we have been largely using bar charts in our work. This chapter will deal with point and figure charting, a system favored by many technicians particularly because of its abilities to yield price objectives for stock and market movements.

Point and figure charts have, as contrasted to bar charts, the following advantages:

(1) They require little physical space to maintain. This makes possible broader market coverage by charting services at lower price and simpler home construction.

(2) In most instances, fewer entries have to be recorded. Only significant price changes require entry.

(3) It is readily feasible to include long periods of stock movement within a given chart.

(4) Intra-day fluctuations are recorded, which can be very significant for active stocks.

(5) Price objectives are readily discerned from the charts.

The limitations involved in point and figure charting arise largely from the absence of volume data, the significance of which has already been reviewed.

Point and figure charts are adaptable to trendline study and in many cases to formation work, although again the lack of volume data frequently renders formation interpretation difficult.

In my own experience, I have found a combined use of point and figure and bar charting most helpful. If I had to express a preference, however, it would be towards bar charting, largely because of volume study considerations. Keep in mind, though, that this is my personal preference—many other technicians do take an opposing point of view. Bar chart and point and figure signals frequently occur simultaneously; sometimes the one or the other renders the more precise signal.

Point and figure charts are, again, simple to construct and to maintain. They can be set up to sensitively reflect daily price fluctuations or to reflect long term trends. All that is needed for plotting is squared graph paper. However, special point and figure charting sheets, marked at five or ten point intervals, simplify construction and study.

Point and figure charts are constructed in the following manner. We will employ, as an example, the use of a one point reversal system. This means that one point changes in price direction are considered sufficiently significant for entry. In a one point system, all fractions of prices are ignored; only price changes to a whole number are entered. Let us assume a stock starting in the $20.00 area. Scale the chart from 15-40. Entries are marked by placing X's within the squares of the graph paper. The squares rather than the lines are scaled.

Price movement of the stock	**Point and figure price changes**
Advances from 19½ - 22	Record 20 - 21 - 22
Declines to 21¼	No recording (Fraction, ignored).
Advances to 22¾	No recording (Fraction, ignored).
Declines to 19	21 - 20 - 19

A price reversal has taken place, that is, a recordable change in direction. Upon a change in direction from down to up or up to down, it is necessary to move to the next column since the square 21 in column 1 has been previously occupied. We will stay now in the second column until a reversal upside takes place. However, when new columns contain only one entry it is the second entry which determines the direction of the column. No column can have only a single entry.

Advance to 20

Record 20 (New column).

The chart now appears as follows:

```
    x
    xx
20  xxx
    x
```

Decline to 19

Record 19 (Same column. Since there was only one previous reversal entry we continue in the same column. Square 19, column 3, was not previously occupied.)

The chart now appears as follows:

```
    x
    xx
20  xxx
    xx
```

Advance to 24

Record 20-21-22-23-24. (New column required. Square 20, column 3, previously occupied).

Advance to 28

Record 25-26-27-28

```
30
        x
        x
        x
25      x
        x
        x
    x   x
    xx  x
20  xxxx
    xx

15
```

Advance to 30-1/2

Record 29-30

Advance to 31-7/8

Record 31

Decline to 30-1/8

No entry (Disregard fractions)

Decline to 26-1/2

Record 30-29-28-27 (New column)

Advance to 36

Record 28-29-30-31-32-33-34-35-36 (New column)

Decline to 34-1/2

Record 35 (New column)

Advance to 40

Record 36-37-38-39-40 (No new column)

The complete chart appears as follows:

```
40      x
        x
        x
        x
        xx
35      xx
        x
        x
        x
      x x
30    xxx
      xxx
      xxx
      xx
      x
25    x
      x
      x
   x  x
   xx x
20 xxxx
   xx
```

For lower price stocks, under $20.00 per share, reversals may be plotted at one-half point intervals in the areas below 20 with a switch to a full point scale above 20. This allows for the determination of more significant price reversals than otherwise would show. For high price stocks, such as I.B.M., three or five point reversal units may be employed. In the latter case, each box will be scaled at the fifth point (300, 305, 310), and only reversals to these five point intervals are considered significant and recordable. A two, three or five point scale for high price or very active stocks eliminates the need for very frequent entries while still preserving the over-all representation. Figure 1 shows a one point reversal point and figure chart of Joy Manufacturing and Figure 2 shows its condensation into a two point reversal chart.

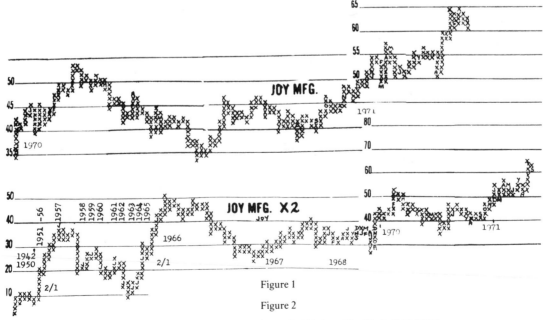

Figure 1

Figure 2

Source: Andrews Technical Studies, 119 Fifth Ave., New York, N.Y. 10003

All recordable intra-day fluctuations are entered into point and figure charts. If you wish, you may mark the first entry for each month with the initial of the month and also mark the changes of year. This will provide some perspective as to the extent of the stock's activity and volatility. *Paflibe*, an excellent point and figure chartbook, records the previous week's activity with diagonal lines rather than X's. This indicates the recent volatility of the stock under investigation.

Points To Remember

(1) Only changes to a full reversal unit are recorded.

(2) Remain in one column while the price direction remains constant.

(3) Change columns when the price direction reverses.

(4) No column can have just one entry in a completed chart, except for the very last entry.

(5) In the event of a price gap between trades, the intervening prices must be filled in with entrees (unlike a bar chart).

The Application Of Trendlines To Point And Figure Charts

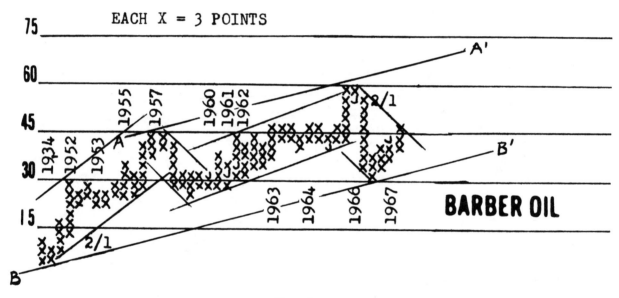

Figure 3

The long term channel of Barber Oil, and shorter term channels.
Souce: Andrews Technical Studies, 119 Fifth Ave., New York, N.Y. 10003

Point and Figure charts are adaptable to trendline and channel study in the same manner as bar charts. Figure 3 demonstrates trendline construction and channeling with such charts.

Point And Figure System #1
Determining The Count

Analysis of congestion areas provides the means for determining the probable extent of market moves. The term "congestion area" refers to sidewise price activity within a trading range which can occur during a base (accumulation), as an interruption of a move (consolidation) or as part of a top (distribution). The fluctuations within the congestion area represent the temporary balance between the forces of supply and demand, until either buying or selling pressures predominate. The direction of the breakout indicates retrospectively whether the process within the congestion area signified distribution or accumulation. However, as we will discuss below, study of the congestion area itself frequently provides clues as to the ultimate direction of the breakout.

There is a definite correlation between the width of the congestion area and the extent of the move to follow the breakout. The wider the congestion area, the more extensive the accumulation or distribution activity signified by its formation, the further will moves subsequent to a breakout carry. This holds particularly true for active trading stocks which often achieve quite precise counts. To establish the price objective following an upside breakout, simply measure the count line, the bottom line (or most occupied row) of the congestion area. Use as a measure its width, measured in the number of squares, including blank squares. Carry this count in squares vertically from the count line. The result is the count or price objective for the move. For downside breakouts, measure across the highest row of the congestion area or a near highest row having the most occupied squares. If the count from the most occupied row is different from the count inferred from the top or bottom row, the price objectives determined will lie within the differing ranges so projected. Figure 4 illustrates this procedure. The arrows point to the row from which the count was taken. Note the exact workout of the objective.

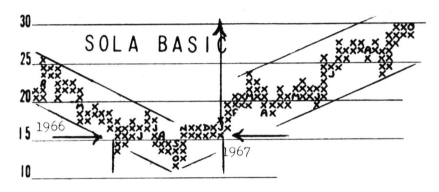

Figure 4

The count is taken across the fifteen line, and is fifteen squares wide. The width, projected vertically, yields a price objective of 30
Source: Andrews Technical Studies, 119 Fifth Avenue,
New York, N.Y. 10003
[Trendlines by author]

Remember, the count that is projected vertically is based upon the width in squares of the congestion area and that is measured vertically *in squares*. Thus, on a one point reversal chart, each square across represents one point of price objective because each vertical square is scaled at one point. In a five point reversal chart each square across will represent five points of objective because each vertical square is scaled at five point intervals.

This procedure is clear for congestion areas bounded by vertical lines or walls. Keep in mind, however, that counts are taken across only one horizontal price line. You do not cross lines to make a count. Many charts do not show clear vertical walls from which to derive counts. Either one or both walls may slant. In this case, use as your count line a line towards the lower center of the congestion area having the most occupied squares. See Figure 5.

Occasionally, a congestion area will develop in the form of a V, either right side up or inverted. These V's will frequently show on either or both sides, a few squares separated from the V formation, neighboring upthrusts or downthrusts, forming adjacent walls. The count in these cases is taken across the lines bounded by these extensions. Such formations often derive as the point and figure representations of head and shoulder formations. In these situations, the side upthrusts or downthrusts represent the shoulder peaks. See Figure 6 and Figure 7 for a point and figure head and shoulders and the same action noted on a bar chart. Note the counting line which should be employed, Figure 7.

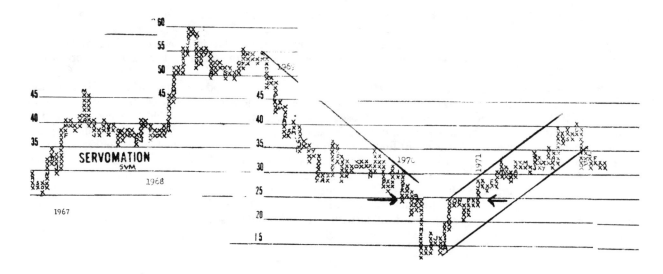

Figure 5

The count in this V formation is taken across the 24 line. The price objective for the upmove was 41.

Source: Andrews Technical Studies, 119 Fifth Avenue,
New York, N.Y. 10003
[Trendlines by author]

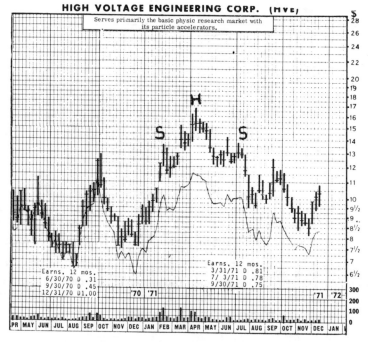

Figure 6

Source: Securities Research Co., 208 Newbury Street, Boston, Mass. 02116

Figures 6 and 7 show the price action of High Voltage Engineering between 1970-1971. The arrows on Figure 7 define the head and shoulders formation marked on Figure 6. The downside count is taken along the 15 line, with a secondary count taken along the 14 line. The average of the downside objectives so determined is 9, which objective was reached in October, 1971.

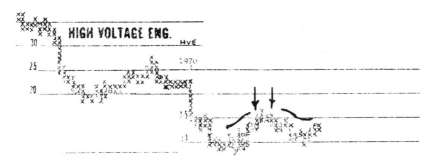

Figure 7

Source: Andrews Technical Studies, 119 Fifth Ave., New York, N.Y. 10003.

Many congestion areas are segmented, that is, the total base is broken up by temporary upthrusts, the stock then retreating back to the base and expanding the congestion area. In this situation the total base represents the ultimate count. Each segment represents possible intermediate or short term objectives, with consolidation likely at the levels indicated by partial counts. Thus, the last segment formed may indicate the first price objective; the last segment plus the one previous a second price objective and the total base, the major objective. Figure 8 illustrates the segmented count and a successful workout.

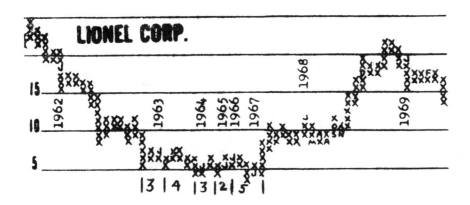

Figure 8

The segments of the base of Lionel have been marked off. An initial rally to 10 was indicated, followed by rallies to 12, 15, 19 and 22. Note how closely the actual upthrusts conformed to these indication. Figure 8 also illustrates the principle of the secondary count, taken across line 9. The primary count along line 5 yielded an objective of 23. The secondary count yielded an objective of 19. The average objective, 21, represented the actual high.
Source: Andrews Technical Studies, 119 Fifth Avenue,
New York, N.Y. 10003

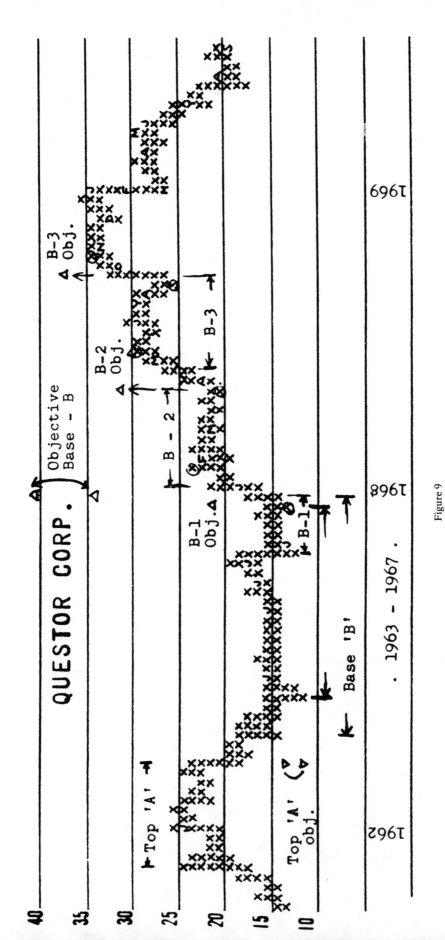

Figure 9

The workout of the primary base was confirmed by the workouts of the secondary congestion areas.
Source: Andrews Technical Studies. 119 Fifth Ave.. New York. N.Y. 10003

Another frequent action is one in which, following a breakout from a base, count partially achieved, the stock pauses in a consolidation, developing a secondary congestion area, rarely as wide as the base. A secondary count taken in this area often confirms the initial count which adds to the odds that the initial count is valid. Occasionally, there is even a third consolidation area, which does likewise. Caution is advised, however, if the secondary congestion area develops a width greater than the base. This may represent a reversal top rather than a continuation consolidation. Figure 9 demonstrates secondary congestion areas, confirming the base count, and their workout.

Very broad base counts may be overly optimistic if the complete base is employed for count study. More realistic intermediate counts, for upside moves, might be achieved if the segment of the base to the right of the lowest downthrust is employed.

Counts should be modified to some extent in the following situations. In strong bull markets, stocks tend to overshoot upside counts and to not quite achieve downside counts. The reverse holds true in bear markets. The presence of heavy supply directly overhead will mitigate against full upside count realization, particularly if the supply exists near the area where the count runs out. For instance, a stock moving up from 35, towards an objective of 50, will have difficulty passing through supply at 48 because its technical condition has already been weakened by the extent of its previous rise. Again the inverse is true regarding support areas and declines.

Point And Figure System #2
How To Predict The Direction Of A Breakout

The first thing to do in coming to a decision regarding the probable direction of the next move from a congestion area is to evaluate whether the stock has achieved its last objective. In other words, should a stock have moved from a long base upwards in three waves, count achieved, and develop a congestion area—the probabilities have increased that the next significant move will be down, particularly if a downside breakout has occurred. Conversely, a congestion area formed far short of the price objective is likely to be resolved in the original direction of the move, particularly if previous counts in the reverse direction have been achieved. Or, to clarify, presume a stock has dropped from 50 to 24, at which level it forms a large congestion area. Check the original top congestion count in the fifty area. Should 24 represent a thorough workout, the percentages favor the move from the 24 area to be towards the upside. This is *probable,* not positive.

Examination of the congestion area itself often provides useful clues as to whether accumulation or distribution is taking place. Accumulation congestions are weighted at the bottom, most reversals taking place near the lower limits of the trading range. This occurs because during the process of accumulation there is little distribution taking place. Retreats from upthrusts are sharp; there is little topside churning. Therefore, look to see that the most occupied row is closer to the bottom than the top of the congestion area. If the congestion area is wide, it is possible for the left side to appear top heavy, while the center of gravity appears to move down as the congestion area develops. This indicates a change in the underlying tone from distribution to accumulation.

The most bullish congestion areas usually slant downwards at a moderate slope, are flat, or appear as a scoop or dish shape. Congestion areas that slant mildly upwards, with most of the work at the top are potentially quite dangerous. We have seen that bullish consolidation formations (flags, pennants) slope downwards while bearish rising wedges slope upwards. The same principles *usually* apply to point and figure formations. A break above the down trendline of a long, mildly declining congestion area can be extremely profitable. (Figure 10).

A third factor to consider is the proximity of nearby congestion areas above the congestion area in formation. If there are nearby congestion areas, wider in scope, directly above, penetration through these is not likely until the most recent trading range develops at least as many squares in width as the supply area overhead. We have seen this principle already in the previous discussion of support and resistance levels. A typical action should a stock attempt to rally out of an insufficient base through heavy overhead is for the rally to fail and for the stock to then retreat either back to the base or near to it for further work. (Figure 11).

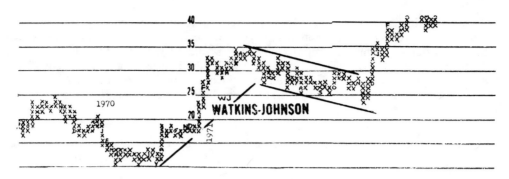

Figure 10

A very bullish, downsloping consolidation. Note the rapid price movement following the breakout.
Source: Andrews Technical Studies, 119 Fifth Ave., New York, N.Y. 10003

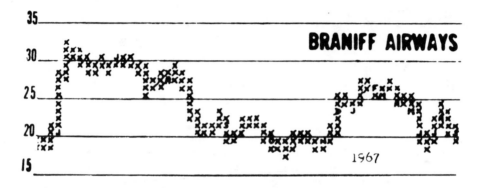

Figure 11

Twice, Braniff had insufficient base accumulation to penetrate overhead
supply. First, it could not penetrate through the 30 area. A subsequent
attempt to rally through supply at 25 also failed.
*Source: Andrews Technical Studies, 119 Fifth Avenue,
New York, N.Y. 10003*

And finally, examination of the market and stocks in the same industry groups usually infers the ultimate direction of a breakout. If other stocks in the same industry are breaking topside, the stock under investigation is likely to follow. Of course, the major and intermediate trends of the overall market carry implications for individual stocks.

Point And Figure System #3
The Safest Method Of Taking Positions

We will assume that you are going to take a long position in a stock. Later on in this chapter we will discuss point and figure formations and breakout signals. But first, we should keep in mind that the loss-cut point remains the same regardless of whether you take your position at the extreme bottom of the congestion area, in the middle or upon a breakout above the area. Your risk, then, increases the higher from the low point you initiate action. Conversely, purchases at the extreme low carry the least risk since your stop will always be placed one or two points under the trading range. Of course, you sacrifice speed for safety in purchasing near the lows, but since the name of the game is to avoid serious loss, this procedure is recommended for at least some of your trades. First, to sum up, evaluate the following:

(1) Has your stock achieved its last downside count, preferably through three downwaves or minimally two?

(2) Is the base now developing at least as wide as the congestion areas above? If not, is the stock sufficiently

active to infer completion of the necessary base-building within a reasonable period of time?

(3) Does analysis of the congestion area indicate that accumulation is taking place?

(4) Is the potential count large enough to make the whole trip worthwhile?

(5) Optional but very positive—have significant downtrendlines been broken?

(6) Are related stocks moving up? Is the market in an early bullish phase?

If the answer to *all* of these questions is "yes", you would be well justified in initiating long positions near the lows of a congestion area in anticipation of an upside breakout. With this procedure, you have reduced your risk to a minimum, increased your risk-reward ratio to its maximum and are operating in the most professional manner. It is well worth scouring your chartbook for situations that meet these criteria. You can be right one-third of the time and still make money. Reverse the above for taking short positions.

Point And Figure System #4
Establishing A Risk-Reward Ratio

Here is where point and figure charting really shines. The procedure is quite simple. We will again assume an initiation of long positions. Take the count from the applicable congestion area. Measure the distance from the current price of the stock to its probable (not fantasy) objective. Result: potential profit. Measure distance from current price to stop loss point. If the stock is within a consolidation congestion area, the stop will be placed just below that range, not beneath the major base. Establish a ratio between potential gain and potential loss. Remember, we haven't included commissions, the house tab. You should shoot for a risk-reward ratio of no less than 3-1, preferably at least 4-1, on your side. Let your winners ride until price objectives are reached or stops are triggered. Take any losses as soon as your stops are hit, quickly and with no regret. This way your winners will be worthwhile and your losses small. Operations will be quite profitable if you are right half the time. In fact, as noted above, you will probably make money if even just thirty-five to forty per cent of your trades resolve favorably.

Support And Resistance Areas

We have already observed that heavy congestion areas above stock impede upwards price movement. The support and resistance rules for point and figure charting are similar to those of bar charting. Each successive congestion area, developed during an uptrend will represent a support level against decline as the move progresses and a support level later on against subsequent decline. Each congestion area left during a decline becomes a resistance area against subsequent advance. In bar charting, we looked to the amount of volume at support and resistance levels to determine the strength of the support and/or resistance zone. In point and figure work, we look to the width of the area, measured by its number of squares. During uptrends, the effective zone of support is usually just above or at the top of congestion areas. However, if a congestion area shows pockets within it at the upper to middle ranges, there is at least a fair chance that tests of support in that area will involve the stock's price, retreating to fill these pockets, down to the levels of the most occupied row. Top formations are frequently signalled by a stock, after a long advance, breaking out upside from a top congestion area and then retreating back within it, right down to the bottom of the trading range. The implications for a false breakout are so strong here that sales may be initiated upon any strength, or certainly should the stock rally to the top of the congestion area once again.

These considerations do not hold true following a long decline. During base building processes, it is common action for stocks to break upside from their base and then retreat to the lows. However, it is *very bullish* if a stock breaks sharply below its base and then rallies back to the top of the congestion area (the reverse of topping formations). It is even more bullish if the stock can directly rally through the congestion area.

Point And Figure System #5
Identifying The Most Bullish Point And Figure Formation

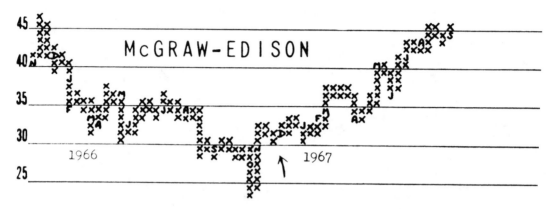

Figure 12

A basic change in trend was indicated as the stock penetrated the supply at 29.
Source: Andrews Technical Studies, 119 Fifth Ave., New York, N.Y. 10003

The most bullish action for any stock is a demonstration of ability to penetrate overhead supply. This is particularly true following a sustained decline. The ability to penetrate overhead following a decline signifies the end of the decline and a reversal of at least intermediate proportions. The characteristic of the chart pattern observed in Figure 12 is the breakdown from a wide congestion area, with severe downside implications. This is followed by an immediate reversal up through the congestion area. Usually, further work is required just above the congestion area, or occasionally within it. However, following this action, the stock will almost always move significantly higher. Occasionally, this pattern is predictable. Prediction may be made if the previous downmove has taken place in two waves, followed by a sidewise congestion movement through the downtrend line. The third and last downwave frequently occurs in the form of a false downbreak, ending at or near the reverse side of the downtrend line. (Figure 13). Look for this formation following severe market declines; it is very profitable. Purchases may be made on the first pullback after supply has been penetrated.

Shows the downtrend to the point where the downtrend was broken. The downside objective of $7 to $13 *has not* been reached. Although this is probably the left side of the base area, the downside objective will very often be reached during the construction of the base area. By extending the downtrend line, the price will very often use the line as a support.

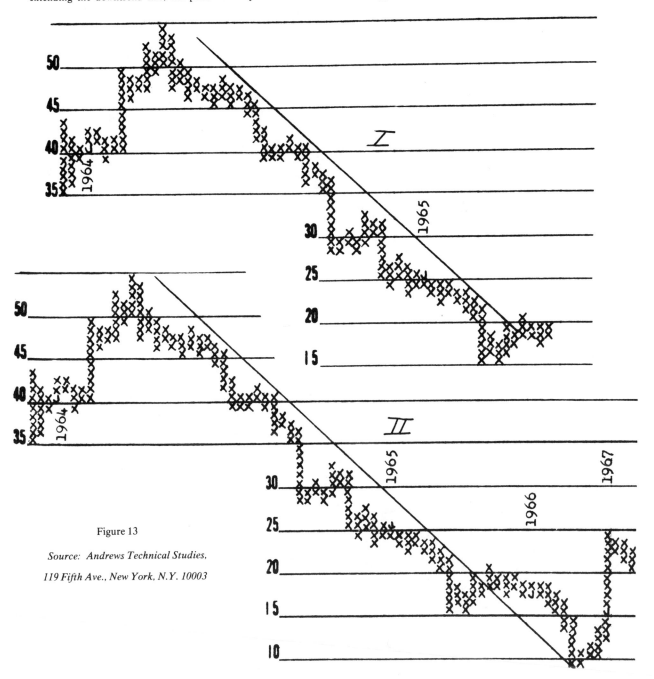

Figure 13

Source: Andrews Technical Studies,

119 Fifth Ave., New York, N.Y. 10003

Shows the price receding to the down-trend line and holding there. The price then reversed itself and for the first time during the long down-trend was able to crash thru supply—$15 to $20—and reach $24 on the move.

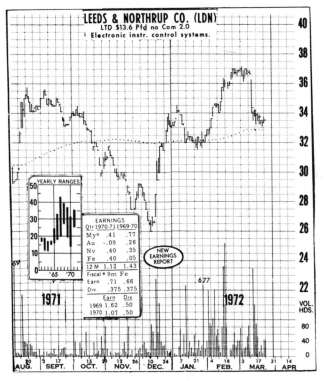

Figure 14

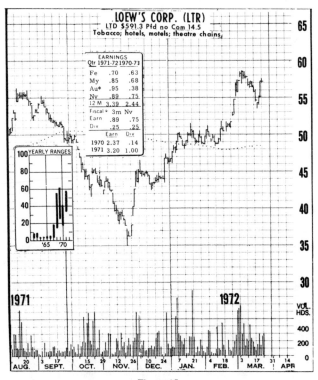

Figure 15

Source: Trendline Daily Basis Stock Charts, 345 Hudson Street, New York, N.Y. 10014

Figures 14, 15, 16 all demonstrate similar bullish action, the ability of stocks to rally directly through overhead supply. Compare to Figures 12 and 13.

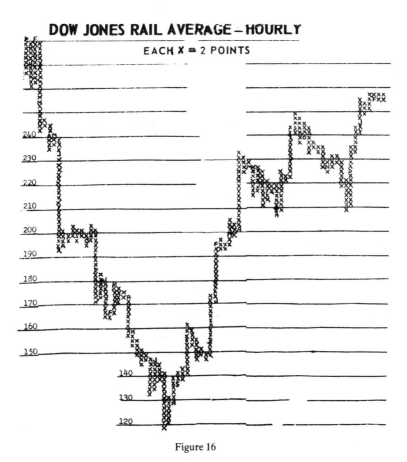

Figure 16

Source: Andrews Technical Studies, 119 Fifth Ave., New York, N.Y. 10003

Figures 14 and 15 are bar chart equivalents of these patterns. They are typical in that the last shakeouts occur with gaps, on light volume and actually present little resistance to subsequent rallies. Incidentally, the market decline from September-November 1971, ended in almost exactly the Figure 12 formation (Figure 16).

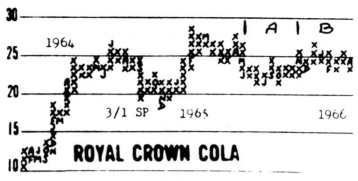

Figure 17

The fulcrum formation lies in the area A. Note the mid-fulcrum rally, the retest of the lows, the additional base building, and the catapult. The work in area B is necessary because the base is not sufficiently extensive for penetration of overhead supply at 25.
Source: Andrews Technical Studies, 119 Fifth Avenue, New York, N.Y. 10003

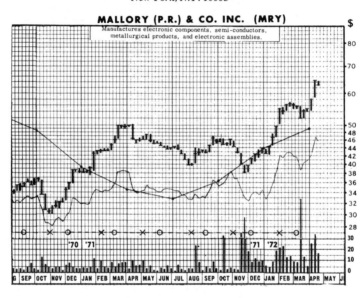

Figure 18

A fulcrum was formed between April and January, the mid-fulcrum rally developing from July-October.
Source: Securities Research Co., 208 Newbury Street, Boston, Mass. 02116

Point And Figure System #6
The Fulcrum

The classic point and figure breakout formation is the fulcrum, illustrated in Figure 17. Figure 18 is the bar chart equivalent. The fulcrum represents an accumulation area (inverse fulcrum; distribution), usually but not always following a market decline. Within this area, stock is being accumulated in preparation for an upmove, the scope of which will depend upon the width of the fulcrum base.

The fulcrum is characterized by (1) a decline in the stock (usual, but optional; sometimes fulcrum formations occur as major consolidation areas); (2) sidewise price movement within a trading base; (3) a short rally out of the base, followed by a retest of the lows; (4) more sidewise action and (5) a breakout above the mid-fulcrum highs by at least one full charting unit. This is a buy signal, called the "catapult". Purchases may be initiated upon the formation of the catapult, upon the first pullback thereafter, or within the base, upon a downtrend break. Figure 19 illustrates buy points, and the count line.

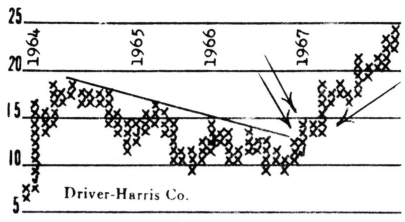

Figure 19

This chart illustrates a classic compound fulcrum. Buy points are marked
with arrows. The upside count, taken across the 10 line, yields a price
objective of 24.
Source: Andrews Technical Studies, 119 Fifth Avenue,
New York, N.Y. 10003

A compound fulcrum is a similar basing pattern involving, however, more than one mid-fulcrum rally,
sometimes several. A catapult following such activity is generally very significant. Catapults following declines
and base developments are more reliable than are catapults following fulcrum formations at the end of major
advances, which more frequently produce false upside breakouts. Following significant declines, breaks below
the base area are more likely to develop into false shakeouts. False shakeouts following major advances are less
common. More frequently encountered are false breakouts. If, following a major advance, a stock develops a
catapult and then returns deeply within its base, it must be considered suspect. A false breakout must also be
suspected if the stock forms a large congestion area just above the catapult point. Inverse fulcrums following a
major advance signal the completion of distribution and represent a sell signal. (Figure 20).

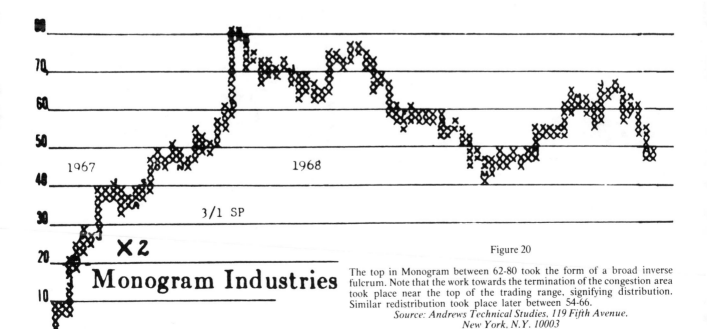

Figure 20

The top in Monogram between 62-80 took the form of a broad inverse
fulcrum. Note that the work towards the termination of the congestion area
took place near the top of the trading range, signifying distribution.
Similar redistribution took place later between 54-66.
Source: Andrews Technical Studies, 119 Fifth Avenue,
New York, N.Y. 10003

Accumulation fulcrum areas are bottom weighted and resemble a W or a compound W. Distribution fulcrum areas are top weighted and resemble an M or compound M.

Point And Figure System #7
Identifying Bottom And Top Formations

On the following pages are charts of other point and figure bottom and top formations. Buy and sell points are marked on the charts with diagonal arrows. Count lines are marked by horizontal arrows.

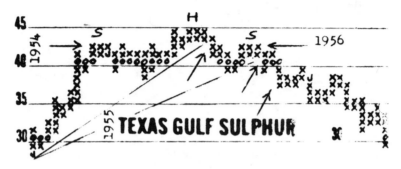

Figure 21

A broad head and shoulders top.
Source: Andrews Technical Studies, 119 Fifth Ave., New York, N.Y. 10003
[Trendlines by author]

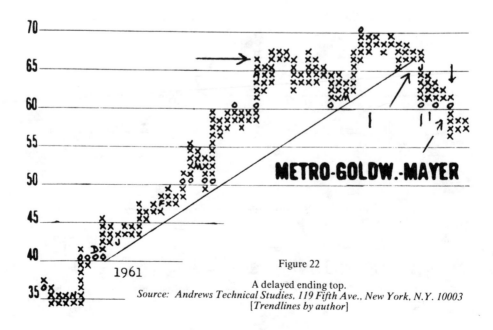

Figure 22

A delayed ending top.
Source: Andrews Technical Studies, 119 Fifth Ave., New York, N.Y. 10003
[Trendlines by author]

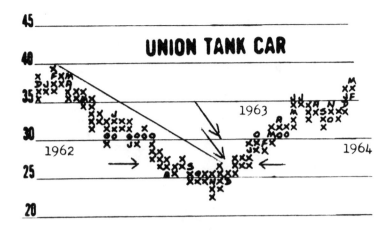

Figure 23

A V bottom.
Source: Andrews Technical Studies, 119 Fifth Ave., New York, N.Y. 10003
[Trendlines by author]

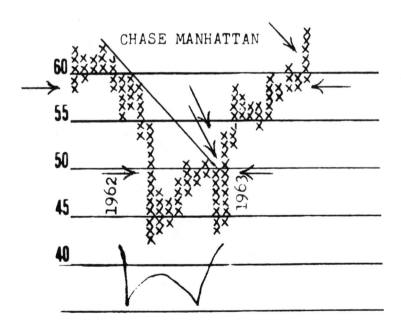

Figure 24

A double bottom. The complete formation also comprises an inverse head and shoulders.
Source: Andrews Technical Studies, 119 Fifth Ave., New York, N.Y. 10003
[Trendlines by author]

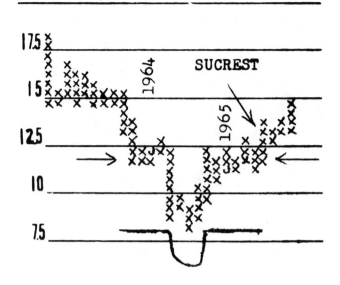

Figure 25

An inverse head and shoulders.
Source: Andrews Technical Studies, 119 Fifth Ave., New York, N.Y. 10003

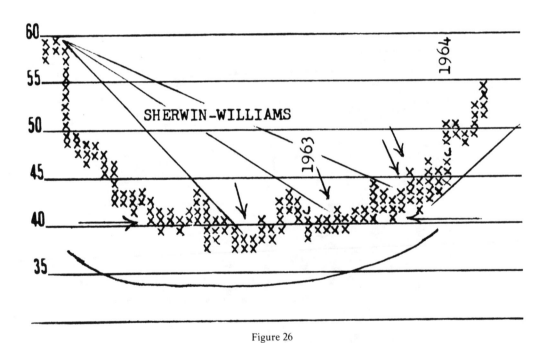

Figure 26

A saucer bottom.
Source: Andrews Technical Studies, 119 Fifth Ave., New York, N.Y. 10003
[*Trendlines by author*]

Point And Figure System #8
The "Chartcraft Method", Three Point Reversal Charts

This is a most readily maintained system of charting, described fully in *The Chartcraft Method of Point and Figure Trading* by A.W. Cohen, published by Chartcraft Inc., Larchmont, N.Y. The manual has been reasonably priced and is recommended for those readers who wish to further investigate this system.

The primary advantage of the three point reversal method lies in the simplicity of its chart maintenance. Because of the entry system, few entries are required and the charts are readily posted without need to subscribe to a chartbook service. Signals are clear and automatic, easily determined. I strongly urge use of this system, at the least, for readers who invest regularly but do not wish to take the time for more complicated chart study.

Entries are made in a manner similar to other point and figure systems, except for the following differences:

(1) Up columns are marked by X's; down columns by O's.

(2) A three point reversal is required for entry. However, an entry consists of a box marked for each single price unit. Each column must have at least three occupied boxes. No reverse columns are started until at least a three point reversal occurs. Then all the boxes represented by that reversal are entered. For example, assume a stock originally entered onto the chart at 25 and rising to 30.

```
30  x
    x
    x
    x
    x
25  x
```

The stock then declines to 28. No entry is made. The stock must decline at least three points to institute a down column. The stock rises to 29. No entry. The stock then declines to 26. Enter four O's; the stock has made at least a 3 point reversal.

```
30  x
    xo
    xo
    xo
    xo
25  x
```

The stock then declines to 24. Add two more O's.

```
30  x
    xo
    xo
    xo
    xo
25  xo
    o
```

The stock rallies to 29. Add five x's. It declines to 27. No entry. Rallies to 28; No entry. Rallies to 32. The chart now appears as follows:

```
      x
      x
30  x x
    xox
    xox
    xox
    xox
25  xox
    o
```

Charts may be scaled in ¼ point units below 5; in ½ point units below 20; in 1 point units between 20-100 and in 2 point units above 100. However, different scales may be used, and five or ten point reversal systems may be employed.

Simple buy signals are given when any ascending column exceeds the previous ascending column by at least one square (double top buy). A sell signal is indicated by a declining column falling below a previous decline. In

International Nickel (N)

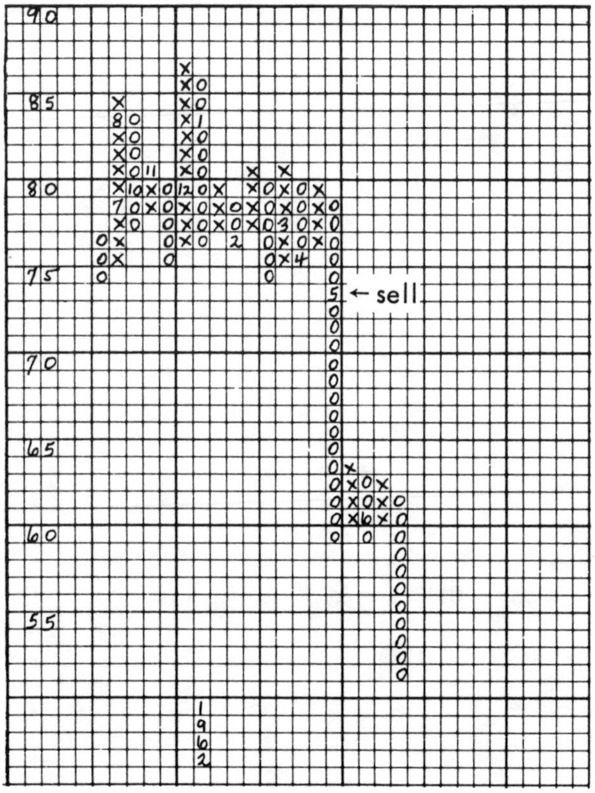

Honeywell, Inc. (HON)

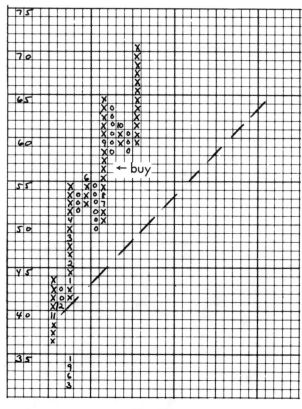

Figure 27

The sell signal is given on a breakdown from a spread formation, reversing a previous buy signal at 81.
Source: The Chartcraft Method of Point and Figure Trading
by A.W.Cohen, Chartcraft Inc., Larchmont, N.Y.

Figure 28

Note that the buy signal reversed a previous sell signal. Since the stock remained above bullish support lines, minor sell signals may be disregarded.
Source: The Chartcraft Method of Point and Figure Trading
by A.W.Cohen, Chartcraft Inc., Larchmont, N.Y.

the chart constructed above, a buy signal was rendered at 31, at which point the price exceeded a previous high. Wide, extended, multiple top formations are more reliable than simple double top and double bottom formations. The wider the formation, the more significant the breakout. Bullish formations are marked by a series of higher lows and higher highs. Bearish formations by lower lows and lower highs. Figures 27-30 illustrate formations with buy and sell points indicated.

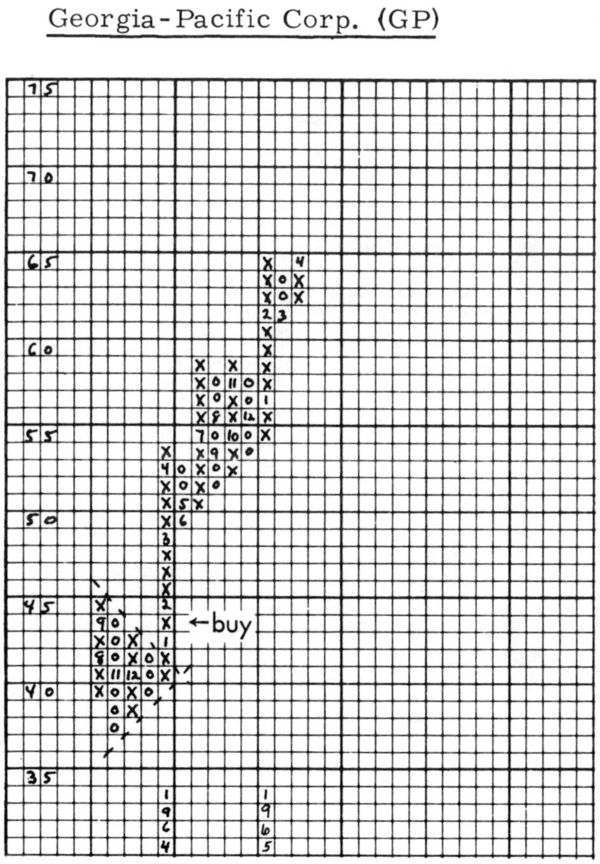

Georgia-Pacific Corp. (GP)

Warner Brothers Pictures (WB)

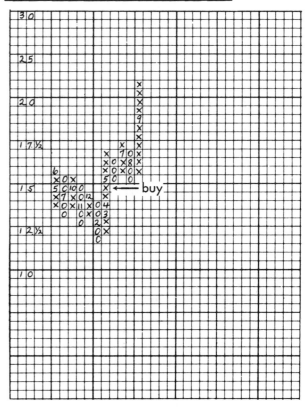

Figure 29

The buy signal developed after a breakout from a symmectrical triangle.

Source: The Chartcraft Method of Point and Figure Trading
by A.W.Cohen, Chartcraft Inc., Larchmont, N.Y.

Figure 30

The buy signal reversed a bear trend. Compare this chart to figure 12.

Source: The Chartcraft Method of Point and Figure Trading
by A.W.Cohen, Chartcraft Inc., Larchmont, N.Y.

THE BEARISH SUPPORT LINE

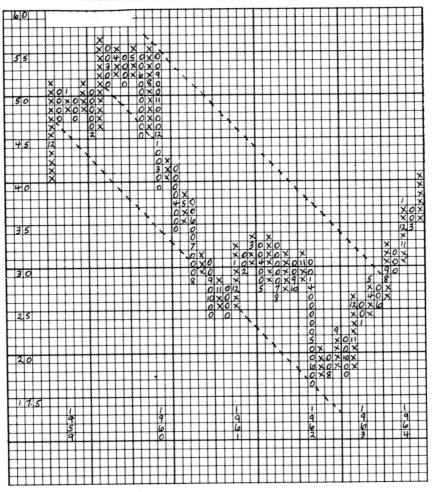

Figure 31

A down channel may be constructed in advance by drawing lines downwards at 45 degree angles, beginning at the last column of X's that preceded the bearish signal. The first such line wil usually act as the mid-channel line, the second as the end channel boundary.
Source: The Chartcraft Method of Point and Figure Trading
by A.W.Cohen, Chartcraft Inc., Larchmont, N.Y.

Bullish support lines are drawn upwards from the square below the lows preceding the bull signal at a 45° angle. Bearish resistance lines are drawn downwards at 45° angles from the high point prior to the sell signal. Bullish resistance lines are drawn following an upside breakout, at a 45° angle upwards from the point where the congestion formation runs into a declining column. This line will tend to halt advances. Bearish support lines are drawn downwards at 45° from the left of the formation where it meets the last row of X's. This will tend to halt declines. Figures 32 and 33 illustrate all these lines. (Many chartists prefer not to use these 45° lines; instead draw regular trendlines connecting bottoms.) Long term investors may disregard short or intermediate term sell signals so long as the market and/or stock remains above the bullish support line. Purchases should be initiated only after all existing bearish resistance lines have been penetrated. Reverse these procedures for short selling.

Support And Resistance Lines

There are three methods of estimating price counts in the Chartcraft System.

THE BULLISH RESISTANCE LINE

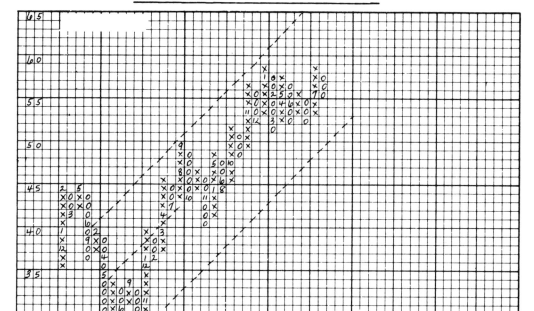

Figure 32

An up channel may be constructed in advance by drawing a line at a 45 degree angle, beginning at the last open column of O's that preceded the bull signal. The first such line so constructed will act as the mid-channel line. The second line so constructed will serve as the top channel boundary.
Source: The Chartcraft Method of Point and Figure Trading
by A.W.Cohen, Chartcraft Inc., Larchmont, N.Y.

(1) The horizontal count method is similar to counting described in previous sections. The width of the base prior to an upside breakout is measured at its lowest point. Since we are employing a 3 unit reversal chart, the width is multiplied by 3. The result is the number of boxes, added to the low point that the move will carry. (Remember, that the price increments will change from ½ point below 20 to 1 point above 20.) The count in boxes has to be converted into a point estimate. If the lowest line is below 20, the width in boxes is multiplied by 1½ points (3 x ½) to yield a price objective.

(2) The vertical count method may be employed. In this method, multiply the first uninterrupted rise in boxes by 3. The result is the number of points from the last previous low that the move will carry. For example, the first move, prior to reversal, in a 30 dollar stock is 13 boxes. Multiply 13 by 3, result 39. Add this to 30. Price objective will be 69.

If the move started below 20, the number of boxes in the move below 20 is multiplied by 1½ points since the chart increments are in half points, instead of full. Combine the increments if part of the move is below 20 and part above. Make similar adjustments for stocks over 100.

THE VERTICAL COUNT

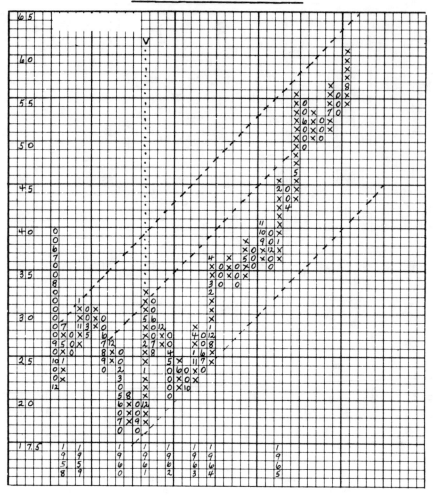

Figure 33

The vertical count objective of 62 was reached in the following manner: There was an initial thrust of 16 squares from 18½ to 33. From 18½ to 20, the chart is scaled at ½ point increments. The 3 boxes advance in this area provide an objective of 4½ points (3 x 3 ÷ ½). The remaining 13 boxes in the upthrust are multiplied by 3 for a 39 point count. We add 39 to 4½ for a total count of 43½. This, added to 18½ where the move began, yields a price objective of 62.

Source: The Chartcraft Method of Point and Figure Trading
by A.W.Cohen, Chartcraft Inc., Larchmont, N.Y.

(3) The first bullish resistance lines and bearish support lines do not usually hold. The second lines, drawn at the next level of walls usually do, and indicate likely stopping places for moves. Figure 33 illustrates both the vertical count and the use of bullish resistance lines.

Results

There is no time limit on counts. My own impression is that vertical counts tend towards overoptimism, but I have statistical verification neither of this nor of the results claimed by Chartcraft. According to Chartcraft, signals based upon their methodologies are profitable approximately eighty to ninety per cent of the time, depending upon the formation involved. The more widely spread the formation, the more reliable its breakout.

THE HORIZONTAL COUNT

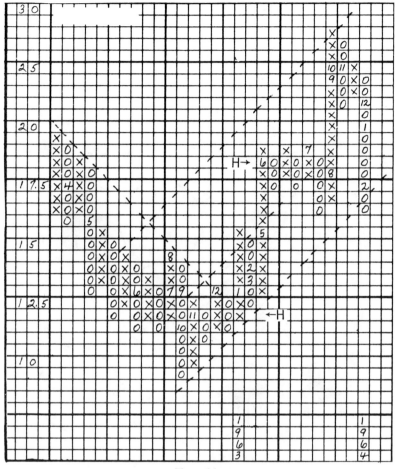

Figure 34

The horizontal count is taken across the 12 line, which is 12 squares wide.
This yields a count of 36 squares, divided by 2 since the chart is scaled at ½
point increments below 20. The resulting count of 18 points is added to the
low point at 9½ for a price objective of 27½.
Source: The Chartcraft Method of Point and Figure Trading
by A.W.Cohen, Chartcraft Inc. Larchmont, N.Y.

Trading profits will be maximized if positions are taken on pullbacks. Long positions should be initiated only if stocks remain above both bullish support lines and bearish resistance lines. Short positions should be initiated only if stocks remain both below bearish resistance lines and bullish support lines.

Disadvantages

The Chartcraft System is not sensitive to short term moves and signals are frequently given only after a considerable portion of a market move has passed. Unless you initiate purchases only upon considerable pullback, stop loss positions do not protect against severe loss. Larry Williams has published a research report showing that from 1966-1968, action on this system's signals would have resulted in a loss. However, his work disregarded suggestions that trades be initiated only upon pullbacks, and on the chartwork that accompanied his report it is clear that purchases initiated upon breakouts from spread formations were indeed profitable. The earlier into a move the action is taken, the more certain the success. Likewise, the Williams research results disregarded the recommendation that buy and sell signals be respected only in regard to major support lines. The Chartcraft system is not recommended for short term traders. It does appear to produce good long and major intermediate term results.

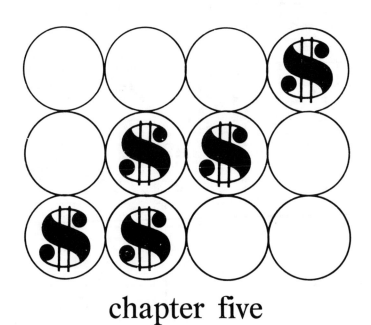

chapter five

MOVING AVERAGE SYSTEMS: HOW YOU CAN BECOME YOUR OWN ADVISORY SERVICE

Have you ever wondered how to construct one of those "proprietory" timing indices that some of the fancy advisories promote? Read on. Most of these "top secret" devices are based upon some sort of moving average study. In this chapter you will learn how to construct market and individual stock timing oscillators which you can use to pinpoint short term moves. We will also discuss what you can and cannot do with moving averages. And finally, you will see before your very eyes, some very popular myths exploded.

First, let's define the terms. A moving average is a mathematical device employed to smooth out rough data. In construction, the initial entry of the moving average is calculated by adding the sum of the units comprising the most recent series length to be averaged and then dividing by the number of units in the series. The second entry is computed by adding the next entry and subtracting the first. The result is then plotted in the next entry space. For example, using stock market data, to compute a ten day moving average of the N.Y.S.E. Composite Index:

(1) Add the first ten days entries, closing prices of the N.Y.S.E. Composite Index:

59.42	
59.99	
59.86	
59.73	
59.68	
59.31	
59.68	
59.82	
60.17	
60.68	Total: 598.34

(2) Divide by the number of entries in the series (ten); result 59.83 (rounded). Now add an eleventh day, 60.93. To maintain the series at ten entries, subtract the first entry, 59.42. Result, 599.85. Divide new result by ten. New moving average entry, 59.99. Add another entry, 61.08. Subtract eleventh entry back, 59.99. Result, 600.94; moving average entry 60.09. A moving average series based upon daily closings is computed daily. Weekly based moving averages are computed weekly, generally based upon end of week closing prices. Moving averages are usually chart-plotted with the latest moving average entry placed at the same perpendicular as the latest stock price or market index entry. (See Figure 1.)

This procedure has its uses but is, in actuality, statistically incorrect since the moving average measures the average price of the series period plotted. For an accurate statistical representation, the latest moving average plotting point should be placed midway in the data series, lagging the last stock or market entry by a period half the length of the moving average span.

To illustrate, presume a seven digit series: 1,2,3,4,5,6,7. Total, 28. Moving average plot of series, 4. The moving average plot, 4, should be placed at the number 4 in the series, not at the last entry, 7. The more usual method of placing the last moving average plot at the last data entry and the midpoint plot, just described, both have their applications which we will examine below.

Applied to the stock market, moving averages smooth widely oscillating price fluctuations so that trends may be more readily identified. Long term stock market movements are usually represented by way of a 200-day moving average. Intermediate trends are reflected by 10-week and 20-week moving averages. Shorter term trends are reflected by 10-, 20- and 28-day moving averages.

General Theory Of Moving Averages

Since moving averages represent the smoothed trend of the market, it follows that a rising moving average represents positive market action and a falling moving average, weakness in the market. The sharper the upslope of the moving average, the more accelerated the market rise. In theory, also, so long as the market (or

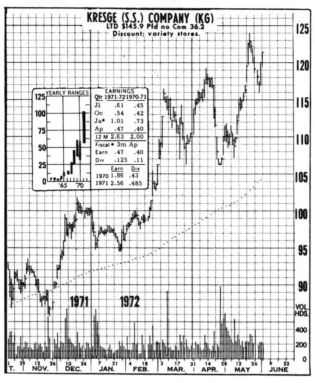

Figure 1

The dotted line represents the 200 day moving average of Kresge,
plotted beneath the last day of price entry. Note how the moving
average smooths Kresge's strong uptrend.
*Source: Trendline Daily Basis Stock Charts, 345 Hudson Street,
New York, N.Y. 10014*

stock) remains above its significant moving averages, its action is bullish since no change has taken place in its
basic trend. Penetration down through a moving average is considered bearish since the shorter term action is
now weaker than the longer term. Many technicians employ penetrations of moving averages as buy and sell
signals and, indeed, moving average lines, *if plotted perpendicularly to the last price entry* do tend to act as
support and resistance levels. If plotted with a mid-period lag, the moving average will bisect price action and
can be employed to project channels. Figure 2 illustrates a moving average plotted to the last data entry and the
same moving average centered to the middle-of-the-period time span (solid line). The moving average shown is
for a ten-week period.

Trading Tactics

Moving average considerations should be taken into account before initiating purchases and short sales.
However, there are no mechanical rules that can be followed as action signals except for those mentioned below
in the discussion of timing oscillators. Some general observations may be made, however.

(1) During a bull phase, reactions will tend to halt at or near significant moving average lines (10 week and
200 day), if these are plotted at the last price entry.

(2) During bear phases, rallies will tend to halt at or near significant moving average lines.

(3) Following a penetration of a moving average line, a reaction back to the line frequently occurs.

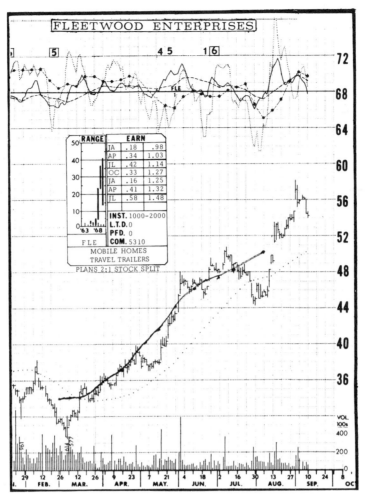

Figure 2

The dotted line is the 10 week moving average of Fleetwood. The solid line
is the same moving average, statistically centered. The centered moving
average bisects the price data and lags the last price by 5 weeks.

Source: Wall Street's Top 50, *P.O.Box 14096, Denver Colorado 80214*
[centered moving average line by author]

(4) A centered moving average line will bisect market moves pertaining to the cycle represented by that moving average (See Chapter 6 and below).

(5) Stocks and the market will usually deviate only so far above and below their moving averages and caution should be exercised when the deviation reaches certain limits. For instance, the daily Dow-Jones Average of 30 Industrials rarely rises and/or falls more than a distance of 100 points from its 200 day moving average. Each stock appears to demonstrate certain deviation probabilities. When these are exceeded, some reaction or consolidation is likely. Study of the stock's history usually reveals its prevailing pattern.

(6) An upward penetration through a rising moving average is very bullish.

(7) A downward penetration through a falling moving average is bearish.

(8) Buy stocks that have remained above their moving averages as soon as their reactions appear complete.

(9) Short only stocks that have remained below their moving averages as soon as corrective rallies appear complete.

We have already noted that moving averages tend to act as support and resistance levels. But do buy and sell signals generated by moving average penetration really work? In strongly trended markets, yes. Within trading ranges, no. Figure 3 illustrates the problems involved.

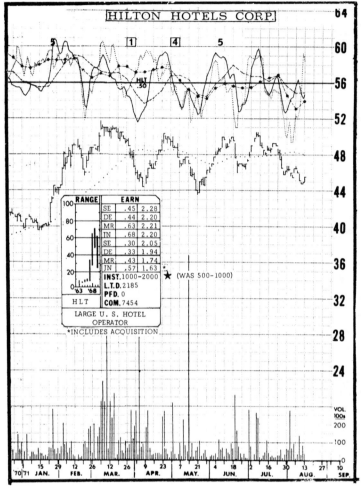

Figure 3

Within trading ranges, action signals based upon moving average penetrations result in whipsaws and provide poor results.
Source: Wall Street's Top 50, *P.O.Box 14096, Denver, Colorado 80214*

The moving average employed in this chart is a ten week moving average. You can observe the number of false signals that were generated by moving average crossings.

The issue of whether moving average crossings can be profitably employed as trading signals has remained unresolved. Some recent computer studies have raised question as to whether this method is indeed profitable. Other studies have validated the technique if certain rules are followed. These investigations will be discussed in subsequent pages. Highly recommended for the serious student is an excellent book, *Consistent Profits in the Stock Market* by Curtiss Dahl (Tri-State Offset Co., Cincinnati, Ohio). It is available through the Dunn and Hargitt Advisory, 124 West State Street, West Lafayette, Indiana 47906. Recent price, $20.00. The basic trading method presented by Dahl involves purchases and sales initiated upon penetration of a lagging ten week moving average. Although his basic methodology is not recommended, Dahl does offer many qualifications and secondary rules to his basic technique—so many in fact as to practically obscure the basic method itself. His discussions of the bases of these qualifications represent in themselves a fine course in technical theory.

Figure 3 illustrates a situation in which moving average crossings presented problems for the trader. Figures 4 and 5 represent situations in which the moving average demonstrates its support and resistance characteristics.

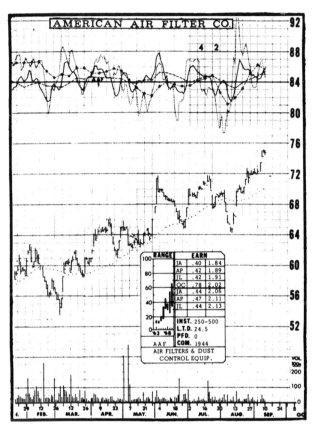

Figure 4

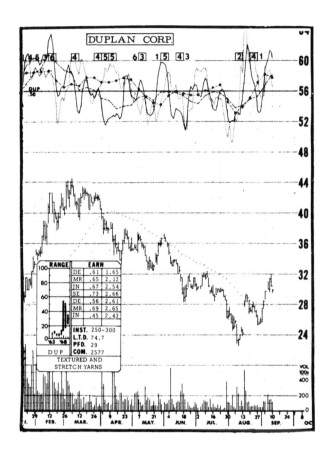

Figure 5

These charts illustrate the support and resistance characteristics of moving averages. The 10 week moving average supported the price of American Air Filter for 5 months. During the same period, Duplan could not rally through its 10 week moving average.
Source: Wall Street's Top 50, *P.O. Box 14096. Denver. Colorado 80214*

Research Attempts

For presentation in this book, a number of trading systems have been isolated from which readers might select for their own operations. Each system has had to meet the following criteria:

(1) Its signals, automatically applied have to exceed the performance of the over-all market.

(2) Preferably, an experienced trader, familiar with the system, could improve upon the automatic signals.

(3) The risk-reward ratio has to be favorable. Profit potential has to exceed loss potential.

(4) The system has to be simple enough to maintain so as to encourage rather than discourage its use.

(5) The results have to be statistically verifiable.

One Unsuccessful Attempt

Some technical theorists hold that action signals based upon crossings of shorter term and longer term moving averages are effective and profitable. For instance, buy signals are generated when a 10-week moving average of a stock or the market crosses from below to over the 20-week moving average; a sell signal is generated when the reverse occurs. In theory, an upwards penetration implies strength in the short term relative to the long term. Therefore, the buy. This is a widely held theory. However, rather than succumb to the temptation to present this methodology as a trading system, untested, I computed the actual results of employing this system, using the 1970-1972 market as the model. Three pairs of moving averages were employed. The 10-week crossings of 20-week moving averages were tested for major intermediate trends, the 5-week crossings of 10-week for lesser intermediate trends, and the 10-day crossings of the 20-day for short term trends.

Results were, in all cases, frankly surprising and disappointing. In no case did this system, automatically applied, outperform the market. In fact, two out of three crossings of the 10- and 20-week moving averages during the study period produced false and unprofitable signals, if market action was measured to the next reverse crossing.

Does this rule out any use of moving average crossings for the trader? No. By and large, the cross of a shorter term over the longer term moving average indicated in the majority of cases that *a continuation of the move was likely.* For example, there were seventeen action signals generated between October 1970 and March 1972, employing the crossings of the 10- and 20-day moving averages. Taking action on the cross and holding to the reverse cross produced only six profitable transactions. However, in fourteen of the seventeen situations, further progress took place after the cross in the direction of the cross; in seven instances this progress was significant. Using the 5- and 10-week crossings from May 1971 to April 1972, action taken upon reverse crossings would have produced results only half as profitable as holding positions long throughout that period. However, positions taken upon crossings and held to the point of highest gain during the period until the reverse cross, produced results twice as profitable as holding throughout the whole period. Therefore, you may initiate long positions upon a penetration of the 10-week by the 5-week moving average with an expectation that at some point during your holding you will show a profit. However, there is seemingly no way to employ the same system for close-out action. The system, therefore, does not meet Criteria #1; it does not provide automatic action signals.

Moving Average System #1
Create Your Own Market Oscillator

Here is the market oscillator that is employed by a variety of advisory services, the formula for which is sometimes kept hidden from subscribers. The system meets all criteria, works automatically, and involves relatively little work. The methodology is straightforward. Compute and maintain a 10-day moving average of the closing levels of the New York Stock Exchange Composite Index. Measure the difference between the last day's closing level and the last moving average entry. Signals are generated on the days that the last NYSE Index daily closing rises above (buy) and falls below (sell) its 10-day moving average. No graph is required.

Interpretation can be improved, however, by plotting the data graphically. Using graph paper, plot the closing levels of the N.Y.S.E. Composite Index. Use a line chart. On a separate scale, above, draw a horizontal zero line. Leave twelve boxes above the line, twelve below. Scale these boxes at .25 intervals, each line representing a .25 differential between the daily close and the 10-day moving average. Mark daily the amount by which the daily close exceeds (plus, above the line) or is below (minus, below the line) the 10-day moving average. Connect the plotting points with lines. Figure 6 illustrates the relationship of the oscillator to the closings of the New York Stock Exchange Composite Index.

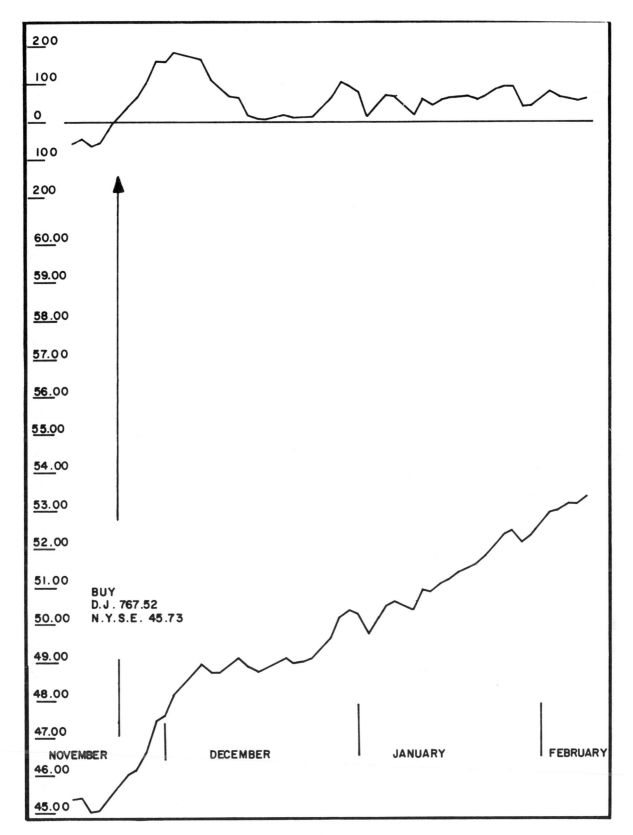

Figure 6

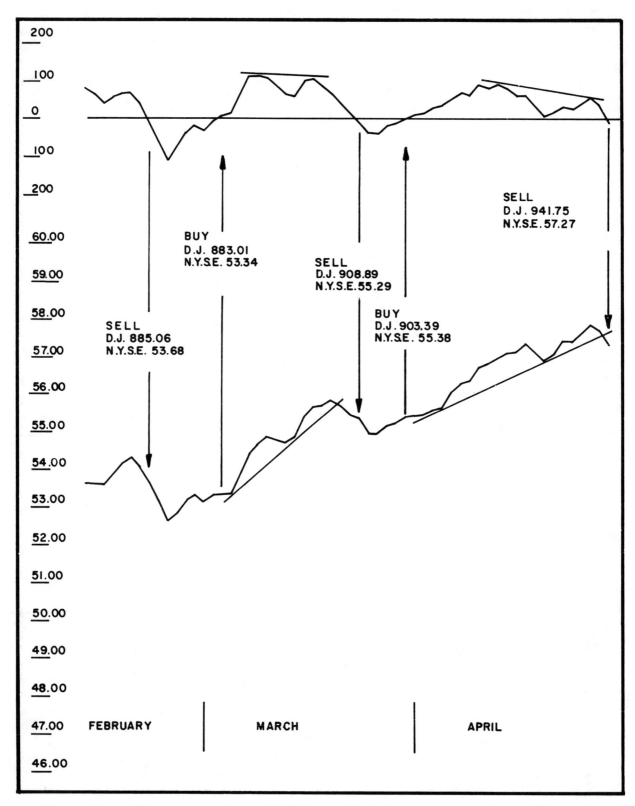

Figure 6A

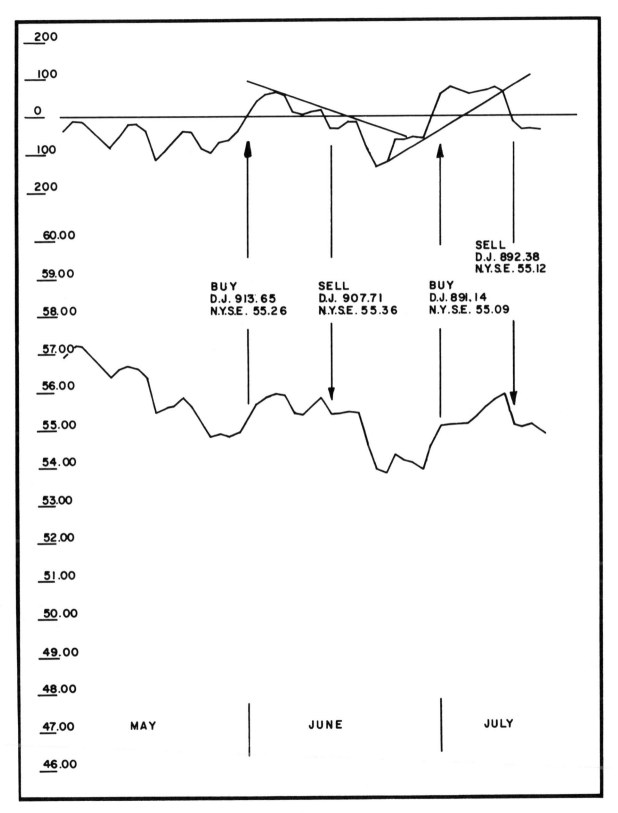

Figure 6B

Comments: Figures 6, 6A, 6B

Figures 6, 6A and 6B illustrate the relationships between the 10 day oscillator (above) and the New York Stock Exchange Index on which it is based. The period illustrated is from November 1970 through mid-July, 1971.

The first buy signal was given in November, 1970 at D.J. 767.52 and remained in effect until late February, 1971, D.J. 885.06 for a gain of more than 117 points. The oscillator reached a maximum height of near plus 200 in December 1970, gradually descended thereafter, but did not penetrate the zero line until one day after the beginning of the sharp February sell-off. The market spent eight trading days basing in early March, but the oscillator, steadily rising, flashed an excellent buy signal two days before the market broke upside. The signal was worth nearly 26 D.J. points.

The descending double top in the oscillator during March as the market continued to advance presaged the sell signal on March 23, which resulted in a gain of 5.50 Dow points but a loss of .09 in the N.Y.S.E. Index. The sell signal on April 30 developed only one day past the actual market peak, resulting in a gain of more than 28 Dow points.

The general weakening of the market's entire intermediate trend was apparent in the action of the oscillator which could not rise above plus 100 throughout April and which showed a series of descending peaks from mid-March on.

The period throughout June and July was marked by repetitive whipsaws as the market vacillated within a trading range. Notice that the buy signal, June 30, was indicated by the failure of the oscillator to dip with the market in late June. Whipsaw periods are difficult to trade profitably and particular attention has to be paid to stock selection and stop loss points, since the resolution of the trading range will carry strong significance. In this case, the trading range resolved downside and the sell signal of July 13 ultimately resulted in a short side gain of 46 Dow points.

There were no serious losses incurred during the periods shown. The total gain was 229.30 Dow points. During this time, the market advanced approximately 125 points.

Results

Results are impressive. Table I shows the results of all signals from September 1970 through April 7, 1972.

Signal Date	Average of 30 Dow Jones Industrials		N.Y.S.E. Composite Index	Points gained (lost) to Reverse signal D.J. Ind.	NYSE C.I.
September 15, 1970	(sell)	750.55	44.39	(7.12)	(.61)
September 17	(buy)	757.67	45.00	(5.75)	(.18)
September 21	(sell)	751.92	44.82	(2.46)	(.45)
September 23	(buy)	754.38	45.27	14.31	1.24
October 9	(sell)	768.69	46.51	10.68	1.07
November 2	(buy)	758.01	45.44	9.99	.37
November 12	(sell)	768.00	45.81	.48	.08
November 23	(buy)	767.52	45.73	117.54	7.95
February 17, 1971	(sell)	885.06	53.68	2.05	.34
March 2	(buy)	883.01	53.34	25.88	1.95
March 23	(sell)	908.89	55.29	5.50	(.09)
March 30	(buy)	903.39	55.38	38.36	1.89
April 30	(sell)	941.75	57.27	28.10	2.01
June 1	(buy)	913.65	55.26	(5.94)	.10
June 14	(sell)	907.71	55.36	16.57	.27
June 30	(buy)	891.14	55.09	1.24	.03
July 13	(sell)	892.38	55.12	46.00	2.83
August 11	(buy)	846.38	52.29	55.05	2.72
August 30	(sell)	901.43	55.01	(11.32)	(.65)
September 3	(buy)	912.75	55.66	(3.36)	(.28)
September 13	(sell)	909.39	55.38	15.41	.72
October 1	(buy)	893.98	54.66	(5.18)	.10
October 13	(sell)	888.80	54.76	46.32	2.41
November 3	(buy)	842.48	52.35	(16.33)	(.77)
November 10	(sell)	826.15	51.58	9.56	1.01
November 26	(buy)	816.59	50.57	80.23	6.20
January 24, 1972	(sell)	896.82	56.77	(3.01)	(.61)
January 27	(buy)	899.83	57.38	11.07	.71
February 14	(sell)	910.90	58.09	(3.61)	(.25)
February 15	(buy)	914.51	58.34	14.15	1.48
March 13	(sell)	928.66	59.82	(16.03)	(.17)
March 23	(buy)	944.69	59.99	(4.97)	(.26)
March 27	(sell)	939.72	59.73	(1.20)	(.09)
April 3	(buy)	940.92	59.82	21.68 incom.	1.25 incom.

Summary of Results:

Total number of action signals: 34

Profitable Signals: 13 long, 9 short

Unprofitable Signals: 4 long, 8 short

Sum of Gains: 25.99 long, 10.74 short (based on N.Y.S.E. Composite Index)

Sum of Losses: 1.49 long, 2.92 short

Net Gain: 24.50 long, 7.82 short

Total Net Gain: 32.36

During this period, the market advanced 16.68.

The Dow Jones Industrial Averages of 30 stocks, during this period, on actions based upon the oscillator signals, produced a net gain long of 347.97 and a net gain short of 135.92. Total gain, 483.89. Average gain per signal, 1.7 per cent. During this time, the market advanced 190 points.

It should be kept in mind that the results of trading by the oscillator are being compared to a strong market period, with the market at its highest level. The oscillator was producing profits during weak markets as well; for instance, during the latter half of 1971. On balance, approximately 90% of signalled movement is profitable. The disadvantage of the system, of course, lies in the high frequency of signals and the amount of whipsaws. These are annoying and appear to be the price for the ability to get early into every major turn. There were no serious losses taken for nearly two years. Traders using this system would have participated on the right side of every important market move. Because of commission costs, however, profitable trading based upon automatic buying and selling at the signal can be done only where commission costs as a percentage of the total round trip transaction can be kept in the area of 1.5% or less. Convertible bonds, no load mutuals, stocks purchased through third market houses (Chapter 10) or very high priced stocks may all qualify for this method. For other stock purchases, where round trip commissions may average 3%, this oscillator has to be used in conjunction with other indicators so that not every signal is acted upon.

In order to evaluate the possible effects of employing different moving average spans, the same technique may be applied, creating oscillators based upon the 20-day, 28-day and 10-week moving averages.

Results

An oscillator based upon the 20-day moving average underperformed the market by approximately 20 per cent and produced a majority of false signals. Its use is not recommended.

An oscillator based, however, upon the 28-day moving average produced a net gain of some 244 Dow points long, 58 Dow points short, therefore outperforming the market, in total by over 50 per cent. It is recommended for those who prefer fewer action signals (22 during this period).

An oscillator based upon the 10-week moving average slightly underperformed the market and rendered a majority of false signals, none, however, producing serious loss. Its use is recommended provisionally: for those traders who are willing to short a bear market as well as stay invested long during bull moves. The relative performance of the 10-week oscillator during bear markets will improve considerably when measured simply against a program of holding stocks. The 10-week oscillator did protect traders against the sharp October-November 1971 sell-off.

The *Dunn and Hargitt Letter* recently published a study showing that from 1948-1972, signals based on penetrations of the 10-week moving average produced a cumulative gain of 828% (commissions not included). There were 167 trades during that period. The service found that better results were achieved by plotting the moving average line *four weeks ahead* of the associated market reading. This reduced the percentage gain to 750% but also reduced the number of trades to 108.

William Gordon, (*The Stock Market Indicators,* Investor's Press, Palisades Park, N.J., 1968) recommends the use of a 40-week moving average oscillator for major signals. Buy when the market penetrates a rising moving average or a moving average that is flattening after a decline. Sell when a falling 40-day moving average is down-penetrated. Bear signals averaged 4% profits; bull signals 27% annually. Study period: 1897-1967.

Trading Tactics: How To Use The Oscillator

The oscillator constructed here is a measure of the overbought-oversold condition of the market. The basic signal is the crossing of the zero line. However, keep the following in mind: (1) The 10-day oscillator is a sensitive, general market timing indicator. It provides many signals, generally valid, but sometimes for only short moves. Not all stocks will move sufficiently with the oscillator to make trading worthwhile. In fact, in view of commission charges, traders operating this system automatically should employ only investment vehicles in which round trip costs can be kept below 1 per cent. Suggestions: no-load mutual funds, convertible bonds, very high priced stocks (see Chapter 10). (2) The oscillator works very well during strongly trended markets. Some whipsaws do occur during consolidation, topping and bottoming activity. (3) Since the average gain per signal is 1.7%, automatic in and out trading should be limited to investment vehicles in which the round trip commission cost can be kept under 1.5%, e.g. no-load mutual funds, convertible bonds, very high-priced stocks, and stocks which you can purchase in the Third Market (see Chapter 10). Otherwise, the oscillator cannot be employed on its own for automatic trading.

Overbought-oversold indicators are subject to trend and to support and resistance study. The initial up-thrust, following a period of base building or a climactic decline, is generally sharp, reaching the overbought zone (+1.50 - 2.50) quickly. This is usually followed by a dip to near and occasionally slightly below zero. A secondary rise in the oscillator follows, to about the level of the first. The oscillator remains in a solidly plus condition, dipping periodically and gradually working its way downwards as the rally loses momentum, crossing zero as the rally ends. Some technicians advise selling action as soon as the oscillator either breaks its uptrend or demonstrates a violation of a previous low. Cash never hurts, but short selling on this sort of action alone is not recommended.

The 10- and 28-day oscillators can be used in conjunction as follows:

(1) Buy only if both oscillators are uptrended, preferably as they cross zero simultaneously or as per observation 4, below.

(2) You may sell on the 10-day signal but do not short unless the 28-day oscillator has also rendered a sell signal.

(3) You may cover shorts based upon the 10-day signal, but do not buy except as per rule 1.

General Observations

(1) Readings of ± 2.00 represent strongly overbought-oversold conditions. A brief consolidation or reaction, at the least, may be anticipated once these levels are reached. The strength of the initial thrust frequently infers the extent of the move to follow. If you missed the early part of a strong move, buy as soon as the oscillator completes its first reaction.

(2) Short term peaks and troughs in the oscillator will occur at four and eight-week intervals. The oscillator will complete significant bottom formations at 20-24 week intervals (See Chapter 6).

(3) The first sell signal after a strong bull move will likely be false. The first buy signal after a severe decline may be false. However, there are probably more false sell than false buy signals.

(4) A series of higher lows and higher highs in the oscillator, even below the zero level, as the market declines, usually indicates that the decline is losing momentum—a rally is in the offing. A series of progressively lower highs and lower lows in oscillator peaks as the market advances indicates that the rally is losing momentum—a correction to follow.

(5) If the oscillator, following an extreme low reading, forms a triple bottom, purchases can usually be made

upon the turn-up from the third bottom, even before the zero line is crossed. Following such a formation, buy instantly as the zero line is crossed.

(6) The oscillator can remain in overbought and oversold conditions for long periods of time. A period of time spent near neutral frequently presages a change of trend.

Moving Average System #2
Constructing A Stock Timing Oscillator

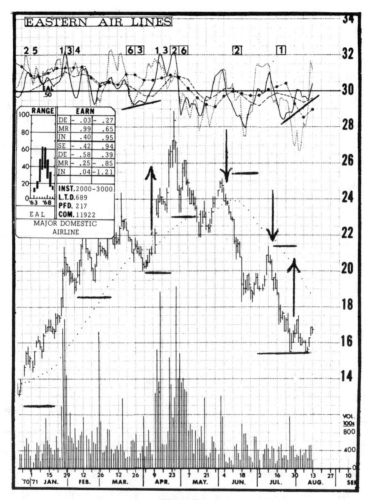

Figure 7

Figure 7 demonstrates the relationship between the stock oscillator and price activity. The stock oscillator is the solid line above the price action. The other lines are superimposed market oscillator and longer term stock lines, all proprietory to *Wall Street's Top 50*. I have marked in buy and sell points. Note the two buy signals generated as the stock oscillator rose from bottoming formations. The heavy horizontal lines indicate the stop loss points, long and short.

Source: Wall Street's Top 50, *P.O. Box 14096, Denver, Colorado 80214*

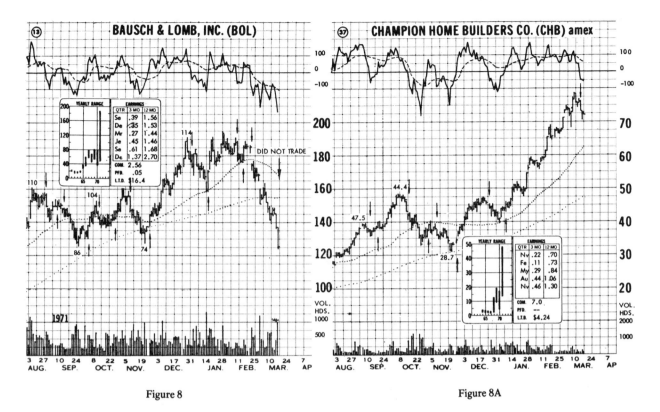

Figure 8   Figure 8A

Figures 8, 8A illustrate the proprietory stock oscillator employed by *Comparative Market Indicators.* Arrows show buy and sell signals. Bausch and Lomb fluctuates sufficiently for profitable trading based upon oscillator signals alone. The oscillator also provided excellent signals for Chamption Home Builders. Notice that serious losses rarely occur with this sytem and that you participate in all major moves.
Source: Comparative Market Indicators, *P.O. Box 1557, Bellevue, Washington 98009*

The basic method involved is quite similar to the construction of the market oscillator, except that instead of plotting the daily vs. a 10-day moving average, you compute the last 3-day moving average and the 10-day moving average. The differential between the two is plotted and becomes the oscillator. Buy when the 3-day moving average crosses above the 10-day. This methodology is employed by a number of stock and commodity services. Figures 7, 8 and 8A represent charts of stocks with their market oscillators. The charts are by *Comparative Market Indicators* and *Wall Street's Top Fifty,* two fine advisories. Their own particular methodologies are proprietory but the chart patterns produced are similar to those arrived at by the stock oscillator method just described.

Trading Tactics

The stock oscillator should be used in conjunction with the market oscillator. For best results, operate with charts showing tandem action. That is, buy at a point when both the market and stock oscillators are crossing up through zero. You can create a longer term oscillator for individual stocks by employing a five-week moving average of the end of week oscillator readings and plotting that with the daily oscillator. A declining five-week moving average of end-of-week oscillator readings carries bearish implications, particularly if it crosses below zero. The best buy signals will be generated when the 10-day and 28-day market oscillators and the short term and five-week stock oscillators are all simultaneously rising through zero, or if the shorter term oscillators are rising through zero while the longer term ones have remained above zero. Reverse for short selling. A series of higher lows in the stock oscillator as the stock declines indicates a potential reversal. Look for double bottoms with the oscillator remaining higher on the second dip. You can usually buy on the turn-up. Some very active and volatile stocks can be bought and sold as soon as their oscillators change direction, providing enough latitude in short term movements for profitable short term trading. A stock blowing off may be sold as soon as its oscillator turns down. This will frequently get you out very close to the top.

I do not recommend a policy of selling and/or buying upon oscillator moves through zero alone. Too many whipsaws. Instead, following your purchases, if not immediately stopped out, place stop orders just below the price level at which the oscillator last started to turn up. Keep raising your stops as the stock rises until stopped out or a significant channel extremity is reached. Reverse for shorts.

Most stocks demonstrate extreme oscillator readings which can be identified as overbought and oversold conditions. Do not initiate long positions until the overbought condition is rectified (usually just a few days) and do not short a severely oversold stock.

Refer again to Figures 7, 8 and 8A. Significant patterns are discernible, which will help you in identifying your own formations. The buy, sell, and stop loss points have been marked.

Moving Average System #3
Using Moving Averages To Project A Stock's Channel

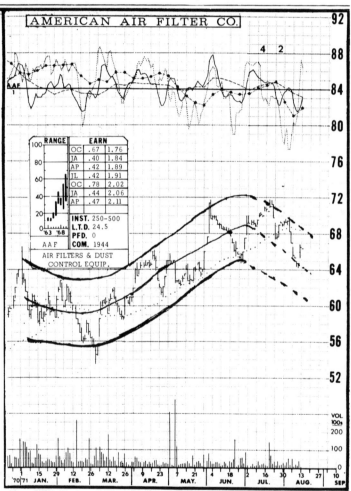

Figure 9

The 10 week moving average has been statistically centered and now acts as the mid-channel line. The complete channel is drawn surrounding it. The down channel is projected in early July. Note how its boundary stops and rallies and how the projected mid-channel line operates as support. Purchases should be initiated near the lower boundaries of channels created by this technique.

Source: Wall Street's Top 50, P.O.Box 14096, Denver, Colorado 80214
[*Channels by author*]

Stocks will usually deviate around their moving averages by just so much before correcting. One way of achieving a prediction of a correction is to center the 10-week moving average (Figure 9, solid line). Create a channel around the centered moving average. The stock will tend to oscillate within that channel. Purchases should be made either at mid-channel, or, preferably at bottom channel. Longer term investors can employ a centered 200-day moving average in the same manner.

Moving Average System #4
Using Moving Averages To Project A Price Objective

COX BROADCASTING

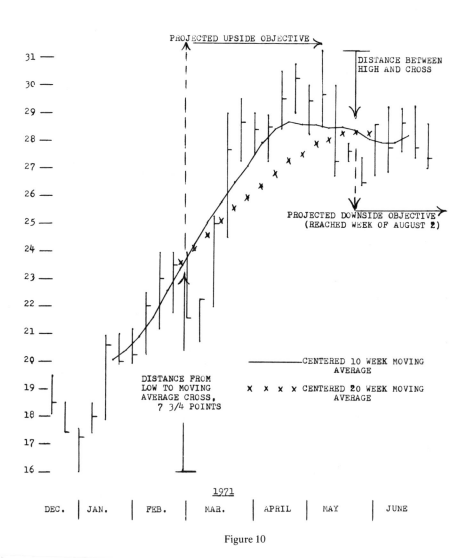

Figure 10

To project the price objectives: Upside—measure from the low at 16 to 23¼, where the 10 week moving average crossed over the 20 week moving average. Project the 7¼ point move up to the cross vertically from the point of the cross. Result, price objective of 31½. Actual high, 31¼.

A downside objective is secured by measuring from the high to where the 20 week moving average crossed to below the 10 week. The downside objective of 25½ was reached in August, 1971.

A price objective for stocks and the market may be projected by the use of centered moving averages through use of a method suggested by J.M.Hurst, author of *The Profit Magic of Stock Transaction Timing*, an excellent book which relates to time cycles and moving averages and is highly recommended.

The basic method involves some work but may be worth the effort to serious investors.

(1) Locate significant intermediate time cycles by which the stocks to be studied operate. (See Chapter 6). The intermediate time cycle is the average time it takes the stock to move from intermediate low to intermediate low. In most cases, you can assume a basic 20-week intermediate cycle for simplified arithmetic. Plot a moving average of the time cycle period and another moving average of the half-time cycle period, e.g. one 20-week and one 10-week. Plot these two moving averages on the stock chart, using the centered statistical plotting system. The plot of the 10-week will lag the last price by 5½ weeks; the plot of the 20-week will lag the last price by 10½ weeks. Measure, vertically during an up cycle from the previous lows to the point where the 10-week moving average crosses over the 20-week. The amount the stock has moved until that point will likely represent half the total move. Figure 10 illustrates the procedure. The solid line represents the centered 10-week moving average; the XXX line, the 20-week. The arrow points to the estimated price objective.

Results

This methodology has frequently produced excellent projections, both of the market (using 10 and 20-week moving averages) and for individual stocks. R.N. Hurst has recommended that a projection of price objective be made as soon as the significant moving averages turn up, or down for a downside projection. I have found this to be a dangerous procedure. Accurate projections can be made only as the significant moving averages actually approach one another very closely. Unfortunately, by this time the move in question is very nearly complete. I have, however, had successful experience in using this system to confirm that tops and bottoms are indeed at hand. Following the achievement of a projected objective, there is usually sufficient time remaining to put out shorts or to initiate long positions for the price reversals to follow.

Moving Average System #5
Larry Williams' Shadow Line

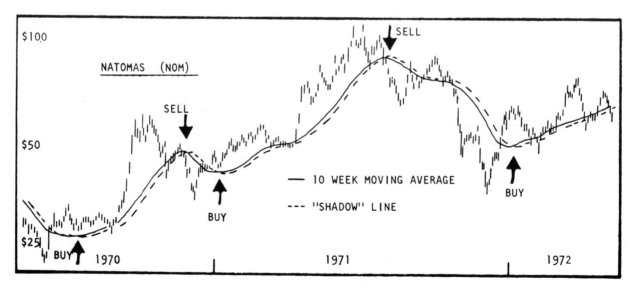

Figure 11

Source: Williams Reports, *Box 1552, Carmel, California 93921*

In the May, 1972 issue of *Williams' Reports*, Larry Williams published a simple intermediate trading technique that appears to produce profitable signals a clear majority of times. Employ a standard ten-week moving average line, plotted at the last price of the series. Draw a second line, parallel to the first but projected one week ahead (the shadow line). A buy signal is generated when the moving average crosses from below to above its "shadow line". A sell signal is generated when it crosses from above to below its "shadow line". See Figure 11 for an example. Results are good, particularly with consideration that this is an automatic system. You do not get in and out at extreme high and low points, but the odds are excellent that your transaction will be profitable. The system works best with strongly trended stocks but does avoid some of the whipsaws that plague other moving average systems.

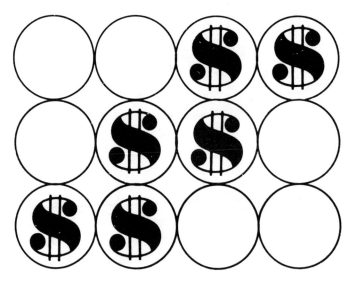

chapter six

TIME CYCLES:
CASHING IN ON THE CALENDAR

How about the possibility that market action is influenced by planetary movements? Larry Williams thinks it a probability (Williams Reports, April 1972).

Planets aside, we can demonstrate that market action is subject to laws of time and calendar cyclicality and that these laws can be used to excellent trading advantage. Why does market action have cyclical features? Frankly, no one is certain. Some cycle characteristics can be linked to quarterly earnings reports. Others seem unrelated to tangible events external to the market. But, again, regular time cycles do exist, for the broad market and for individual stocks. And money is to be made by checking your calendar before you buy.

A complete cycle of movement consists of an upmove and a downmove, the period betwen the start and finish representing the time duration of the cycle. Each cycle in turn, is composed of smaller cycles which, in combination, make up the larger cycle. These are composed of even smaller cycles. Therefore, any market cycle is in itself part of a larger, longer cycle and in itself is composed of small cycle units. This principle is illustrated below, in Figure 1.

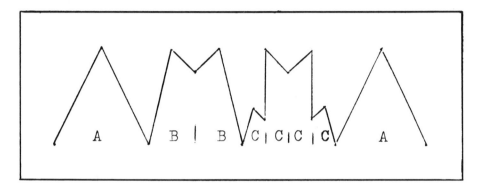

Figure 1

Cycle A, it can be seen, consists of two half cycles B and these in turn consist of two half cycles C. Cycle A consists of four cycles C. This is an idealized model. The time between crests and troughs remains constant. This model applied to the stock market would indicate a long term flat market with intermediate and short term fluctuations within a broad trading range. In actuality, when measured long term, the market is relatively flat, with some upward bias. Most of the violent moves are of major intermediate proportions.

The length of a cycle is measured in time by the period between troughs. So long as the peaks and troughs for that cycle occur at successively higher levels, that cycle must be considered in an uptrend. It is possible for a longer term cycle to be pointing up while one or more of its shorter term components are trending down. In market terms, we would think of the major trend as still pointing up while the intermediate trend is down. This concept is illustrated in Figure 2.

In the above chart of Loews Corporation Wts. we can see that although the stock remained in its major uptrend, an intermediate cycle turned down from July through November, 1971. The eight-week cycle rally in October showed a failure, resulting in a series of declining eight-week low points. Incidentally, throughout the whole period shown on this chart, Loews regularly rallied every 12 to 14 weeks. It could have been purchased at any time, thirteen weeks from bottom to bottom, with profitable results.

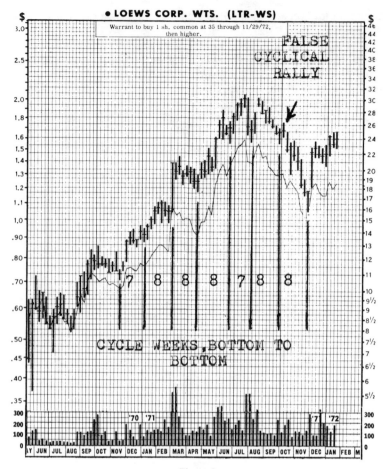

Figure 2

The eight week cycle in LTR-WS. The 8 week cycle turned down in
October 1971, after more than one year of rising 8 week cyclical lows.
Source: Securities Research Co., 208 Newbury Street, Boston, Mass. 02116
[Cycles by author]

Market Cycles

Figure 3 illustrates significant market cycles. A dominant cycle of approximately four to four and one-half years appears to exist from bear market bottom to bear market bottom (October 1953-December 1957, December 1957-May 1962, May 1962-October 1966, October 1966-May 1970). Next bear market bottom due: autumn 1974? The last cycle, from 1966 to 1970, was a few months shorter in time than the series of bottoms which preceded it. This wrought havoc among many cyclical technicians, who expected the decline to run into early 1971. Nothing's perfect.

A major 70 to 75 week cycle appears to exist also as a significant component. This last bottomed in November 1971, which accounts for the pronounced market weakness at that time.

Intermediate traders can make particular use of somewhat shorter cycles. There is a quite regular 20 to 28 week cycle of tops to tops and bottoms to bottoms, which can be profitably traded.

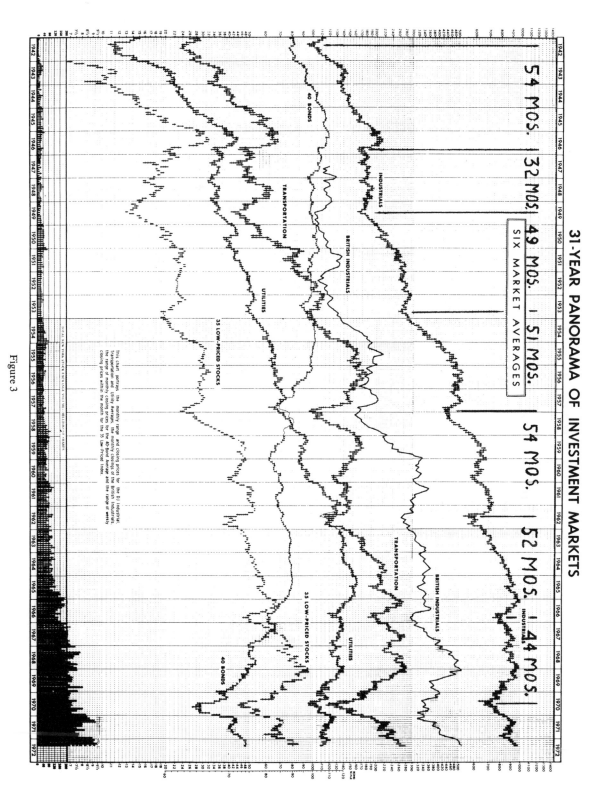

Figure 3

The long term market cycles, measured from bear market low to bear market low.
*Source: Securities Research Co., 208 Newbury Street, Boston, Mass. 02116
[Cycles by author]*

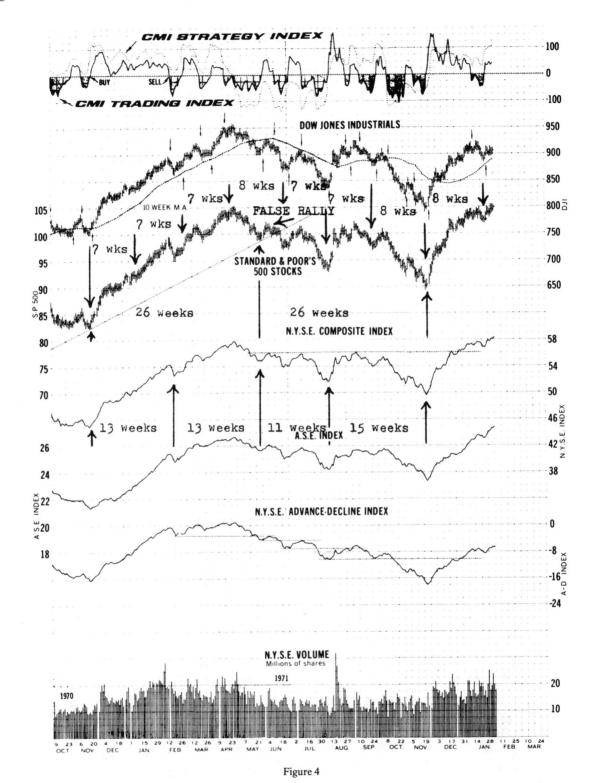

Figure 4

Sources: Comparative Market Indicators, P.O. Box 1557, Bellevue, Washington 98009
[Cycles by author]

A thirteen-week market cycle also exists, as do an eight, a four and a two-week cycle. The 26-week, 13-week and eight-week cycles are marked on Figure 4.

The shorter in duration the cycle, the less meaningful it is to the intermediate trader, although for fine timing, it helps to know exactly where you are. Periods where two cycles merge are the more significant; periods where three, four or more cycles coincide are very significant. For instance, let us presume that the market is in position where it is due for its four-week, eight-week, thirteen-week, six-month and eighteen-month cycle bottoms, simultaneously. The confluent influence of these combined cycles is likely to result in a severe decline. Should the thirteen-week, the six-month and the eighteen-month cycles still be in an up-phase, the influence of the eight and four-week cycles will be less severe. Review Figure 4. You may observe that in November 1971, the eight-week, thirteen-week, and six-month cycles all bottomed simultaneously. Besides, a 70-week cycle, not shown, bottomed then. The confluence of these cyclical bottoms deepened and lengthened the October-November decline.

Time Cycle System #1
Predicting Major Intermediate Turning Points In Advance

Employ the six-month cycle, with the thirteen-week cycle as a back up. Count six months from the preceding market low point. The next major low should occur roughly at that projected time period. During bear markets, to predict high points, measure six months from peak to peak. (This works well in bull markets also.) The results are excellent. In recent years, low points were spaced from February-July 1969, July 1969-January 1970, January 1970-May 1970, May 1970-November 1970, November 1970-May 1971, May 1971-November 1971. High points during the 1969-1970 bear market occured in May 1969, November 1969, April 1970—all six months apart!

J.M. Hurst in, *The Profit Magic of Stock Transaction Timing,* previously mentioned, suggests that envelopes be drawn through significant cycle extremities as a tool for the identification of the direction and slope of cycles. The application of this technique is demonstrated below, Figure 5.

So long as the longer duration cycles remain up, the long term investor need not overly concern himself with short term cycles. The direction of cycles may be determined by study of the moving average of that cycle (See Chapter 5). So long as the moving average of that cycle is in an accelerating rise, the cycle may be considered uptrended. However, the moving average will not begin to turn down until the cycle is approximately halfway through its declining phase. The shorter term components of a larger cycle will change direction before the longer term and will provide advance warning of an impending major shift in trend. It usually takes some time to reverse a major trend. Tops, in particular, usually round off. Bottoms tend to be sharper, so the investor usually has more time to sell than to buy.

Identifying True Cycle Bottoms

Cycle tops and cycle bottoms do not always coincide with the exact top or bottom of market movement. This is illustrated in Figure 6. To establish the true cycle, locate two or more cyclical extremities in which the tops or bottoms are clearly defined—the more cycle points you can isolate, the better. Measure the distance in time between these points. If you have two or more cycles from which to measure, use the average time distance between them to derive a cycle length.

From time to time, the distance so projected will not match the actual peak or low of your stock or the market. This has predictive implications. For instance, in Figure 6, on the daily chart of Loews Corporation, the four week cyclical low at 43 in December was actually higher than a mid-cycle low at 36, three weeks previous. The validity of the four-week cycle could be established from the measurement of previous low points, all almost exactly three and one-half weeks apart. The stock, in effect, changed direction in the middle of a minor cycle. The previous cyclical bottom was at 38. My own experience has led me to conclude that the employment of the calendar cycle rather than the actual stock lows provides better results than rearranging your time cycle locations to suit price action.

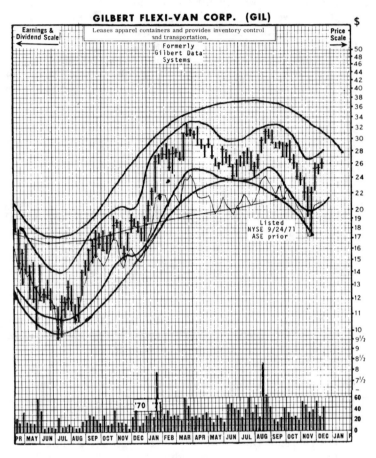

Figure 5

Envelopes drawn surrounding major and intermediate moves clarify the direction of the cyclical trend. The intermediate envelope touches the lower rim of the long term envelope at 6 month intervals, illustrating the six month cycle.
Source: Securities Research Co., 208 Newbury Street, Boston, Mass. 02116
[Envelopes by author]

If a stock's time cyclical bottom ends up above the actual low during the cycle, bullish action may be predicted. If a stock's cyclical high point develops below the actual high peak reached during the cycle, we may draw bearish implications.

The sharp drop of October-November 1971 was predictable in this manner. The market had been operating

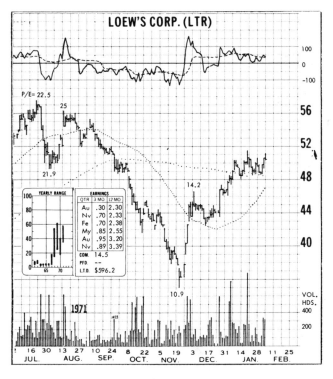

Figure 6

*Source: Comparative Market Indicators, P.O.Box 1557,
Bellevue, Washington 98009*

on a regular six-month peak-to-peak cycle. The previous peak had been reached late April, implying a six-month top during October. By early October, it was apparent that the August peak was not to be surpassed within the cycle period; the market stood lower than the month previous with only two weeks remaining of the projected up cycle. This was in itself a sell signal, into which traders could sell short. Sometimes, cyclical peaks will match actual peaks; at other times they will match into formation conclusions. The October 1971 cyclical top was the right shoulder of a head and shoulders formation. In 1970, a six-month measurement from January yielded a cycle objective not into the low of May but rather into July, where the last bottom of the triple bottom that ended the bear market developed.

The Relationship Between Market Cycles And Stock Cycles

Market cycles and individual stock cycles will tend to coincide, though not exactly. Individual stocks should be traded on their individual cycles. Both bull and bear markets are characterized by group and stock rotation. During a good bull move, individual industry groups and stocks correct sharp advances as other groups temporarily assume market leadership. Some stocks will lead the market up; some will lead it down. For the most part, however, the rule of operating in harmony with the major and intermediate trend remains applicable. Nimble traders can hop from group to group as cyclical tops are approached by the one and cyclical bottoms are approached by the other.

Cycle System #2
The Basic Cycle And Trendline Method

This is essentially the method described by R.N. Hurst. When employed in conjunction with other techniques, it is quite effective. If I had to pick one single method for trading operations this would be the technique I would select. It is simple in concept and execution, protects against serious loss and provides quick profitability when you are correct. The method consists of the following steps:

(1) Decide upon the type of trading you wish to do. Long term investors can try operating on the 70-week cycle, and upon bull and bear market initiation signals, but I prefer and suggest operation on the six month cycle. Intermediate traders should operate on the six-month and thirteen-week cycles. Shorter term traders can operate on eight-week and four-week cycles. If you miss the more important turns, try to take positions upon the next minor cycle bottom. It will usually pay to get into the six month move even if you miss the exact turning point. Research has shown that moves beginning at six month bottoms have averaged approximately ninety Dow points or better than eleven per cent from six month bottom to subsequent cycle high. It is risky to stay in stock past the six month cyclical peak. Declines from six month peaks to subsequent mid-cycle lows have averaged approximately ten per cent or ninety points. This data included the 1965-1972 period.

(2) Select your stocks. Look for stocks preferably in new uptrends, showing strong relative strength and demonstrating solid earnings growth. After a severe intermediate decline, stocks in new uptrends will be scarce. Use volume and oscillator methods to select picks.

(3) As your potential selections decline to and approach their projected cyclical bottoms, track them with tight downtrendlines, preferably on daily charts.

(4) Buy on the first break of the downtrendline, particularly if the stock is at or near a supporting longer term uptrendline, near a major channel bottom.

(5) Immediately place a stop-loss order a point or so below the lows just made. Occasionally, a cyclical rally will be minor, a new cyclical downleg developing after a brief, abortive cyclical rally attempt. Review Figure 2. Loews attempted its thirteen-week rally in August 1971 but the attempt was weak and the stock collapsed to its next thirteen-week low in November.

(6) Follow the stock's rise with trailing stop-loss orders. As the stock approaches its channel extremity and/or its point and figure objective, employ a tight trendline and sell either upon the trendline break or upon a buying climax.

Figure 7 demonstrates the application of this method to the eight-week short term cycle. The procedure for the application of a thirteen or 24-week cycle would be similar except that weekly charts would be employed to determine the larger cycles, with a switch to daily charts for the fixing of the tight terminal trendline.

The idealized cycle consists of one-half length up and one-half length down. During bull moves, the cycle is skewed so that the upwards thrust is longer than the down thrust. In bear moves, the down thrust is of longer duration. A cyclical rally that aborts early implies that the greater part of that cycle will consist of a

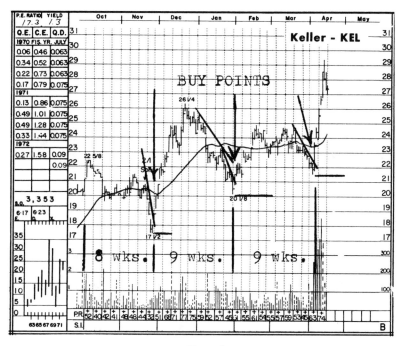

Figure 7

As the end of the nine week cycle approaches, draw in very tight trendlines.
Buy on the trendline violation with a tight stop (horizontal lines) just
beneath the previous lows.
Source: R.W.Mansfield Co., 26 Journal Square, Jersey City, N.J. 07306
[Cycles and trendlines by author]

downmove—bearish. Conversely, a cyclical rally that continues well past the mid-point of the cycle implies a subsequent minor decline or a sharp but not serious correction. Occasionally, the downthrust portion of the cycle seems almost absent, the conclusion of the cycle marked perhaps only by sidewise action or even by only a slowing of the uptrend, with just a few days of softness. This presages a strong move to follow.

Other Trading Hints

As an intermediate cycle lengthens, the probabilities of abortive shorter cycle rallies increase. To clarify, a twenty-four week cycle ideally consists of twelve weeks up, twelve weeks down. During a bull thrust, it will likely consist of perhaps, eighteen weeks up, six weeks down. The last eight week cycle of the three that comprise the twenty-four week cycle will then be likely to turn down prior to or certainly at its mid point. The first and second eight-week cycles will maintain their upthrust periods for longer portions of their cycle life. You can usually initiate positions even at the midway point of the first eight week cycle. The second eight-week cycle will have a longer downthrust than the first, but may still have more than half its length up. The last cyclical rally, as I said, has to be approached cautiously, since its downthrust will be subject to the four, eight and twenty-four week cycle downside influences.

When considering the initiation of positions, pay attention to the status of the shorter time cycles of the stocks you are investigating. A stock may be early in its twenty-four week cycle but at a four week cyclical peak. A wait of a few days until the stock troughs into its four week low can frequently save a point or two.

When I find a stock I like, I often take a pilot position a few days before the cycle is due to expire. Cycles are not exact in length and breakouts can be quite explosive. Initiating positions early, particularly within flat congestion areas, costs me a little time but gets my position established, usually at cheap levels. A second position can be taken at the breakout.

Wave And Cycle System #3
The Elliott Wave Theory

The Elliott Wave Theorists comprise one of the more exotic Wall Street cults. Their tabula rosa includes such romantic language as "irregular tops", "minute" and "sub-minuette" waves and zig-zag corrections. Interpretations of Elliott Theory can be subject to interminable philosophic debate and quibble. All this is by way of suggestion that the Elliott mystique has its uses, but that I do not advise putting your last buck on Elliott interpretation.

Briefly stated, according to the writings of R.N. Elliott, who originated the theory some thirty odd years ago, a full wave or progressive cycle consists of three waves in the primary direction, interrupted by two corrective waves. Each of the primary waves consists of three smaller waves, interrupted by two corrective waves. And each of those smaller waves—ad infinitatum. The corrective waves consist of three legs, two in the corrective direction and one in the primary direction, correcting the correction. Figure 8 illustrates the configuration.

Figure 8

Source: Andrews Technical Studies, 119 Fifth Ave., New York, N.Y. 10003

Intra-day, not closing prices, determine the waves, and hourly and even half-hourly market postings are required to maintain the charts of smaller wave configurations. However, broader market movements can be determined from standard charts. My preliminary remarks to the contrary, the frequency with which the number "three" appears in stock price movement can be startling, and I have, myself, done some successful trading based upon Elliott considerations.

Figure 9 demonstrates the application of the Elliott model to the action of a particular stock. Compare again, to the basic model. Great. Now all we have to do when a stock begins a move is to count waves. Until three are complete we hold positions. As soon as the third ends, we go short. If only... The sad truth, however, lies in the complications. First, it is often difficult to tell whether three identifiable up waves complete the total move or are components only of the first of three larger waves. In the latter case sales are likely to be premature and short sales positively disastrous. Second, Elliott was able to observe that in many instances, following the third up wave, and preceding a decline, stocks frequently take off on a fourth up wave, higher than the third.

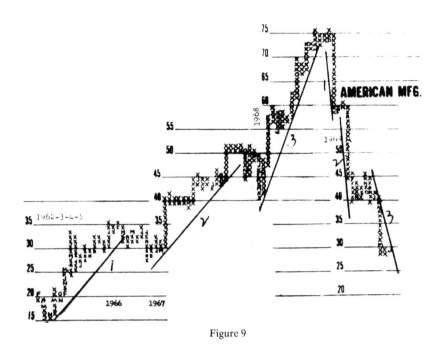

Figure 9

American Mfg. conformed almost exactly to the Elliott model.
Source: Andrews Technical Studies, 119 Fifth Ave., New York, N.Y. 10003

Undaunted, Elliott referred to this action as an "irregular top", with the new high actually representing a corrective movement (Fig. 10). Small consolation if you're short.

However, Elliott does note that following "irregular tops", the "C" wave is quite extensive. Maybe those shorts will work out yet. Figure 11 illustrates other applications of the Elliott Theory.

Trading Tactics

The basic Elliott Wave tactics have already been implied, above, and in Chapter 1. Examine your stock's price history, intermediate and long term, to determine its position in terms of wave count. Keep in mind, however, that the wave count is taken, after a change in trend, from the base or top breakout point. Do not include the basing or topping activity in the wave count. Point and figure charts are very useful in determining longer than intermediate term wave movements. The second of the three waves *should not be* the shortest if your waves have been accurately defined. In a strong market, each up-wave will probably increase in scope over the one previous. In a weakening market, the waves will become progressively truncated. Conversely, a progressive truncation of down waves indicates an imminent end to the decline.

The length of the third upwave may be roughly projected by averaging the lengths of the first two upwaves. This system frequently provides a close estimate of the actual resulting last move.

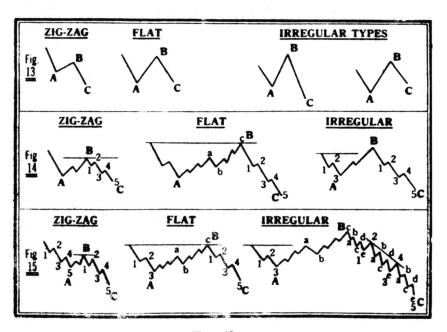

Figure 10

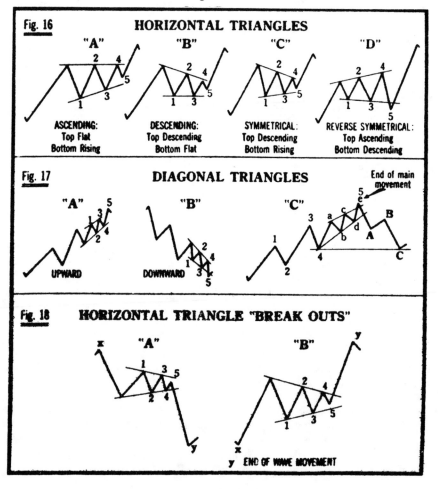

Figure 11

Source: Andrews Technical Sudies, 119 Fifth Ave., New York, N.Y. 10003

The basic tactic, of course, is to make certain before initiating positions, that there is sufficient wave room remaining in the move to provide a sensible risk-reward ratio, keeping in mind that primary moves consist of five waves in total, corrective moves, three.

Elliott interpretation frequently appears more accurate in hindsight than as foresight. Nonetheless, wave count should not be ignored as a major technical tool.

Wave And Cycle System #4
Establishing Price Objectives From Bar Charts

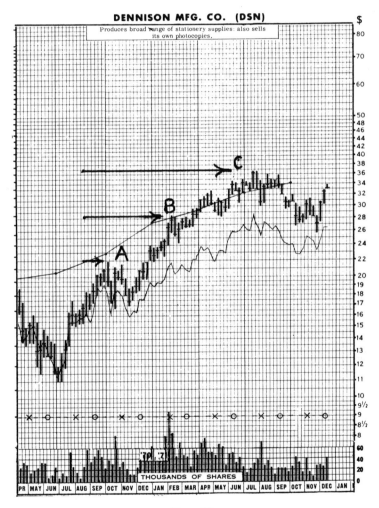

Figure 12

The difference between top A and top B was 6½ points. Top C would have been projected at 35 (6½ points plus 28½).
Source: Securities Research Co., 208 Newbury Street, Boston, Mass. 02116

This method is based upon the tendency of stock movements to repeat themselves in length and time. To estimate the projected end of an up-move, intermediate and short term, measure the difference in points between the most recent top and the one previous. This difference is likely to be repeated at the next top. To estimate potential low points during a decline, measure the distance from the most recent to the previous bottom. The next low should fall approximately as far from the last low as that low was from the low previous.

Make certain that you are relating like highs and lows, that is, that you are comparing short term high to short term high, intermediate high to intermediate high. Short term projections can be made from daily charts and will measure moves arising out of the four and eight week cycles. Use weekly charts to project intermediate top and bottom lows.

Wave And Cycle System #5
A Method For Establishing Time And Price Objectives

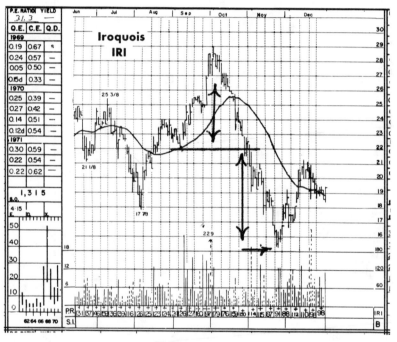

Figure 13

Source: R.W. Mansfield Co., 26 Journal Square, Jersey City, N.J. 07306

Should a stock fail in a cyclical rally, measure from the previous base point to the peak of the last rally. Upon the violation of a previous low, there is a strong possibility that the decline below the base will be equal to the distance between the base and the last high. The estimated time for this decline can be projected using a low to low cyclical time count. Reverse for upside breakouts.

Wave And Cycle System #6
A Second Method For Establishing Time And Price Objective

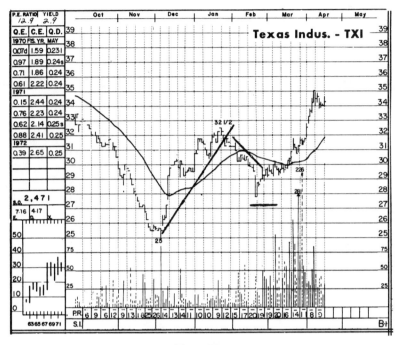

Figure 14

The rise in Texas Industries of 7½ points took 7 weeks. The corrective decline was a 50 per cent retracement and took just under 4 weeks. The loss cut point will be placed at 27.
Source: R.W.Mansfield Co., 26 Journal Square, Jersey City, N.J. 07306
[*Trendlines by author*]

From a study by Larry Williams, *Market Trends and The Price/Time System*, published by Williams Reports.

It is well known that stocks tend to correct approximately fifty per cent of primary moves during corrective action. Not so well publicized is the tendency for the correction to occupy fifty per cent of the time spent on the move to be corrected. For example, suppose a stock rises ten points in eight weeks. The corrective decline should last four weeks and amount to five points.

A trader can pretime his purchases at the points where both the price and time objectives are met, placing close stops as the stock attempts to rally. Should a downside price objective be met in advance of the time objective, caution is indicated. The stock may be weakening. However, should it firm and base throughout the period, positions can be taken.

A decline of further than fifty per cent of the previous up-move may indicate weakness or the onset of a consolidation formation. This method works best with strongly trended stocks, and, of course, does produce some false signals. Figure 14 illustrates the method and the correct placement of loss-cut points.

Cycle and wave theory lends itself to fascinating study and interpretation. I strongly suggest that you secure a chart book or two, daily and weekly, and apply the concepts within this chapter. To emphasize, you will notice the regularity with which rallies and declines arrive "on schedule". Application of time cycle concepts will certainly improve your timing. Properly executed, a cyclical trade usually provides quick profits, with minimal risk—if you employ protective stop-loss precaution. Do not be afraid to take a small loss if the trade goes against you.

Wave And Cycle System #7
Trading By The Clock

The following is reprinted from the *1972 Stock Trader's Almanac,* by Yale Hirsch, The Hirsch Organization, Inc., 6 Deer Trail, Old Tappen, N.J. 07675.

"Certain obvious trading patterns that have evolved over the years provide the professional with many trading opportunities. Here are the typical patterns you will see if you watch the market closely:

Opening

a. A strong opening, accompanied by a late tape, rarely lasts more than a half-hour. Good opportunity for selling.

b. A weak opening, accompanied by light volume in market leaders, usually lasts less than a half-hour. Good opportunity for buying.

c. A mixed opening may last longer than a half-hour—and any action should be delayed.

10:30 to 11 A.M.

a. A sell-off may develop if opening has been strong.

b. A rally can form if opening has been weak.

c. A mixed opening could continue here.

11 to 11:30 A.M.

a. If sell-off started before 11, this could be a good time to do some buying.

b. If rally began before 11, sellers should become interested.

11:30 to Noon

a. Any sell-off started earlier may be losing its steam.

b. Any rally started earlier should be slipping at this time.

Noon to 12:30 P.M.

a. In strong markets, this period becomes perceptibly weaker.

b. In weak markets, this period could be made even weaker by distress selling of over-extended margin accounts.

c. Generally, this time of day is attractive to day-traders buying for a quick turn.

12:30 to 1 P.M.

   a. Lunch deprives the market of normal support and resistance, making this period treacherous for traders.

   b. Professionals normally avoid action during this period.

1 to 1:30 P.M.

   a. A lunch-time rally here could cause a sell-off near the close.

   b. A lunch-time sell-off could spark a good rally near the close.

1:30 to 2 P.M.

   a. Any rally started before 1 P.M. may be dwindling.

   b. Any sell-off started before 1 P.M. could be letting up.

2 to 2:30 P.M.

   a. Important pivotal time when trading decisions must be made.

   b. Traders tend to take profits and cover shorts.

2:30 to 3 P.M.

   a. Calls are cashed in during this interval, adding to any market weakness and/or dampening any rally.

3 P.M. to Close

   a. Rallies begun after 2 P.M. can encounter selling. But if rally starts here, close will be higher.

   b. Sell-offs started after 2 P.M. could reverse sharply, ending in better prices. But if sell-off starts here, close could be much lower.

   Investors and traders should profit from Mr. Hirsch's observations, not by many points on any one trade to be sure, but by eighths and quarters here and there, all of which add up over the course of the year.

   Mr. Hirsch does not mention it, but the market tends to open in the direction it closed the day previously. A strong close usually leads to a strong opening the day after; a weak close to a weak opening. If you suspect an imminent turn, but do not wish to anticipate, employ the short term trading index (Chapter 2, System #10). Buy as soon as the index drops from above 1.0 to less than 1.0, or else upon climactic readings (-1.50 to -2.00). The glamours will usually rebound first. Reverse for selling or shorting. It usually does not pay to act on the opening euphoria unless you wish to sell into strength. Wait for the mid-morning pullback. I have found that after a strong opening, on a *top reversal* day, I get my best sell prices at about 10:20 to 10:30. If it is a bottom reversal point, and the market is starting a sustained rally, don't play too much. We are in an era of instant rally; the early phases of bull moves can be explosive. On bottom climax days, a drop on late tape, look to buy at about 10:20 to 10:30.

The Best Months To Buy Stock

   Also according to the *Stock Trader's Almanac,* the best months to buy stock, based upon their rank order of profitability for various holding periods are as follows: (Table reprinted from the *1972 Almanac*).

	Average Percent Gain	Rank for 30 day holding	Average Percent Gain	Rank for 60 day holding	Average Percent Gain	Rank for 90 day holding	Average Percent Gain	Rank for 6 months
January	0.1%	10	0.7%	10	2.4%	6	4.2%	10
February	0.6	7	2.2	4	2.8	4	4.9	8
March	1.6	3	2.2	4	2.4	6	4.4	9
April	0.5	8	0.1	12	1.5	11	3.3	12
May	-0.6	12	1.0	9	1.9	10	4.0	11
June	1.6	3	2.5	3	2.7	5	6.5	3
July	0.9	6	1.1	8	1.3	12	6.3	4
August	0.2	9	0.3	11	2.0	9	5.7	6
September	0.1	10	1.8	6	3.6	2	6.1	5
October	1.7	1	3.5	1	4.9	1	7.8	1
November	1.7	1	3.2	2	3.5	3	6.7	2
December	1.5	5	1.8	6	2.4	6	5.0	7
	0.8%		1.7%		2.6%		5.4%	
	Average 30 day change		Average 60 day change		Average 90 day change		Average 6 month change	

Summary

October, November and June, in that order, are the best months to pick up stock. Short selling? Try April, May, January and August. But be careful; only May showed an average net loss for holding and that only for the thirty day holding period (-0.6%).

Wave And Time Cycle System #8
First And Last Half Hour

Here's another little system from *Key-Volume Strategies*. This forecasts 30-40 point moves, usually reactions from the primary trend. If the market rises during the day, but falls during the first and last half hour periods, expect a 30-40 point decline to begin within 1-4 trading days. If the market falls during the day but rises during the first and last half hour of the session expect a 30-40 point rally to being within 1-4 trading days. The complete rally or decline we are expecting is generally complete within 10 trading days from the "contrary signal", including the 1-4 day waiting period.

Publisher Conrad also points out that when the market declines during the final half hour 4 or 5 days in a row, a rally can be expected to begin within 5 trading days. Conversely, should the 3-3:30 period show a rise 4-5 days running, a decline may be anticipated within 5 trading days.

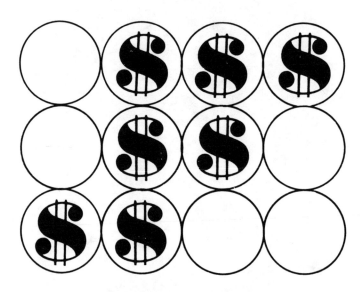

chapter seven

THE A-D LINE TELLS IT LIKE IT IS

What do you do if you want to check out the state of the market? Look at the Dow Jones Industrial Averages? Not too bad, but the Dow tells you about 30 blue chips, not the market as a whole. A hot day for DuPont can throw everything out of perspective. The broader based averages such as the New York Stock Exchange Index or the Standard and Poor's 500 Stock Index represent considerable improvement.

It is the Advance-Decline line, however, that shows what most stocks are doing and what the going odds really are that you'll be able to pick a winner. During market tops, the Dow sometimes keeps moving up while most stocks are turning down. Even the broader based averages occasionally diverge from what the majority of stocks are doing as interest becomes concentrated in a diminishing number of swingers, which get pushed up as traders crowd onto the last train out.

The Advance-Decline line measures the difference between the amount of stocks rising and the amount of stocks falling. For instance, if 800 stocks advance for the day, and 450 fall, the A-D reading for that day is +350. The A-D line is plotted as a cumulative line chart, each day's result added (if plus) or subtracted (if minus) from the previous cumulative total. You can start your chart at any time with any arbitrary number.

The A-D line should be plotted on the same chart sheet as the Dow and preferably the N.Y.S.E. Composite Index as well. If all averages are rising in gear, fine. If all are falling, you're in bear country. However, an early warning is given if the Dow rises while the A-D line does not. The market will usually end up following the A-D line, which should confirm at least intermediate new highs made by the Dow.

Virtually all major market tops have been signalled by a divergence between the A-D line and the Dow regardless of the direction of the divergence. Generally, the A-D line peaks anywhere from one month to over one year before the Dow top. Should the Dow make more than one new high peak while the A-D line continues to drop (a double divergence), a serious decline is almost a certainty. A single divergence, the Dow making one new high while the A-D line fails, is usually good for at least an intermediate decline. The market drop during 1971 was presaged by the Dow making new highs during April while the A-D line was flattening out. At bottoms the A-D line and the Dow tend to hit lows simultaneously.

Figures 1 and 1A show the market action from 1970-1972. Notice how during the period from late January into April 1971, the Dow and the broader averages maintained the slope of their advance, while the A-D line flattened out, and how during the Spring of 1972, the A-D line weakened dramatically compared to the other Indices. The averages to the contrary, the real top to the winter 1972 rally developed in March, not May. The period from March through May showed a double divergence, the Dow twice making new highs with the A-D line dropping below previous support levels.

For those readers who prefer to do their own charting, I suggest that you employ the following relative scales. For every 5 point unit on the Dow, scale your graph for 250 units on the A-D line and .25 on the N.Y.S.E. Composite Index. Arrange your charts similarly to Figures 1 and 1A, so that all readings can be compared the one to the other, with any trading oscillators employed placed above the market averages. Mark in, also, on your charts, in advance, the due date of significant time cycle tops and bottoms.

Number Of Issues Traded

Frequently overlooked as an indicator is the total number of issues traded. This should expand as the market rises for bullish action, fall as the market declines. The implications are clear. An increase in the number of issues traded implies an increase in the breadth of participation of stocks in the advance. However, a climactic bottom may be signified if, following a sharp decline, the number of issues traded suddenly spurts—the public is finally throwing in the towel.

Unchanged Issues

The total of unchanged issues should remain below 300-350 on a daily basis during bull phases. A mounting

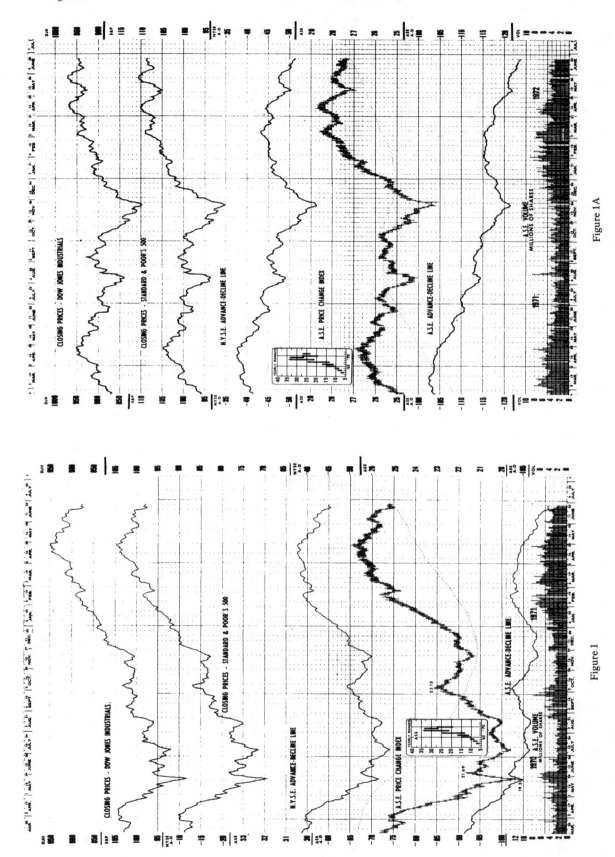

Figure 1A

Figure 1

Source: Trendline Daily Basis Stock Charts, 345 Hudson Street, New York, N.Y. 10014

number of unchanged issues as the market advances indicates sluggishness in an increasing number of stocks. Conversely, a very large number of unchanged issues, say over 375-400, as the market declines indicates that the decline is nearning an end; an increasing number of stocks are giving ground grudgingly. A small number of unchanged issues as the market declines bodes for further decline.

Advance-Decline System #1
How To Recognize Breadth Climaxes

Buying Climaxes

Generally, the market will put together no more than two consecutive days having 1000 or more issues up, without some correction following.

A breadth Selling Climax occurs when the following conditions are met:

1. At least 70% of the total issues traded decline.

2. No more than 15% of the issues traded have advanced.

3. Fewer than 150 issues are unchanged.

4. These units are computed on a daily basis.

Should the market rally after a single day's selling breadth climax, a retracement of approximately 50% of the preceding decline may be expected. Should the market rally after a double selling climax (two climactic days with at least one day intervening), a retracement of 67% may be expected.

Advance-Decline System #2
Constructing An Overbought-Oversold Indicator

An Advance-Decline overbought-oversold oscillator may be constructed in a manner similar to the 10-day moving average stock timing oscillator described in Chapter 5, with one change. Plot a 10-day *moving total* of the advances minus declines, rather than a 10-day moving average. A moving total is simply the total of the last ten days advances minus declines. No division step is required. On the eleventh day, add the figures for that day; subtract the first day's figures.

During bull markets, overbought readings may reach as high as +3000 to +5000 with oversold readings, except for severe declines, reaching between -2000 to -3000. The market will generally reverse direction as these levels are reached. In bear markets, readings of -3500 to -5000 are more common; rallies are truncated. Treat the A-D overbought-oversold index as you would any such device. Look for descending peaks as the market advances for early signs of a decline. During down-moves, look for a gradual upturn in the oscillator as a precursor to an impending advance. Figure 2 demonstrates the relationship of this oscillator to the A-D line and to the Dow averages.

I studied the period from 1970-1972 to establish whether this oscillator might be used similarly to the 10-day moving average oscillator to generate market timing signals. It did not function nearly as well. Use of a crossing of the zero line to generate buy and sell signals produced thirty-two signals from September 1970-March 1972. Ten of sixteen long signals were profitable—net gain, 197.58 Dow points. Six of sixteen sell signals were profitable—net gain, 20.48 Dow points. Total net gain, 218.06 Dow points. This compares to a gain of 189.24 Dow points achieved by the market during this time. Therefore, during bull markets, considering commission costs, you would probably do better holding stock rather than trading on these signals. During bear markets, however, this system would probably produce profits on the short side or would keep you in cash. The major problem lies in the high percentage of false signals which do eat up commissions. The system does catch all major moves. Suggestion: Use the 10-day moving average oscillator for short term timing, the A-D oscillator as a confirming indicator.

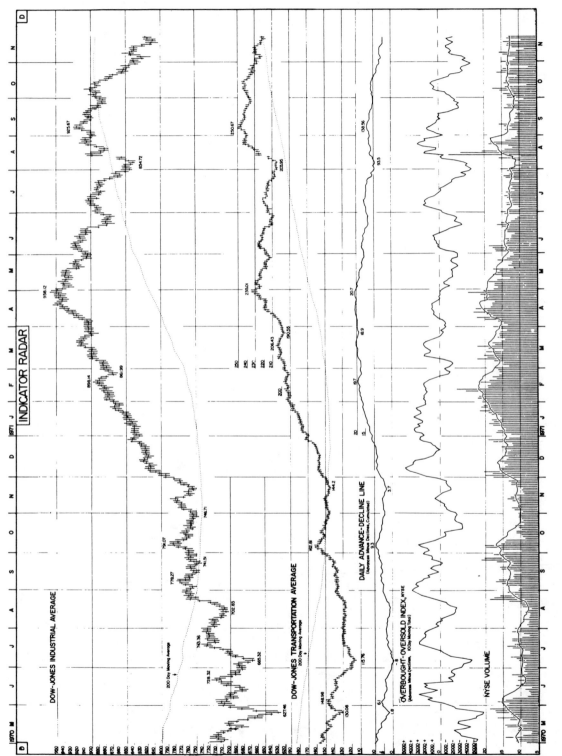

Figure 2

The Overbought-Oversold Index: Note how the index peaked in December
1970, and drifted downwards as the market reached its spring, 1971, top.
Reprinted from *The Paflibe Chartbook*, a weekly publication of
Dines Chart Corporation, *18 East 41st Street, New York. N.Y. 10017*

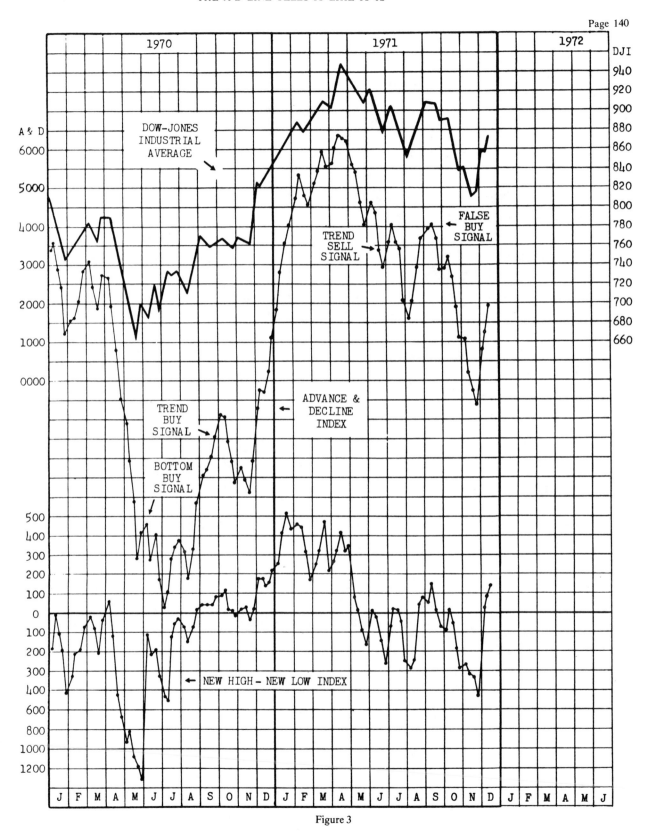

Figure 3

The Haller System gave an excellent major buy signal in September 1970 and an excellent major sell in June 1971. The false buy signal in September 1971 is shown, but not the fine buy in December 1971 or the sell in the spring of 1972.

Source: The Strongest Stocks, *P.O. Box 2048, Stateline, Nevada 89449*

Advance-Decline System #3
The Haller Theory For Determining Major Tops And Bottoms

Gilbert Haller has devised an excellent method for determining major market tops and bottoms. The methodology is described by him in his book, *The Haller Theory of Stock Market Trends* which is available, along with his advisory, *The Strongest Stocks*, based upon his methods. For further information write to Gilbert Haller, P.O. Box 2048, Stateline, Nevada 89449.

The system requires only a few minutes per week to maintain and is highly recommended. Very few unprofitable signals have been provided over its thirty-year history, and it is the most straightforward indicator of major market trend that I know. The system includes five basic signals. Weekly figures are employed, all readily available—in *Barron's* and in other financial publications.

Signals are as follows:

Major Buy Signals [Trend Buy]

1. The weekly Advance-Decline line must turn upwards from its lowest point by an amount of units equal to the number of issues traded on the N.Y.S.E. plus 1000, at this time approximately 2860 units in all.

2. The weekly New High-New Low Index must register 80 or more net new highs.

3. There can be no Trend Buy Signal until after there has been a Trend Sell signal.

Bottom Buy Signals [Alternate Signal]

1. There must be a selling climax, identified by 600 or more net weekly new lows.

2. After the selling climax, buy when the weekly A-D Line rises for more than two weeks and 500 units.

Major Sell Signals

Trend Sell Signals

1. The yield on the Dow Jones Industrial Average must be less than 5% at the time of the signal.

2. The weekly A-D line must turn downward by an amount of units equal to the number of issues traded on the N.Y.S.E. plus 1000.

3. The weekly New High-New Low Index must register 80 or more net new lows.

4. There can be no Trend Sell Signal unless there has previously been a Trend Buy Signal.

3% Yield Top Indicator

1. The weekly yield of the Dow Jones Industrial Average must have declined to less than 3%.

2. After the yield has declined to less than 3%, sell when the weekly A-D line declines for two weeks and 300 units.

Top Sell

1. The yield of the Dow Jones Industrials must have reached a level of less than 4% at some time during the year.

2. The bull market should have been under way for a year or more.

3. The weekly A-D line must have had a failure. A failure is a leg which dips below a previous low. Each leg must be at least two weeks long. A leg may consist of a zig-zag, the whole comprising a leg.

4. The first peak is the highest point reached by the A-D line before its failure.

5. The second peak is the next top of the A-D line.

6. The A-D line must rise for at least three weeks to form the third peak.

7. Sell when the A-D line has declined for two weeks from the third peak and at least 300 units.

8. Weekly net new highs must be less on the third peak than earlier in the bull market. On the third peak, the weekly net new highs should not be much more than half as much as the greatest number of weekly net new highs recorded earlier in the bull market.

9. Volume must be lower on the third peak than earlier in the bull market. Use a six-week moving average to measure volume.

That's all there is to it. Any of the above signals may be acted upon, although in recent years the Trend Buy and Trend Sell signals have appeared most frequently. False bottom buy signals were recorded in 1966 (an older method) and in 1969. A false Trend Buy signal was recorded in September 1971 (also an older method). Use stops on Bottom Buy signals. Occasionally, sell signals have occurred below the level of the buy signals previous, but in the large preponderance of situations, these signals have proven quite profitable and only one Trend Buy (1971) in thirty years did not result in a sizeable move thereafter.

The advantages of this system lie in its reliability, its simplicity, and in the small effort required for maintenance. With this system, you will be into every primary and significant intermediate move relatively early. A major Trend sell was signalled in February 1969. The new bull market buy was signalled in September 1970. A sell was recorded in June 1971; a new buy in September (false) and again in December 1971 (Dow 873). A sell was flashed in June 1972 at Dow 929.03. The disadvantage, inherent in any long term signalling device, lies in the lag between the actual bottom and/or top and the long term signal. Take your pick. Short term signals cost commissions and whipsaw. Long term signals lag.

Advance-Decline System #4
The Harulan Index—A Short, Intermediate And Long Term System Rolled Into One

The Trade Levels, Inc., a technical advisory, has originated a very fine system which doubles for both short and long term investing. Unless you subscribe to the service, the data requires daily updating which takes a few minutes, but the methodology is not complicated.

The long, intermediate and short term components of the system are computed as follows:

Long Term:

Today's index $= C + .01 (P - C)$

where $C =$ yesterday's Long Term Haurlan Index

$P =$ today's N.Y.S.E. advances minus declines

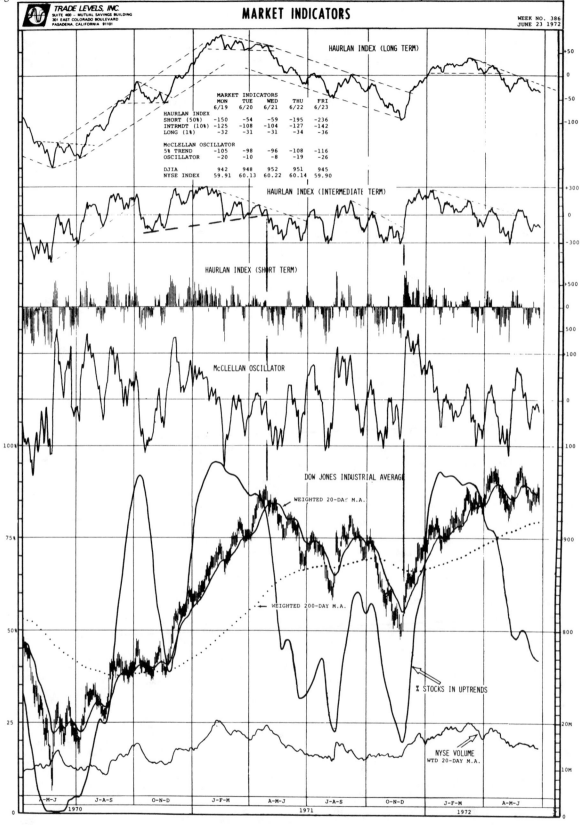

Figure 4

Source: Trade Levels, Inc., Suite 400, Mutual Savings Building, 301 East Colorado Boulevard, Pasadena, California 91101

In other words, first you secure an initial plotting figure to initiate your data. Either secure a trial to *Trade Levels* which carries this material, or for the long term index, carry the process from back issues of *Barron's*, for instance, 200 days to stabilize the data. Presume a reading of 50 on the long term index. Next day, there are 800 advances, 400 declines. Net advances minus declines, +400. The difference between +400 and +50 is 350. One per cent (.01) of 350 is 3.5. We add the 3.5 (or 4, rounded) to the 50. Result, new long term reading, 54. You have to be able to handle negative numbers in these calculations. It is not complicated; a little review with a simple math text should suffice. This is a fine system, and I recommend strongly that you familiarize yourself with its operation.

Intermediate Term

Today's index $= B + .1 (P - B)$

where $B =$ yesterday's intermediate term index

$P =$ today's N.Y.S.E. advances minus declines

In this case, the stabilization period required is 20 days, if you are initiating your own data. The methodology is otherwise similar to the above, except that we use 10 per cent instead of one per cent. For example, yesterday's intermediate reading is +250. Today there are 400 advances, 800 declines. Advances minus declines equals -400. The difference between -400 and +250 (P - B) equals -650. One tenth of -650 equals -65. 250 plus (-65) equals 185, the new intermediate reading.

Short Term

Today's index $= A + .5 (P - A)$

or $\dfrac{A+P}{2}$

where $A =$ yesterday's short term index

$P =$ today's N.Y.S.E. advances minus declines

The stabilization period is 3 days if you are initiating the data. This is a simple formula to apply. Simply add the last short term reading to the latest advances minus declines and divide the result by two. For example: latest short term index, 260. Today's advances minus declines, 140. $\dfrac{260 + 140}{2} = 200$, new short term index.

For each of these, the basic buy and sell indicator is a cross over and below the zero line, except that in the case of the short term index, the reading must remain above or below zero for two days to confirm the signal. Figure 4 illustrates the relationship of the long, intermediate and short term indices to the market.

Although the basic signal is the crossing of the zero line, these indices are quite susceptible to trendline study. The chart shows significant trendlines. Note how trendline breaks create fine action signals, particularly with the long and intermediate term indices. The short term index has the following applications: (1) It provides a measure of the strength of short time buying and selling pulses. As a bull move weakens, its reversal becomes indicated by steadily decreasing peaks in the short and intermediate term indices. (2) The short term index is a sensitive overbought-oversold indicator. Readings of ± 550 almost always indicate the imminence of a short term market reversal or consolidation. (3) Frequently, when short term time cycles are difficult to identify on conventional charts, study of the short term index reveals the underlying minor two- and four-week cycles. This can be a fine help in timing operations.

The long term index provides accurate primary and major intermediate signals. Review Figure 4. Note how in April 1971, the May decline was presaged by a turn down in the long term indicator, its uptrend broken very early in the decline. Also, note the downtrend break that indicated the bull move beginning in November, 1971.

The intermediate index provides effective intermediate signals, upon which the most profitable trading takes place. Again, note significant trendline violations. Traders should attempt to employ trendline violations rather than zero crossings alone to determine action. Strongly overbought-oversold intermediate readings occur when the intermediate index rises or falls to ± 300.

The McClellan Oscillator

This was originally developed by Mr. and Mrs. Sherman L. McClellan of Los Angeles, California and is an integral part of the *Trade Levels* trading system. The indicator makes use of the Haurlan 10 per cent intermediate index plus a less sensitive intermediate indicator. It measures the degree to which a shorter term trend differs from a longer term trend.

The procedure for calculation is as follows:

1. Update the 10 per cent intermediate indicator as described above.

2. Create a 5 per cent intermediate indicator according to the formula:

Today's index equals $B + .05 (P - B)$

where B = yesterday's index (5 per cent basis)

P = today's N.Y.S.E. advances minus declines

Use a 40-day period to stabilize the data if you are initiating your own charts.

3. Subtract the value of the 5 per cent index from the value of the 10 per cent index to determine the value of the McClellan Oscillator.

Mathematically, the formula is as follows:

Let yesterday's 10 per cent index value be A.

Let yesterday's 5 per cent index value be B.

Let today's net N.Y.S.E. advances minus declines be C.

Today's 10 per cent index is $A + .1 (C - A)$

Today's 5 per cent index is $B + .05 (C - B)$

Today's McClellan Oscillator is the new A - B.

Presume that previous day's values were 10 per cent (60), 5 per cent (30) and McClellan Oscillator 30. We get 250 more advances than declines today. The new 10 per cent index equals 79; the new 5 per cent index equals 41. The new McClellan Oscillator reading is 38. Do the complete computation yourself.

Application Of The Oscillator

The McClellan Oscillator is quite sensitive and is a good short to intermediate term indicator. Its characteristics are:

1. Oversold readings are in the area of -100; overbought readings are in the area of +100. Expect some reaction or consolidation as these areas are reached.

2. The Oscillator should move with the market averages. Divergences presage a turn in the market.

3. The Oscillator will make major bottoms at 20 to 24 week intervals, lesser bottoms at 10 to 13 week intervals. Look for multiple formations.

4. At the beginning of a strong surge, up or down, the Oscillator will quickly reach peaks and troughs of +100 or -100 respectively. As the market move loses momentum it will drift towards zero.

5. Like any overbought-oversold indicator, it will vacillate near zero in an indecisive market.

6. The Oscillator is subject to trendline study. Be prepared to buy as soon as it turns up from a multiple bottom formation, particularly at its 24-week cyclical low.

Examine Figure 4 for the effective use of the Oscillator.

Advance-Decline System #5
The Use Of Market Plurality

Market plurality is defined as the daily difference between advancing and declining stocks. It does not matter whether there are more advancing or more declining stocks. For example, on a day in which 800 stocks advance and 300 decline, the plurality is 500. On a day that 450 advance and 650 decline, the plurality is 200. Compute a 10-day moving total of market plurality. Any total under 2000, particularly following an advance, usually indicates a trend reversal.

Advance-Decline System #6
Study The Per Cent Of Industry Groups Rising And Falling

Barron's and other financial publications carry group listings and group performance each week. Evaluate the percentage of groups in upswings and the percentage in downswings. Run a line chart of each week's result and note the trend. This will provide an indication of where the market is heading, particularly as trends reverse.

chapter eight

FUNDAMENTAL SYSTEMS: IF YOU WANT MORE THAN PRETTY CHARTS

Bear markets bring out the fundamentalist in all of us. When stocks are zooming and the sky's the limit, brokers and traders alike lose sight of real value—the name of the game is not to be the last sucker on line. Comes the deluge, everyone repents, promises never again to sin and for a while there's a run on utility stocks.

The 1969-1970 crash did accomplish one thing. It put the Federal Reserve Board in the spotlight as never before. The tight money crunch of 1970 really hurt, and suddenly everyone became money supply conscious. The fact is—and it cannot be denied—as money supply goes, so goes the market. And as earnings go, in the long run, so goes the price of stocks. The end of the 1970 crash could have been predicted by a variety of technical devices (Chapter 1, The Trendline Measuring System; Chapter 5, Time Cycles). However, fundamentally, the market had become dirt cheap. As soon as the Fed began to prime the money pump, we were off and running.

There are times when the cats and dogs fly and the Amex and over-the-counter are the places to be, the more fantastic the price-earnings ratio the better. By and large, though, I recommend that you stick to fundamentally sound companies. They can be small—sometimes the smaller the better, to a point. Look into promising situations where earnings growth and potential appear dynamic. These situations are the really explosive vehicles in good markets. If your fundamental assessments turn out badly, get out. We will be discussing below how to identify promising growth situations, and some ways of determining whether or not the market as a whole is cheap or expensive.

Should you sell on the news of earnings reports? Some traders do, particularly on good news, on the theory that the good news has already been discounted and the stock will sell off on the report. I do not recommend this practice unless the technical situation is weak. In many cases, the stock will settle back for a few points after the news, providing that the report matched expectations. If the earnings report exceeds expectations, the stock may take off on a nice run. If the earnings report fell below expectations, it may be difficult to get out alive. Don't hang on if earnings turn down, particularly if you bought in for a trade. If you're stopped out, go. A declining stock may be sometimes purchased on a bad earnings report, *if the report was no worse than Wall Street anticipated*. Some bounce frequently occurs in hopes of a turnaround. Interestingly, research has shown that, generally, profitable purchases may be made when a company announces a dividend cut. Be leery of broker's tips based on inside contact with corporate officials. As often as not, these officials can't be trusted. They have an investment in good-mouthing their outfits. Sometimes they have stock of their own to feed out. Highly unlikely that they'll tell it like it is.

Fundamental System #1
Identifying The Growth Pattern Of A Stock

Growth Stocks

The charts employed here, published by the Securities Research Company, are highly recommended for the purposes of identifying earnings movement, dividend payout and relative strength. The earnings plot is the heavy black line on the chart, with black dots, spaced quarterly. The earnings and dividend scale is on the left of the chart.

Figure 1 is a chart of I.B.M., the king of the growth vehicles. Notice, however, the recent flattening of the earnings curve and with it the flattening of I.B.M.'s price movement. As earnings go, so goes the price of a stock. Apart from that, the earnings pattern is typical of a solid growth company, albeit now a mature one. The earnings growth as well as dividend growth is steady. The stock moves essentially in a smooth uptrend. Does this chart tell you anything about whether to buy I.B.M. now as a dynamic growth vehicle? It tells me to stay away at this point. Compare to McDonald's and Coca-Cola. (Figures 2 and 3).

Reverse Growth Situation

Here's a sad sack chart. Sprague Electric, a real swinger in the mid-sixties, has had its earnings knocked clear off the chart, reporting deficits since 1968. From time to time the stock rallies as investors, recalling the glory days, try again. Notice again the correlation between earnings and price.

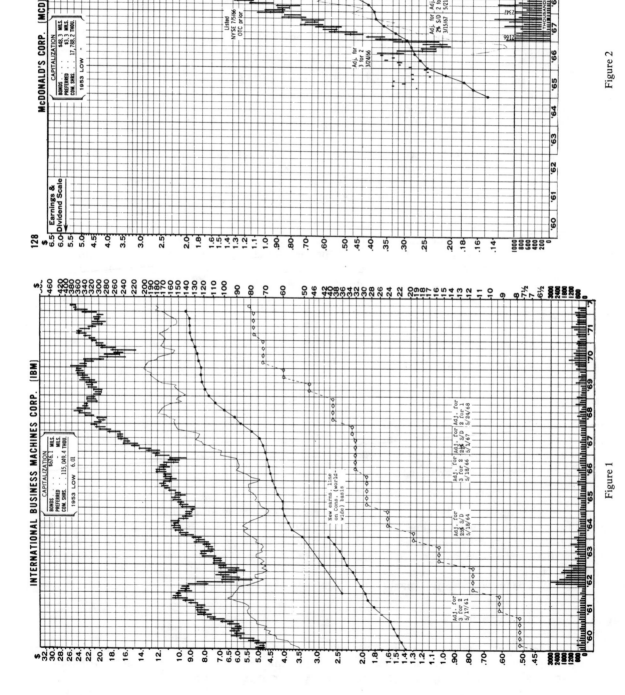

Figure 1

Figure 2

Source: Securities Research Co., 208 Newbury Street, Boston, Mass. 02116

Source: Securities Research Co., 208 Newbury Street, Boston, Mass. 02116

Cyclical Situation

A cyclical situation is just that, a company whose earnings rise and fall somewhat erratically—in gear with the economy (auto makers), or in gear with crops, their own industry or whatever. These companies do not command the high multiple of growth companies, but timed properly, can be excellent trading vehicles. Notice the swings in Stokely-Van Camp, in tune to its fluctuating earnings. Do not confuse a cyclical company with a growth situation. During hot times many people who should know better do precisely that. In the late 1960's, Stokely introduced a new energy drink, Gatorade. Suddenly, it became a "concept" stock and the funds were in buying—and many of them got bagged. As a point of fact, Stokely is a solid but cyclical situation, no more, no less.

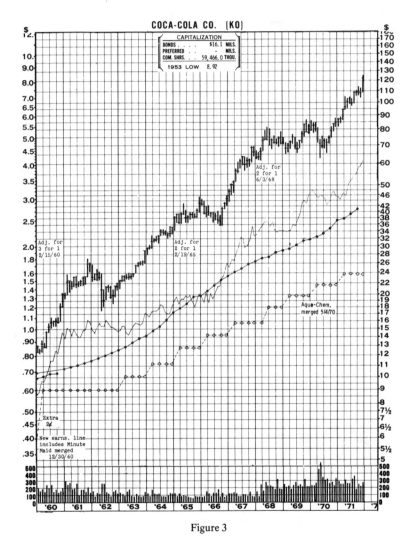

Figure 3

Source: Securities Research Co., 208 Newbury Street, Boston, Mass. 02116

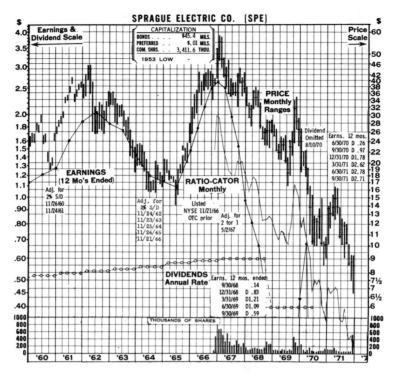

Figure 4

Source: Securities Research Co., 208 Newbury Street, Boston, Mass. 02116

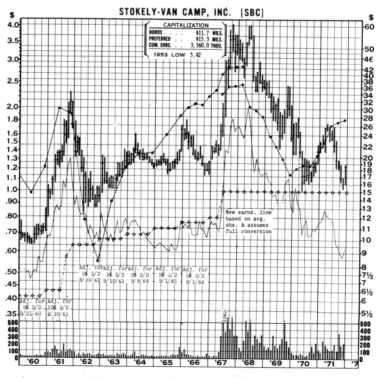

Figure 5

Source: Securities Research Co., 208 Newbury Street, Boston, Mass. 02116

Income Situations

These are characterized by a high dividend payout, a slow but usually steady earnings growth. In recent years these stocks have been out of favor and despite steadily rising earnings the bulk of utility stocks show the same slow price erosion since the mid-60's as the Long Island Lighting Company. Income stocks have generally not been good buys for years, since price erosions have eaten up whatever dividend benefits investors have received. In early 1972, American Telephone was trading at a ten year low.

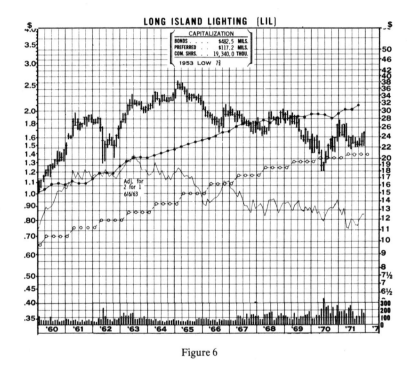

Figure 6

Source: Securities Research Co., 208 Newbury Street, Boston, Mass. 02116

Fundamental System #2
A Quick Way To Estimate Whether A Stock Is Expensive

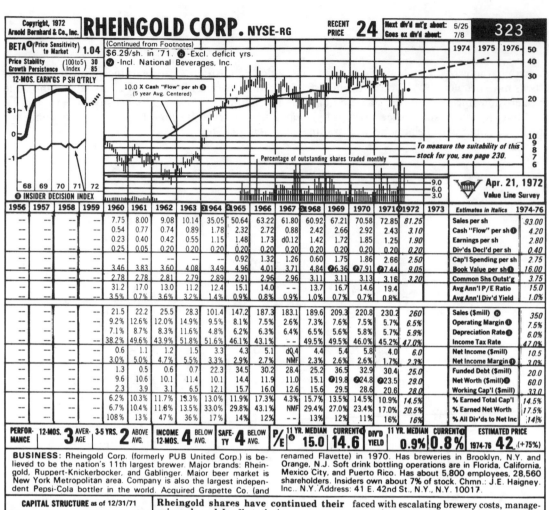

RHEINGOLD CORP. NYSE-RG

Copyright, 1972
Arnold Bernhard & Co., Inc.

RECENT PRICE **24**

Next div'd mt'g about: 5/25
Goes ex div'd about: 7/8

323

BETA (Price Sensitivity to Market) **1.04**

Price Stability (100 to 5) 30
Growth Persistence (Index) 85

(Continued from Footnotes)
$6.29/sh. in '71. ⑥-Excl. deficit yrs.
⑦ -Incl. National Beverages, Inc.

1974	1975	1976

10.0 X Cash "Flow" per sh ①
(5 year Avg. Centered)

To measure the suitability of this stock for you, see page 230.

Percentage of outstanding shares traded monthly

68 69 70 71 72

① INSIDER DECISION INDEX

Apr. 21, 1972
Value Line Survey

	1956	1957	1958	1959	1960	1961	1962	1963	1964	1965	1966	1967	1968	1969	1970	1971	1972	1973	Estimates in Italics	1974-76
	--	--	--	--	7.75	8.00	9.08	10.14	35.05	50.64	63.22	61.80	60.92	67.21	70.58	72.85	81.25		Sales per sh	93.00
	--	--	--	--	0.54	0.77	0.74	0.89	1.78	2.32	2.72	0.88	2.42	2.66	2.92	2.43	3.10		Cash "Flow" per sh ①	4.20
	--	--	--	--	0.23	0.40	0.42	0.55	1.15	1.48	1.73	d0.12	1.42	1.72	1.85	1.25	1.90		Earnings per sh	2.80
	--	--	--	--	0.25	0.05	0.20	0.20	0.20	0.20	0.20	0.20	0.20	0.20	0.20	0.20	0.20		Div'ds Decl'd per sh	0.40
	--	--	--	--						0.92	1.32	0.60	1.75	1.86		2.66	2.50		Cap'l Spending per sh	2.75
	--	--	--	--	3.46	3.83	3.60	4.08	3.49	4.96	4.01	3.71	4.84	⑥6.36	⑦7.91	⑦7.44	9.05		Book Value per sh ①	16.00
	--	--	--	--	2.78	2.78	2.81	2.79	2.89	2.91	2.96	2.96	3.11	3.11	3.13	3.16	3.20		Common Shs Outst'g	3.75
	--	--	--	--	31.2	17.0	13.0	11.2	12.4	15.1	14.0	--	13.7	16.7	14.6	19.4			Avg Ann'l P/E Ratio	15.0
	--	--	--	--	3.5%	0.7%	3.6%	3.2%	1.4%	0.9%	0.8%	0.9%	1.0%	0.7%	0.7%	0.8%			Avg Ann'l Div'd Yield	1.0%
	--	--	--	--	21.5	22.2	25.5	28.3	101.4	147.2	187.3	183.1	189.6	209.3	220.8	230.2	260		Sales ($mill) ⑥	350
	--	--	--	--	9.2%	12.6%	12.0%	14.9%	9.5%	8.1%	7.5%	2.6%	7.3%	7.6%	7.5%	5.7%	6.5%		Operating Margin ①	7.5%
	--	--	--	--	7.1%	8.7%	8.3%	11.6%	4.8%	6.2%	6.3%	6.4%	6.5%	5.6%	5.8%	5.7%	5.9%		Depreciation Rate ①	6.0%
	--	--	--	--	38.2%	49.6%	43.9%	51.8%	51.6%	46.1%	43.1%	--	49.5%	49.5%	46.0%	45.2%	47.0%		Income Tax Rate	47.0%
	--	--	--	--	0.6	1.1	1.2	1.5	3.3	4.3	5.1	d0.4	4.4	5.4	5.8	4.0	6.0		Net Income ($mill)	10.5
	--	--	--	--	3.0%	5.0%	4.7%	5.5%	3.3%	2.9%	2.7%	NMF	2.3%	2.6%	2.6%	1.7%	2.3%		Net Income Margin ①	3.0%
	--	--	--	--	1.3	0.5	0.6	0.7	22.3	34.5	30.2	28.4	25.2	36.5	32.9	30.4	25.0		Funded Debt ($mill)	20.0
	--	--	--	--	9.6	10.6	10.1	11.4	10.1	14.4	11.9	11.0	15.1	⑦19.8	⑦24.8	⑦23.5	29.0		Net Worth ($mill) ①	60.0
	--	--	--	--	2.3	3.9	3.1	6.5	12.1	15.7	16.0	12.6	15.6	29.5	28.6	20.6	28.0		Working Cap'l ($mill)	33.0
	--	--	--	--	6.2%	10.3%	11.7%	15.3%	13.0%	11.9%	17.3%	4.3%	15.7%	13.5%	14.5%	10.9%	14.5%		% Earned Total Cap'l	14.5%
	--	--	--	--	6.7%	10.4%	11.8%	13.5%	33.0%	29.8%	43.1%	NMF	29.4%	27.0%	23.4%	17.0%	20.5%		% Earned Net Worth	17.5%
	--	--	--	--	108%	13%	47%	36%	17%	14%	12%	--	13%	12%	11%	16%	16%		% All Div'ds to Net Inc	14%

PERFOR-MANCE	12-MOS. **3** AVER-AGE	3-5 YRS. **2** ABOVE AVG.	INCOME 12-MOS. **4** BELOW AVG.	SAFE-TY **4** BELOW AVG.	P/E **15.0** 11 YR. MEDIAN	CURRENT **14.6**	DIV'D YIELD **0.9%** 11 YR. MEDIAN	**0.8%** CURRENT	ESTIMATED PRICE 1974-76 **42** (+75%)

BUSINESS: Rheingold Corp. (formerly PUB United Corp.) is believed to be the nation's 11th largest brewer. Major brands: Rheingold, Ruppert-Knickerbocker, and Gablinger. Major beer market is New York Metropolitan area. Company is also the largest independent Pepsi-Cola bottler in the world. Acquired Grapette Co. (and renamed Flavette) in 1970. Has breweries in Brooklyn, N.Y. and Orange, N.J. Soft drink bottling operations are in Florida, California, Mexico City, and Puerto Rico. Has about 5,800 employees, 28,560 shareholders. Insiders own about 7% of stock. Chmn.: J.E. Haigney. Inc., N.Y. Address: 41 E. 42nd St., N.Y., N.Y. 10017.

CAPITAL STRUCTURE as of 12/31/71

Debt $30.4 mill. Interest $1.9 mill.
Incl. $15 mill. 6 1/2% sub. debs. due 1994 conv. into common at $30 a share.

Pfd Stock None   Pfd Div None

Common Stock 3,156,107 shares

Cal-endar	QUARTERLY SALES ($ Millions)				Full Year
	Mar. 31	June 30	Sept. 30	Dec. 31	
1968	38.2	49.4	55.7	46.3	189.6
1969	40.3	55.6	62.0	51.4	209.3
1970	45.4	57.3	63.0	55.1	220.8
1971	48.1	80.6	68.3	53.2	230.2
1972	52.0	67.0	76.0	65.0	260

Cal-endar	QUARTERLY EARNINGS (per sh.)				Full Year
	Mar. 31	June 30	Sept. 30	Dec. 31	
1968	.05	.41	.61	.35	1.42
1969	.08	.57	.70	.37	1.72
1970	.16	.60	.68	.41	1.85
1971	.09	.42	.60	.14	1.25
1972	.10	.60	.80	.40	1.90

Cal-endar	QUARTERLY DIVIDENDS PAID ②				Full Year
	Mar. 31	June 30	Sept. 30	Dec. 31	
1968	.05	.05	.05	.05	.20
1969	.05	.05	.05	.05	.20
1970	.05	.05	.05	.05	.20
1971	.05	.05	.05	.05	.20
1972	.05				

Rheingold shares have continued their price rebound. In effect, the investment community has seemingly forgotten about last year's disappointing results and is looking forward to possibly record earnings this year. From our vantage point, however, this equity now seems rather fully priced. We expect it to parallel the market averages in the coming 12 months. For the longer 3- to 5-year pull, with more soft drink acquisitions likely, the stock's appreciation prospects are good.

A weak final quarter diminished last year's results. Reasons: the East Coast dock strike, which hurt beer sales in Puerto Rico, and, also on the Island, a shortage of soft drink cans... Rheingold's slim dividend is probably not in jeopardy, but another acquisition could require more financing.

An earnings recovery seems likely this year. The highly-leveraged brewing operation, the major earnings swing factor, could benefit from a government-approved 3.42% overall price increase. Moreover,

faced with escalating brewery costs, management is requesting union leadership to forego automatic wage increases and other benefits which are scheduled to go in effect on June 1st.

Rheingold may sue two of its major competitors, presumably Anheuser-Busch and Schlitz, to prevent "discriminatory price practices". Whether or not management goes to court, Rheingold's 1972 earnings are not likely to be affected.

Long-term growth will primarily be in soft drink operations, which contributed 78% of pre-tax income on only 31% of sales last year. (Comparable figures for 1970 were 59% and 30%, respectively.) The recent acquisition of National Beverages, Inc., which has a 15-county soft drink franchise in Central Florida (including Disney World), augurs well for earnings beyond 1972. R.S.G.

INVESTMENT COMPANY HOLDINGS ①

3-31-71 (5 fds)	6-30-71 (4 fds)	9-30-71 (2 fds)	12-31-71 (2 fds)
427,700 shs.	342,500 shs.	225,000 shs.	250,000 shs.

GROWTH	Per Share	15 Yrs.	10 Yrs.	5 Yrs.	Estimated to '74-'76
	Sales	--	30.7%	5.4%	6.0%
	Cash "Flow"	--	17.0%	6.1%	9.5%
	Earnings	--	22.2%	2.8%	11.5%
	Book Value	--	6.6%	12.1%	17.0%
	Price	--	19.1%	3.8%	20.5% ①

①-See Explanation of Terms on p. 355. ②-Div'd payment dates: Jan. 19, Apr. 30, July 30, Oct. 29. ③-Incl. Rheingold Breweries from 5-64. ④-Incl. Jacob Ruppert & Co. ⑤-Incl. Pepsi-Cola Bottling Co. of Santa Ana. ⑥-Incl. excise tax. ⑦-Excl. intangible assets of $14.3 mill., $4.58/sh in '69; $14.8 mill., $4.73/sh in '70; $19.9 mill. (Continued on Chart)

Simply review a sound fundamental publication, Standard and Poor's, Moody's or an advisory such as *Value Line*. Figure 7 is a fundamental report of Rheingold Corporation. Notice that the price oscillates around the cash flow which is in a steady uptrend. The median price-earnings ratio for the stock has been 15.0. Current P-E ratio, 14.6. The stock at the moment, appears slightly undervalued. Standard and Poor's carries price-earnings ratios for stocks for a period of years. Evaluate: (1) have earnings remained steady, declined or continued to grow and (2) compared to past years, is the stock selling at a high or low multiple? Relate the current price-earnings ratio to the history of that particular stock. If it is selling at ten times multiple (price equals ten times annual earnings), is this ratio average, low, or high historically for that stock? Has the multiple for the stock gradually declined or has it remained within a constant range over the years?

This technique can be applied to the market averages as well. For instance, the Dow Jones Price-Earnings ratio, in April 1970, stood at 13.7, very cheap. Before the April 1971 decline, it had stood at 18.3. Earnings rose over the year. By April 1972, despite higher prices it stood at 17.6, still not historically at a peak. In 1961, the Dow price-earnings ratio reached 24. The Amex median price-earnings ratio reached a high of 26.3 in December 1968, declining then to a low of 11.5 at the May 1970 bottom. Figure 8 illustrates price-earnings relationships for several market indices. Note the historic high and low points.

P/E Ratio

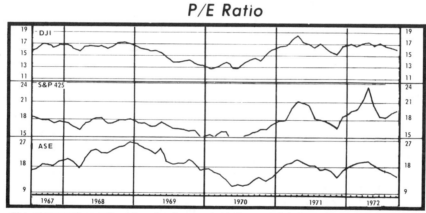

The price-earnings ratio of three leading market indexes, updated monthly, are plotted jointly on the chart above.

Figure 8

Source: The Media General Financial Weekly, 119 North Third Street
Richmond, Virginia 23261

Actually, in recent years, investors have not been willing to pay as much for earnings as in the past. From 1951-1961 the multiple for the Dow group rose from under eight times earnings to the peak of twenty-four times earnings, reached in 1961. Although the actual earnings recorded remained relatively flat during this decade, the period was marked by optimism in America's future. Actual earnings rose strongly from 1961-1966; however, investors have never again been willing to pay as much as twenty times earnings for Dow stocks again. The market seems to top now when the Dow multiple stands at about 18 and the multiple for the Standard and Poor's 425 Index reaches 20-24.

Fundamental System #3
How To Tell If A Stock Is Cheap At Thirty Times Earnings And Expensive At Ten Times Earnings

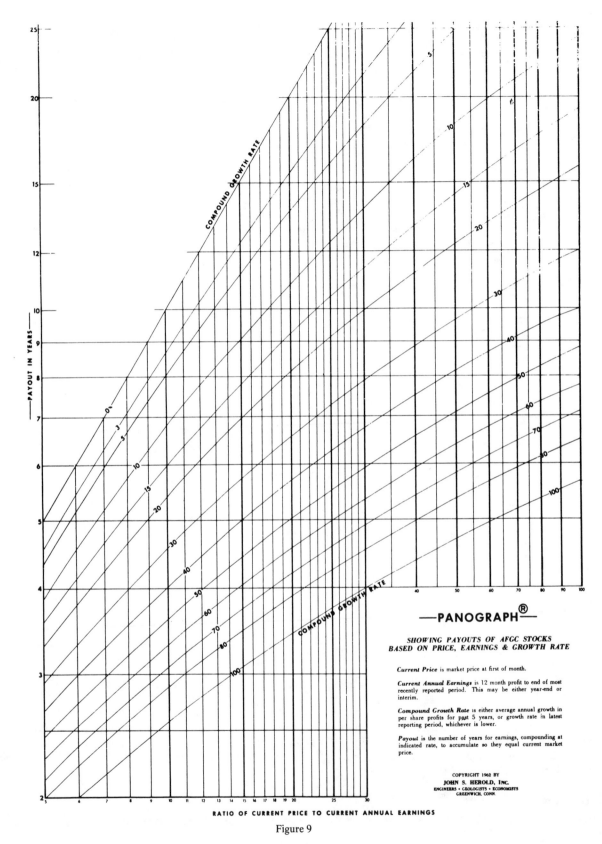

PAYOUT IN YEARS

COMPOUND GROWTH RATE

COMPOUND GROWTH RATE

—PANOGRAPH®—

SHOWING PAYOUTS OF AFGC STOCKS
BASED ON PRICE, EARNINGS & GROWTH RATE

Current Price is market price at first of month.

Current Annual Earnings is 12 month profit to end of most recently reported period. This may be either year-end or interim.

Compound Growth Rate is either average annual growth in per share profits for past 5 years, or growth rate in latest reporting period, whichever is lower.

Payout is the number of years for earnings, compounding at indicated rate, to accumulate so they equal current market price.

COPYRIGHT 1962 BY
JOHN S. HEROLD, INC.
ENGINEERS · GEOLOGISTS · ECONOMISTS
GREENWICH, CONN.

RATIO OF CURRENT PRICE TO CURRENT ANNUAL EARNINGS

Figure 9

Source: John S. Herold, Inc., 35 Mason Street, Greenwich, Conn. 06830

The following is abstracted from *A Doctor's Simple Scientific Approach To Stock Market Profits* by Joseph D. Sutton, M.D. (Executive Reports Corporation, Englewood Cliffs, N.J.) This is a fine book for fundamental investors.

This investment technique is based upon the concept of "payout time", the number of years required for earnings per share, compounded at a given growth rate, to total the present price of the stock. For example, presume a stock selling at $60 with current earnings of $2.00 annually, compounding at a 30 per cent growth rate. It would take approximately eight years for cumulative earnings to total $60.00. By comparison, assume a company selling for $60.00, earning $6.00, but compounding at a growth rate of only one per cent. The payout time required will be approximately 9½ years. The stock selling at 30 times earnings is "cheaper" than the stock selling at ten times earnings. The rapid growth rate of the "high multiple" stock means that investors will pay a premium in price, and should the growth continue, will receive a premium in price appreciation. If the growth trend should reverse? Run fast.

Growth rate can be determined by a study of a series of annual earnings reports. For instance, presume the following series of reports:

1967	1.00	
1968	1.20	growth rate, 20% from previous year
1969	1.50	growth rate, 20% from previous year
1970	1.75	growth rate 16-2/3% from previous year
1971	2.10	growth rate 20% from previous year

We divide the total, 77% (rounded), by four annual periods for an annual growth rate of 19.25%.

Once the growth rate is established, a simple method for determining payout time is available. Employ Figure 9, a panograph. Locate the price-earnings ratio of the stock at the bottom of the panograph. Locate its growth rate. On the left will be the payout time in years. Less than eight years payout time is excellent. The most likely situations will be found among small, aggressive and rapidly growing companies. Investors may purchase stocks providing a payout exists of less than eight years, preferably six, and hold until earnings growth stops or the growth rate slows sufficiently to expand the payout time above eight years.

A second method of selecting from among stocks on a fundamental basis involves the use of another panograph (Figure 10).

By use of this panograph, an estimate can be made of the potential rate of price appreciation of a given stock. Locate the current growth rate and current price-earnings ratio on the panograph. To the left of the intersection of these co-ordinates can be found the potential annual gain of the stock. Stocks falling within the upper boundaries of the panograph are likely to show the best price appreciation.

WHERE TO LOCATE INFORMATION REGARDING HIGH GROWTH RATE STOCKS

The information required for this work is readily available from a variety of sources. *Value Line Investment Survey* now carries this data for the stocks it reviews. *America's Fastest Growing Companies* selects stocks with rapid growth rates. *Paflibe*, an excellent chartbook published by the Dines Chart Corporation does likewise. Figure 11 is from *Paflibe*. If at all possible, select your technical picks from among high growth stocks.

In evaluating earnings reports make certain that you are dealing with "real" earnings, not non-recurring

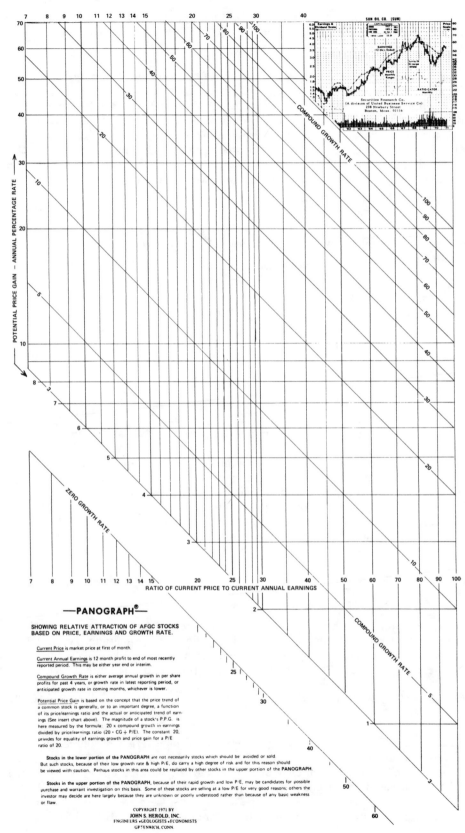

Figure 10

DINES' LISTING OF AMERICA'S SMARTEST MANAGEMENTS - FOR INVESTORS

Growth Stocks - Cream of the Crop

Latest Growth Rate %	4 Year Ave Earn Growth Rate %	Paf-libe Page No	Cross-chart Page No	Name - (Exchange-Price)	1966	1967	1968	1969	1970	1971	Latest 12 Mos	Latest Quarter Reported	P/E Last 12 Mos Earn	Adj* Earn	Adj** P/E Ratio
194	73	69	107B	Winnebago Indus (NYSE-62)	—	.05	.13	.21	.38	—	.94	Nov	65.9	2.76	22.5
167	119	84	125	Lennar Corp (ASE-38)	d.004	.08	.21	.39	.62	1.66	1.66	Nov	22.9	4.43	8.6
122	93	85	127A	Devel Corp of Amer (ASE-36)	.06	.11	.30	.39	.73	—	1.29	Sep	27.9	2.86	12.6
109	98	84	125	Punta Gorda Isles (ASE-19)	.09	.13	.28	.67	.86	1.80	1.80	Dec	10.6	3.76	5.1
103	133	65	98	Ponderosa Systems (ASE-88)	—	.04	.06	.19	.35	—	1.50	Nov	58.7	3.05	28.9
88	72	69	108	Champion Home Builders (ASE-57)	—	.11	.13	.38	.52	—	1.30	Nov	43.8	2.44	23.4
77	444	21	28	Scottex Corp (ASE-16)	.02	.34	.51	.60	1.24	—	1.72	Sep	9.3	3.04	5.3
77	52	103	154	Weight Watchers (OTC-19)	.06	.10	.18	.30	.39	.71	.69	Dec	27.5	1.22	15.6
75	49	62	92	Levitz Furniture (NYSE-136)	—	.18	.25	.39	.57	.87	1.33	Oct	102.3	2.33	58.4
64	30	69	107A	Mobile Homes Industries (ASE-44)	—	.49	.71	.85	1.00	1.35	1.61	Nov	27.3	2.64	16.7
63	44	—	90A	Family Dollar Stores (ASE-37)	.10	.20	.33	.44	.53	—	.91	Nov	40.7	1.48	25.0
59	346	103	154	McKeon Construction (ASE-27)	.02	Nil	.04	.11	.95	—	1.51	Nov	17.9	2.40	11.3
55	72	103	154	Hycel Inc (OTC-30)	.04	.07	.10	.17	.34	—	.45	Jun	66.7	.70	42.9
55	62	103	154	Bandag Inc (OTC-62)	.05	.14	.23	.40	.60	—	.93	Dec	66.7	1.44	43.1
54	39	60	88	Edmos Corp (ASE-18)	.35	.63	.67	.69	1.16	—	1.45	Sep	12.4	2.23	8.1
51	74	103	154	Minnesota Fabrics (OTC-42)	.07	.08	.18	.22	.35	.66	.74	Dec	56.8	1.12	37.5
49	45	103	154	Colonial Penn Group (OTC-78)	.50	.52	.79	1.45	2.03	—	1.29	Sep	60.5	2.05	38.0
47	67	103	154	Liberty Homes Inc (OTC-20)	.08	.11	.25	.40	.61	—	.72	Sep	27.8	1.06	18.9
47	67	72	108	Coit International (ASE-26)@	.01	.11	.21	.28	.53	—	.53	Oct	49.1	.78	33.3
47	72	102	154	Baker Bros (OTC-39)	.37	.45	.68	1.03	1.33	1.52	1.52	Nov	25.7	2.22	17.6
46	40	40	54	Kaufman & Broad (NYSE-43)	.19	.22	.25	.41	.57	.82	.82	Nov	52.4	1.20	35.8
46	41	72	109	House of Fabrics (ASE-43)	.21	.31	.43	.54	.80	—	.98	Sep	43.9	1.41	30.5
44	72	103	154	Westchester Corp (OTC-23)	—	.08	.32	.70	.84	1.24	1.58	Oct	14.6	2.13	10.8
44	122	108	154	Fleetwood Enterprises (NYSE-39)	.06	.09	.18	.35	.50	.66	.85	Oct	45.9	1.13	34.5
35	67	103	154	Horizon Corp (NYSE-52)	.74	1.14	1.65	2.78	4.06	5.48	6.24	Sep	8.3	8.30	6.3
33	48	48	64	Telecor (OTC-38)	.16	.27	.45	.67	.90	1.30	1.54	Nov	24.7	2.05	18.5
33	44	48	64	Electronic Data Systems	.01	.03	.14	.30	.61	.89	.98	Oct	46.9	1.28	35.9
33	103	48	63	Automatic Data Proc (NYSE-83)	.17	.27	.38	.46	.57	.87	.98	Dec	84.7	1.27	65.4
31	158	103	154	Church's Fried Chicken (OTC-57)	.06	.16	.37	.70	1.22	—	1.37	Sep	41.6	1.77	32.2
31	34	102	154	Programming Methods (OTC-23)	.07	.17	.36	.48	.66	—	.78	Sep	29.5	1.00	23.0
29	115	80	120A	Damon Corp (NYSE-52)	.07	.17	.38	.55	.71	.90	.96	Nov	54.2	1.23	52.3
28	82	65	98	McDonald's Corp (NYSE-83)	.29	.39	.57	.77	.99	—	1.22	Sep	68.0	1.45	57.2
28	56	72	107A	Arctic Enterprises (NYSE-29)	.01	.07	.21	.62	1.19	1.82	2.23	Dec	13.0	2.83	10.2
27	80	63	93	Circle K Corp (ASE-30)	—	.28	.34	.42	.50	.68	.73	Oct	41.1	.92	32.6
26	65	25	33	General Battery Corp (ASE-20)	—	.18	.40	1.04	1.40	2.17	2.11	Oct	9.5	2.64	7.6
26	135	61A	90	Caldor Inc (ASE-38)	—	.37	.54	.75	.96	1.16	1.20	Oct	31.7	1.50	25.3
25	63	103	120A	Flagg Indus (ASE-13)	—	.02	.18	.27	.72	1.38	1.18	Oct	11.0	1.44	9.0
25	25	102	128A	Midwestern Financial (ASE-23)@	.27	.35	.47	.67	1.16	—	1.26	Dec	18.3	1.51	15.2
25	93	84	127	General Development (NYSE-27)	.54	.86	.99	1.30	1.73	—	1.92	Sep	14.1	2.30	11.7

*Latest earnings growth rate applied to latest 12 months' earnings in a strictly mechanical fashion, not an earnings estimate.
**Price/Earnings Ratio of adjusted earnings. @ = Newly Listed. # = Delisted. e = Reinstated Earnings. d = Deficit. Average price per share, America's Smartest Managements = 42.46. Average Price/Earnings Ratio = 37.79. Average Adjusted Price/Earnings Ratio = 25.04.

Figure 11

Source: The Dines Chartbook, Dines Chart Corporation, 18 East 41st Street, New York, N.Y. 10017

earnings such as derived from the sale of assets. Assess sales, profit margin, net income, the debt structure, book value and cash flow. Note whether earnings are constant or erratic, and the trend of growth.

Fundamental System #4
How To Use Money And Credit Indicators To Forecast Market Action

We saw above that the investment community is becoming increasingly aware of the effects of money supply on the market. The underlying theory is readily understood. Easy money means easy cash for expansion, investment, and speculation. Tight money means that everyone has to pull in his horns. The Federal Reserve Board can tighten money by increasing the Discount Rate, the amount banks pay the Fed to borrow from the Fed. Also, Member Bank Reserves may be increased, the amount of cash banks have to keep against deposits, thereby reducing the amount of money available for lending. Margin requirements, the per cent in cash a stock purchaser must put up to make a securities purchase, may be increased. The prime rate is now floating, but remains an indicator of the availability of credit.

Other Indicators

Free Credit Balance

Monthly, the New York Stock Exchange issues figures on the total of uninvested cash left in customer accounts. This represents potential buying power, the higher the total the better. The data is available in *Barron's* as it is released. Changes in trend frequently forecast the direction of the market. According to a study by William Gordon (*The Stock Market Indicators*, Investor's Press Inc., Palisades Park, N.J.), this is a rather fine primary trend indicator, reaching lows an average of 1.3 months prior to major market lows and peaking an average of 4.3 months ahead of the market.

New York Stock Exchange Margin Debt

This is the amount of margin debt owed by customers of member firms. Inasmuch as margin customers are usually the more sophisticated, higher margin debits generally imply higher prices to come. Data available in *Barron's*. The amount of margin debt tends to peak and bottom roughly in tandem with the market, although on some occasions it has peaked many months in advance of market tops. Be wary if the amount of margin debt proceeds for four months without making a new high.

Bond Yields

An examination of Figure 12 will reveal the relationship between market prices, margin requirements, free credit balances, margin debt and bond yield. As interest rates rise the market has tended to weaken.

The Three Step And Stumble Rule

By Edson Gould, editor of *Findings & Forecasts*, a very prestigious advisory. Whenever any one of the three rates set by the Fed—the discount rate, rate for bank reserve requirements or the margin requirements set for stocks—increase three times in succession, the stock market has subsequently suffered a severe decline. The decline may be delayed, but the rule has not failed in over 50 years.

Fundamental System #5
How To Use Municipal Bond Yields To Forecast Market Action

Another one from Larry Williams.

We have already seen that the market and interest rates move in opposite directions (interest rates up, market down). *Barron's* carries weekly the current Municipal Bond Yield Index. The Index tends to lead the market by four to six weeks, and may be used to forecast the market according to the following rules:

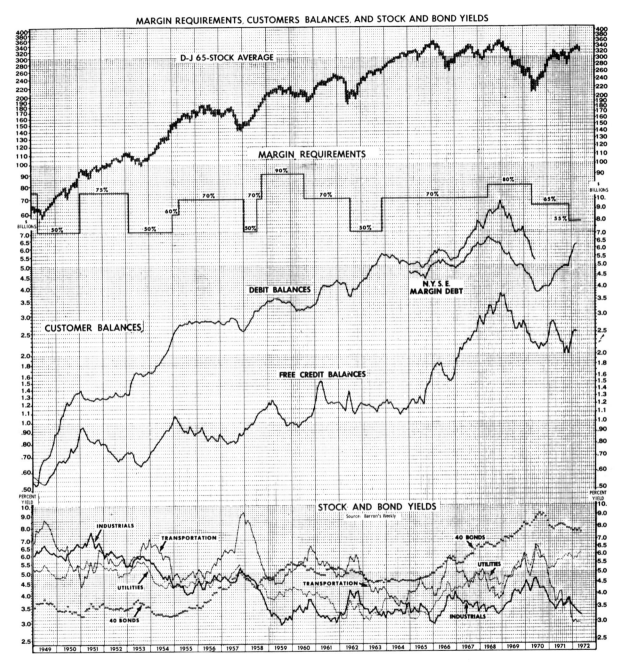

Figure 12

Source: Securities Research Co., 208 Newbury Street, Boston, Mass. 02116

1) If the market makes a new high while Municipal yield rates fail to drop to a new low, a decline will follow in the market in four to six weeks.

2) If the market makes a new low while Municipal yields fail to climb to a new high, a rally will follow in four to six weeks.

3) A trendline break in the plot of the Municipal Bond Yield Index indicates a related trendline break in the market.

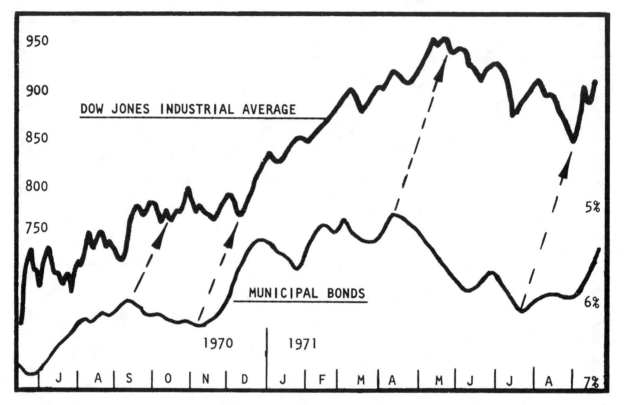

Figure 13

Source: Williams Reports, P.O. Box 1552, Carmel, California 93921

Fundamental System #6
How To Use Mutual Fund Cash Position To Forecast Market Action

Mutual funds have been accounting for an increasing percentage of market activity. Does it follow that these "pros" have been smart enough to get into cash at market tops and into stock at the bottom? Sad to say, no. The funds have been up to their ears in stock at major tops and loaded with cash at bottoms. It figures. If the funds are out of money, who's to do the buying? In any case, as Figure 14 reveals, a mutual fund cash position of less than five per cent has resulted in important market declines. High cash positions of near ten per cent (1966, 1968) and near twelve per cent (1970) have marked significant market bottoms. Recently, mutual funds have begun to periodically suffer net redemptions as opposed to sales. There is a possibility that they will become more cautious and keep larger cash reserves. If so, the bear signal per cent may rise.

MUTUAL FUND CASH POSITION

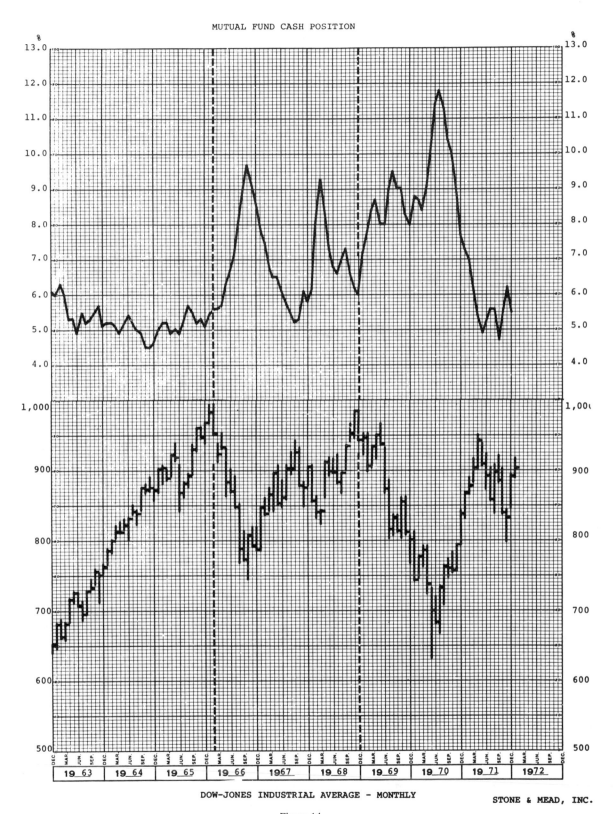

DOW-JONES INDUSTRIAL AVERAGE - MONTHLY

STONE & MEAD, INC.

Figure 14

Source: Long Term Technical Trends, *Stone and Mead, Inc., 15 Broad Street, Boston, Mass. 02109*

Fundamental System #7
How Dow Yields Can Be Used To Forecast The Market

Whenever the cost per $1.00 dividends for the Dow Jones Industrial stocks has risen to over $30.00, a decline has shortly followed. Or to restate another way, whenever the Dow stocks yield under 3.3% and particularly under 3.0%, an important top has been always at hand. The figures are available weekly in *Barron's*.

Fundamental System #8
Using Money Stock Data To Forecast The Market

Technical Trends, P.O. Box 228, Chappaqua, N.Y., publishes the above chart of money stock. Larry Williams has found that changes in money stock peaks about seven weeks before market tops and troughs about nine weeks before market rallies. The length of rallies in the money stock indicator are matched by the length of rallies in the stock market. Similarly for declines; a four-week decline in the rate of change of money stock will produce a four-week market decline.

Fundamental System #9
Using The Dow Jones Utilities To Forecast Market Action

The Dow Jones Utility Group has a history of leading many market moves by turning up or down in anticipation of the rest of the market. The basis for this lies in the relationship between utility stocks and the availability of credit. Utility companies have to frequently borrow for expansion. Tight money increases their costs and impedes profit. Concurrently, investors buy utility stocks for income. Should interest rates rise, utility dividends will not compare favorably with other forms of yield. Therefore, the strength of the utility group carries implications for the general availability of money. The more available is credit, the stronger the utility stocks. We have already discussed the correlation between money supply and market action. Strength in the utilities, therefore, implies subsequent broad market strength. The Dow Utility Average bottomed with the Industrials in May 1970 and again in November 1971. However, the April 1971 top was forecast by the topping action in the Utilities during January 1971; the Spring 1972 decline was likewise predicted by a breakdown of the Dow Jones Utilities Average that January.

The Confidence Index

From time to time, the *Barron's* Confidence Index has come into high popularity, mainly because of its touted ability to predict future market developments. The Index shows the ratio of yield on high-grade bonds to that of speculative bonds. In theory, sophisticated bond investors will switch from low-grade to high-grade bonds if they suspect difficulty on the financial scene. This results in a drop in the Confidence Index. If low grade bonds are in demand, the Index rises.

The usual rule applied to the Confidence Index is that it will lead market action by two to four months, but gives no projection of the price objective of the move it is signalling. In other words, if the Confidence Index rises to a new peak, the market should rally in two to four months. There have been times in recent years when this has worked quite well, when the market did, indeed, follow the Index's signals. At other times, the Index has proven valueless.

William Gordon, in *The Stock Market Indicators*, mentioned previously, did careful research into the results of using the Confidence Index as a leading indicator. He has established that a 10-month moving average of the Index can be somewhat useful. Buy signals are generated by a 1½ point penetration up through the moving average, sell signals by the same penetration down. Another signal is generated when the Index remains above or below its 10-month moving average for a period of at least three months.

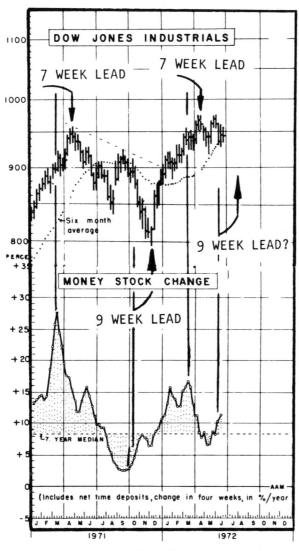

Figure 15

Source: Technical Trends, P.O. Box 228,
Chappaqua, N.Y. 10514

It was found that the Confidence Index, based upon the above formula, produced poor buy signals (losses resulting), but somewhat effective major sell signals. As a short term indicator, its use is highly doubtful, popular misconception notwithstanding. This concurs with my own observations. For those readers who wish to experiment themselves, the data is available weekly in *Barron's*.

The Seven Early Warning Signals

The following is an abstract of a report prepared by Len Cedar, publisher of *The Wall Street Survey*. These seven signals scream caution to the wary investor, so pay heed.

Early Warning Signal No. 1 — Insider Trading

By law, every officer, director and owner of ten per cent or more of a company's securities that are listed on an Exchange, are required to report, to both the S.E.C. and the particular Exchange, any trading they may do in that company's securities.

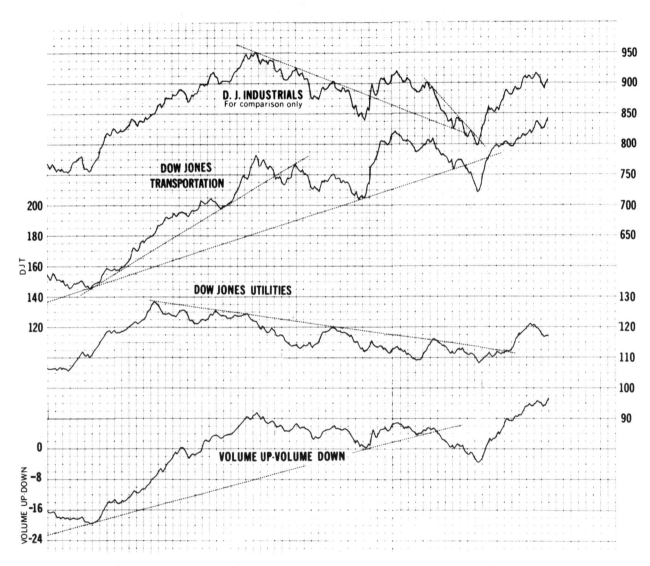

Figure 16

Source: Comparative Market Indicators, P.O.Box *1557, Bellevue, Washington 98009*

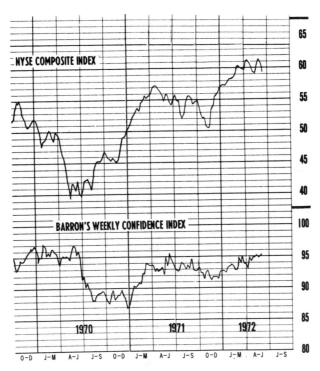

Figure 17

*Source: Trendline Daily Basis Stock Charts, 345 Hudson Street,
New York, N.Y. 10014*

There have been several cases in which the price of a particular stock collapsed, apparently without warning. Yet, in many of these instances, large insiders had disposed of huge holdings shortly before the break. (Author's note: Insider transactions are not always significant. The timing of insider purchases is frequently very premature on the buy side, and on the sell—well, anyone can have gambling debts. Still, it pays to keep your eyes open. Data widely available.)

Early Warning Signal No. 2 — Accounting Techniques

Editor Cedar warns against companies that manipulate accounting to keep earnings high and cites the conglomerates and some computer companies in particular. Be on the lookout for "restated earnings," "poolings of interest," "profits from continuing operations," sudden shifts in the company's fiscal year or depreciation schedules and other "artful tricks" of the accounting game.

Early Warning Signal No. 3 — Diversification

Diversification, carefully planned and soundly implemented, has helped many companies to grow and prosper. However, badly timed or ill-conceived overexpansion can stick in a company's throat. Watch out for unprofitable companies, attempting to bail out by swallowing more than they can chew. (Author's note: Where to get data? Try *Barron's* and *Forbes*.)

Early Warning Signal No. 4 — Litigation

Watch out for potentially costly legal suits. These frequently appear in the financial press in small letters, many of them inconsequential. Be careful, however; some can really hurt.

Early Warning Signal No. 5 — Who Minds The Store?

Watch out for the reputation of the company's management or, if a takeover is in the works, the reputation of the management of the surviving company. Many corporate powers are known for their ruthlessness and unreliability not to mention past credibility gaps. (Author's note: Where? Try *Forbes* again.)

Early Warning Signal No. 6 — Trading Volume

Borrowing a leaf from our book, Editor Cedar alerts his readers to the significance of climax volume, accompanied by little or no price movement. As he puts it, "this is the kind of … situation professionals love … thousands of shares changing hands with hardly a ripple … before the public catches the scent."

Early Warning Signal No. 7 — Common Sense

When interest rates, go-go funds, multiples and prices go out of sight, it's time to lock up your profits and run.

To these, I would add the following:

Early Warning Signal No. 8: A series of earnings forecasts off target.

Early Warning Signal No. 9: Resignations of key top executives.

Early Warning Signal No. 10: Failure to innovate new product lines.

On the other side of the ledger, sound companies show resourceful management, new product lines (e.g. Polaroid), know how to thwart competition (IBM), and produce consistent earnings growth at least in the area of 10 to 15% annually.

Investment Planning vs. The Random Walk

From time to time, some computer or other "proves" that future market action cannot be forecast on the basis of facts currently known or by charting techniques. Any number of technical systems already presented in this book, and the tables and charts of actual results, should have put the random walk hypothesis to rest, at least insofar as technical analysis is concerned. What about fundamental analysis?

Arnold Bernhard, Research Director of *The Value Line Investment Survey* and President of *The Value Line Funds*, dealt the random walkers a blow in a paper presented at the Eighteenth Annual Management Conference, The Conrad Hilton Hotel, Chicago, March 19, 1970. I don't take sides with the purpose of the paper: to defend mutual fund management fees and sales commissions. Of interest, however, are the potential results of solid fundamental investigation. *The Value Line Investment Survey* ranks 1400 stocks into five categories (I, best; V, worst), by computer evaluation of price-earnings ratios relative to historical norms, relative momentum of earnings by comparison to the market, and by price momentum. The results of the *Value Line* program are conclusive. Rank I stocks increased by 102% between 1965-1969; Rank V stocks declined 26%. The tally of all five groups matched perfectly to the *Value Line* rankings. The average investor, of course, cannot duplicate the complete system but by careful fundamental research and use of the payout system—well, you just might build an even better mousetrap.

Fundamental System #10
Evaluating A Balance Sheet

Hopefully, after evaluating each of the below, some of the mystery surrounding corporate reports and balance sheets will be dispelled.

Earnings:

Evaluate the "quality" of earnings. Real earnings growth is that which is created by increased sales, the introduction of new products, better operating margins, etc. Evaluate the degree to which accounting reports allow credit for mergers, research costs, non-recurring gains. Do the earnings represent the actual flow of funds or are certain future accounts receivable credited as earnings where a substantial risk exists that debtors to the company may default? Land companies, for instance, have, in the past, credited to current earnings future time payments on parcels sold, despite the risk that purchasers of land will not meet payments.

Payout Time:

Previously discussed. The payout time should result in a growth rate equal to or better than competitive investments. Shoot for a payout time of six to eight years or 12 to 16 per cent return on average each year.

Price Earnings Ratio:

Previously discussed. Investors have to be increasingly cautious as the P-E ratio exceeds 40. Compare to historical and industry norms.

Dividends and Yields:

Mature companies tend to pay out a larger portion of earnings to shareholders in the form of dividends rather than to plough these back into research and the development of new product lines. Growth corporations have provided more profit over the years to shareholders than have high dividend paying concerns, but many investors do prefer to receive current income and regular dividends do support the price of a stock. Evaluate the security of dividends: are current and projected earnings sufficiently ample to cover dividends or is the dividend itself insecure?

The Number of Shares Outstanding:

Evaluate possible increases due to conversion of bonds or the exercise of warrants. The larger the number of shares outstanding, the less potential the stock has for volatility. Volatility generally involves small float, thin supply. A large number of shares outstanding also retards the possibility of dramatic earnings per share explosions.

Debt:

Companies heavily in debt are not necessarily poor investments. Heavy debt magnifies the leverage of the situation. During good times, the owners of the corporation will benefit, inasmuch as earnings derived from borrowed money will exceed the interest and other costs involved in the loan. During bad times, the company will suffer not only from reduced earnings but from having to pay charges on its debt as well. Companies borrow in the hope that they will secure a higher return on borrowed funds than they will have to pay out. Since this works both ways, conservative investors will seek situations in which debt is minimal.

Bond Ratings:

Check the bond ratings of the corporation. A high rating implies solvency, ability to meet obligations and a sound financial structure. Where? Try the Moody's and Standard and Poor's Bond rating services. Several investment advisories (Chapter 10) carry this data.

Book Value:

The shareholders' equity if the corporation were to be liquidated. This consists of the total assets minus liabilities, divided by the number of outstanding shares. Assets include cash, marketable securities, accounts

receivable, inventories, owned real estate, patents, etc. Liabilities include debt, accrued interest, wages, taxes and undelivered items or services. Book value may be somewhat illusory since owners cannot actually count on receiving projected value for assets. However, experience has shown that shares priced below book value do usually represent fine investments. *Forbes* has reported on such situations periodically.

Balance Sheet:

The ratio of current assets to liabilities. The total assets should be at least twice total liabilities. Ratios much below that raise question as to corporate solvency.

Corporations having a high book value, particularly if large portions of assets are in cash, have been prime targets for takeover attempts—the insurance companies are one example. This sometimes does and sometimes does not ultimately resolve in the shareholder's favor. However, some price appreciation almost always takes place during takeover negotiations. Should you own shares in a corporation which is being approached for takeover, consider selling into the price rise that accompanies the spread of rumor. Prices will rise usually to a level approximately 10% below what the corporation's shareholders will receive should the takeover be consumated. Should the deal fall through, prices will usually drop sharply. There has been less takeover fever recently; this sort of insanity peaked with the conglomerate craze, 1967-1968. *Do not* buy on takeover rumors unless you feel that the current price of the stock represents fair technical and fundamental value in the absence of such an occurrence.

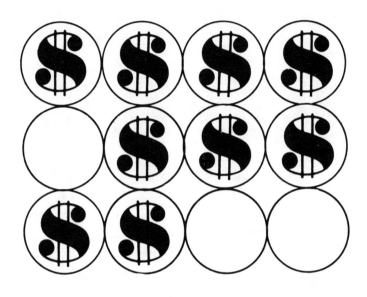

chapter nine

A POTPOURRI OF PROFITABLE PLOYS

As the title implies, this chapter deals with a variety of systems and indicators that appear to stand on their own, rather than readily group within previous categories. For the most part, these should be employed as backups to the basic trading tactics discussed in previous chapters. Each system, of course, will be evaluated as to results and basic tactics.

Miscellaneous System #1
Pick The Strongest Stocks In The Strongest Industry

Research has shown consistently that investors profit greatest from the selection of stocks operating within the strongest industry groups, based upon the industry group action relative to the total market. Over the years, of course, certain consistent winning groups stand out—the mobile homes during 1970-1972, for one. Periodically, different groups swing into favor. During the early sixties, everyone was going bowling. In the mid-sixties everyone was going to fly to buy a color T.V., providing they didn't buy a computer first. In 1970, the world was going double-knit. (As this is written, in May 1972, take a look at those stocks—the world is apparently going nudist.) 1971 was a great year for warehouse furniture, soft contact lenses, anti-pollution devices and, after half a decade, airlines once again. Alaska got a good play, the first since 1968, during early 1972, but Florida land was out, witness Punta Gorda and Amrep.

The moral is clear. Get into the swinging groups while they're hot, but do not overstay your welcome. Today's hero is tomorrow's flop—a few outstanding groups notwithstanding.

Typically, groups rotate in and out of favor in three ways:

1) During any bull phase, a certain amount of healthy group rotation takes place. By and large, new market advances are led by current market favorites. These groups frequently anticipate turns in the market, sometimes beginning their rise slightly before the pack. The initial surge is sharp, but profit taking inevitably sets in. The money then looks for other vehicles and as the one group recedes slightly a new one comes to the head of the parade. Sometimes, the old leaders come back during the same move for a second and third ride; sometimes not—they may turn out to be only short distance runners.

A good speculative intermediate move is led by the flyers, the stocks that lend life and color to the market. I consider a blue chip led rally suspect, on the basis that only cautious money looks for big profits in Allied Chemical. The exception lies in cyclical economic turnarounds when, occasionally, Chrysler growls like a tiger. Following the initial flyer led surge, the money turns to the secondary stocks—the $20.00, $30.00, and $40.00 numbers—which comprise a large bulk of the publicly traded market (the pros like the biggies—Burroughs, I.B.M., etc.). Finally, the tertiaries have their day in the sun, the cats and dogs of the Amex and O-T-C. When the $4.00 stocks begin doubling, it's time to get out. The declines that follow often start under cover of the Dow making new highs. This chapter is being written in the midst of such a decline (May 1972). Two weeks ago, the Dow hit a yearly high, but the A-D line failed to follow suit. Now, the market as a whole is being hit, in most cases real hard.

The basic trading tactic is clear. Try to anticipate which groups haven't joined the play yet. Evaluate whether the group has been relatively weak all year (avoid those). If not, see how quickly and precisely you can hop aboard a strong group early in its move or preferably just before it starts.

2) Group rotation occurs over a longer pull for very real fundamental reasons. Lower interest rates and an incipient housing boom boded very well for Fannie Mae during 1970-1971. The new jets and the travel explosion helped the airlines during the mid-sixties, but over-capacity made Pan Am's going not so great later in the decade. Cutbacks in government spending bode badly for defense stocks during the late sixties and early seventies. We all know what air travel did to Penn Central and other railroads. New fashions have helped the textile and clothing manufacturers from time to time; these are real roller-coaster groups. And of course, Japanese imports haven't helped American office equipment companies lately. (Remember the glory days of SCM?). Gold stocks, of course, rise and fall with the monetary situation.

Evaluate the fundamental picture. Are these economic developments of major significance which are likely to effect the earnings and therefore price of any one or group of industries. Where to get the poop? *Barron's* is

Preferences in Leading Groups

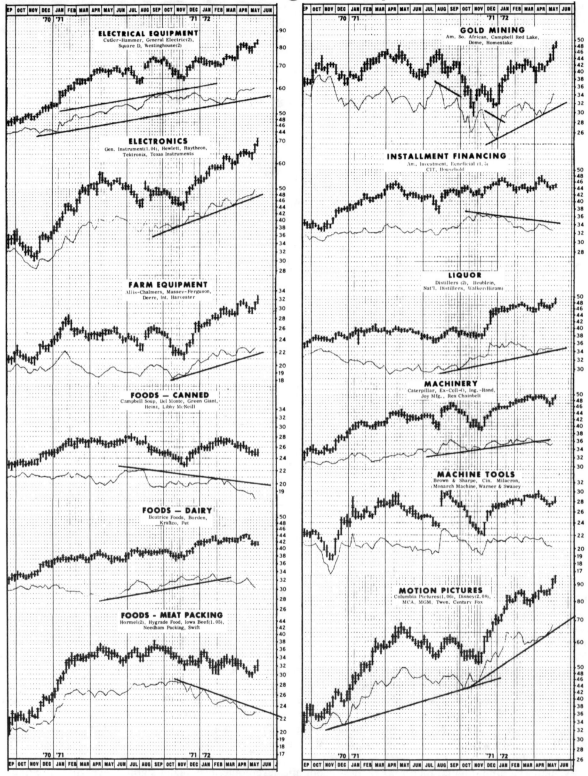

Figure 1

Group strength charts: The relative strength lines compare the strength of the group to the strength of the Dow.

Source: Securities Research Co., 208 Newbury Street, Boston, Mass. 02116

[Trendlines by author]

good. So are some of the better fundamental advisories.

3) Concept. That's always good for a 900% rise until someone actually totes up the balance sheets or figures out how far into eternity the market has already discounted earnings. Concept stocks usually show little earnings, or at least no earnings that can stand any kind of scrutiny. It's the future that sells. Examples? During the late sixties, computerized education was the thing. An outfit called Cybern Education ran to around 20 while showing deficits, subsequently went bankrupt. Something called Educational Computer lifted off to near 400 and split a few times along the way. On the way down, it dropped some fifty points a day. Alaska was a big concept in 1968 until someone realized that it would take years to bring the oil down. Medical technology has recently been big, nursing homes and such. I recently received a prospectus for a new issue. The company's developing a sperm bank. The stock doubled shortly after issue.

Are concept stocks bad risks? Not necessarily. Just be ready to run. Technically traded, they can be hot as pistols. Some concepts, of course, do come to fruition. Xerox was once a concept. So were I.B.M. and Redman. The good concepts stay strong over the years. Good growth industries are fine trading and investment vehicles. However, if high price-earnings multiples develop, watch out for the first bad quarter.

Where To Get The Data, Trading Tactics

I have already discussed *Barron's* for fundamental data. The technical data is available from a variety of sources. *Barron's* carries group progress reports. A variety of advisory services carry group strength data, usually including the best performing stocks within groups. The cheapest source of this data is the *Media General Financial Weekly*, which carries a whole slew of technical and fundamental information, including charts of every listed stock.

Several chartbooks carry group strength material. Figure 1 is from one such chartbook. The bar chart represents the price action of the group. The thin line graph below the bar chart represents the strength of that group relative to the market. Note the strong relative strength of the motion picture group, the weak relative strength of the food groups. Relative strength lines are subject to trendline and channel study. You can readily see that during the period from mid-1971 to early 1972, a purchase of MGM stood a better chance than a purchase of Swift.

Stock ranking data can be found in a variety of places too. Not every source of group strength data carries individual stock rankings. Does it pay to check beyond group rankings? Just compare the relative strength ratings of National Airlines and Pan Am (Figures 2 and 3), two companies in the same industry. On these charts, the thin line under the price bars represent the strength of that particular stock relative to the market.

The ideal time to enter an industry group is upon an upside penetration of a relative strength downtrendline, or upon the group's first entrance into the top ten or so groups. Look for groups rising rapidly in relative strength. I do not recommend jumping onto groups that have been among the top three for any length of time because of the risk of being last on line. However, top groups can continue their leadership for surprising periods of time and if you enter while a group is running, you don't have to wait for the mark-up to begin. Use your judgment. Even very strong groups undergo corrective reactions. Volatile groups, during reactions, will temporarily appear weaker than the market. Look for the turn. Track the strong groups throughout the year. Research has shown that the strongest groups in any six month period will outperform the market the next six months. They're your best bet, long. As usual, reverse the above for short selling.

A Quick Way To Determine A Stock's Relative Strength

This is no exact measure but works quite well enough for most trading purposes. For selecting longs after a market decline, simply seek out stocks which have not made a new low with the last market downleg. For example, the market made a lower low in November 1971, the November low violating the previous August low.

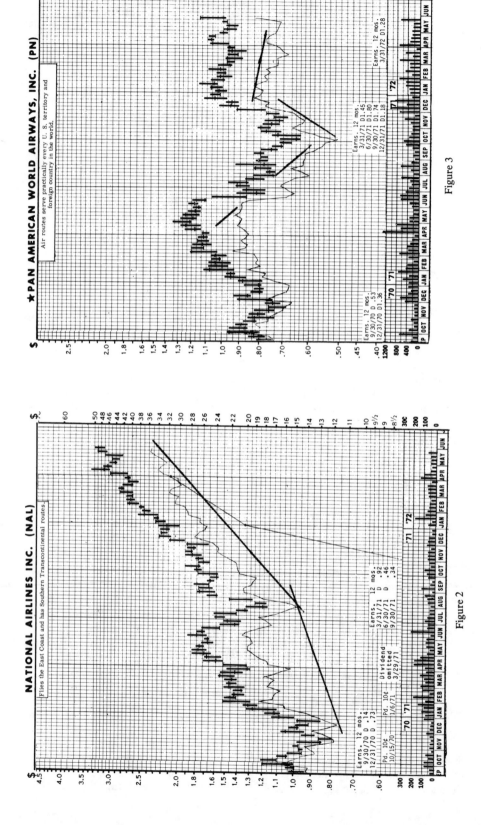

Figure 2

Figure 3

Although both were in a strong airline group, National showed much greater strength relative to the market than Pan-Am.

Source: Securities Research Co., 208 Newbury Street, Boston, Mass. 02116

[*Trendlines by author*]

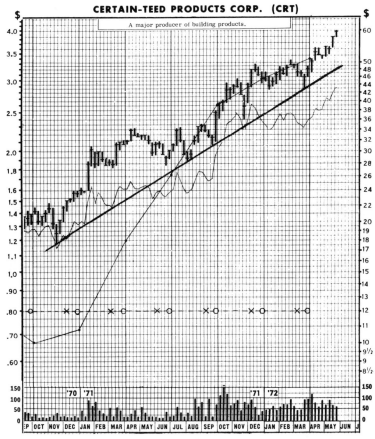

Figure 4

Certain-Teed showed excellent relative strength by maintaining its uptrend
despite the market decline in November, 1971.
Source: Securities Research Co., 208 Newbury Street, Boston, Mass. 02116
[Trendline by author]

Notice, however (Figure 4), that Certain-Teed did not make a new low with the market. In fact, its uptrend was never disturbed. Showing such fine relative strength, Certain-Teed figured to rally strongly with the turn.

To short, look to stocks that have not made new highs with the market. These are weaker than the market and will most likely turn down as the market declines.

Miscellaneous System #2
Short Sale Systems

There are two varieties of short sale systems. The first measures the total amount of short selling taking place. In principal, every short sale represents potential demand since each short seller must one day replace those shares that he is short. The second variety measures the relative amount of short selling done by unsophisticated traders (the public, particularly the odd-lotters) against the sophisticated traders (specialists and members of the exchanges). The systems, of course, involve tracking and interpretating the various data, and setting your market course accordingly.

The New York Stock Exchange Short Interest Ratio

RATIO OF SHORT INTEREST TO AVERAGE DAILY VOLUME - NYSE

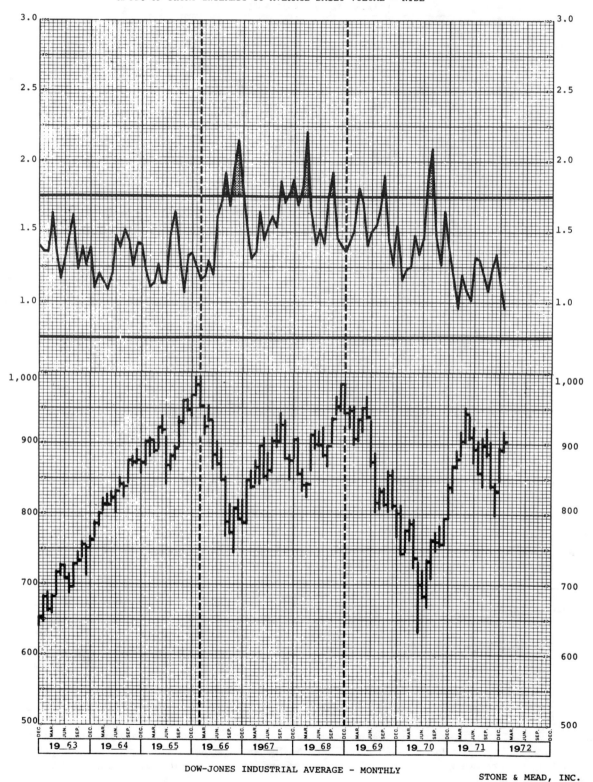

DOW-JONES INDUSTRIAL AVERAGE - MONTHLY

STONE & MEAD, INC.

Figure 5

Source: Long Term Technical Trends, *15 Broad Street, Boston, Mass. 02109*

As I mentioned above, a short sale represents potential demand. This is most apparent at major bottoms where the short sellers are "squeezed", that is, forced by suddenly rising prices to scramble and cover at any price. A person long on a stock can lose only so much. A wrong short can become complete calamity; there is no limit to how high a stock can go. A high public bearish contingent is almost always bullish, sooner or later. Conversely, the best time to short is usually when no one else wants to keep you company.

The short interest is released monthly by the exchanges, in the total amount of shares short outstanding. This figure by itself is relatively inconclusive. Of more significance is the per cent of recent volume represented by the actual number of short sales, which in itself has had an upward bias over the years because of the general increase in absolute trading volume.

Figure 5 illustrates the relationship between the ratio of short interest to average daily volume on the New York Stock Exchange. This data is available upon release, in a variety of sources including but not limited to *Barron's* and *The Wall Street Journal*. Incidentally, study also the rate of short selling for individual stocks, which is usually included and which is available in certain chartbooks.

Study of Figure 4 reveals that major rallies almost inevitably follow upon the achievement of a short sale ratio of 2.0 or higher. The ratio is computed by dividing the total monthly short interest by the average daily volume during that month. Readings near 1.0 are bearish, albeit frequently somewhat premature. Readings of 1.75 or better are generally considered bullish, but I consider any reading between 1.25 and close to 2.0 as neutral. Study the chart and decide for yourself.

The Specialist Short Sale Ratio

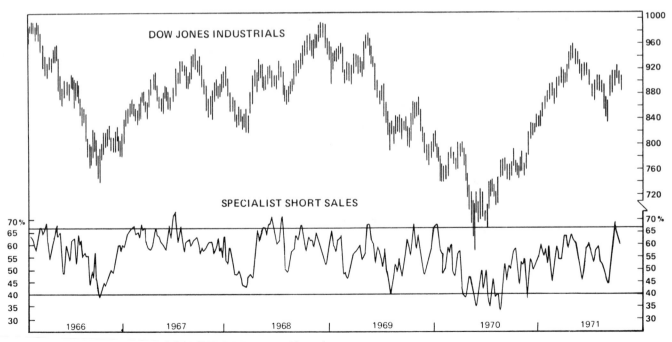

Figure 6

Source: Indicator Digest, *Palisades Park, N.J. 07650*

The specialists as a group, have an excellent record of going heavily short at market tops—not particularly because of any special astuteness but because of the structure of the specialist system. During strong markets, the specialist is gradually forced to go short as demand for stock exceeds his own inventory. At the first opportunity, he covers and usually at a profit. Don't expect the specialist to support prices if he is heavily short.

The specialist short sale data is released weekly and represents the percentage of total shorting done on the exchanges by the specialists. Very bullish readings are represented by specialists doing less than 45 per cent of the total short selling done on the New York Stock Exchange. Declines usually follow a rise in this reading to over 67 per cent. This is a highly reliable market indicator, data available weekly in *Barron's*. However, a major difficulty arises because the data is released about three weeks after the fact, by which time declines or rallies may already have started. You can project the potential reading with some accuracy. If the reading reaches a high level and the market continues to rise, you can usually assume that for the weeks you do not have, the figures remain high. Do not make this assumption if the market has declined or has consolidated since the publication date of a high reading. Reverse for down markets. A low specialist reading combined with a still declining market almost always indicates a major upside reversal.

Odd-Lot Short Sale Ratio

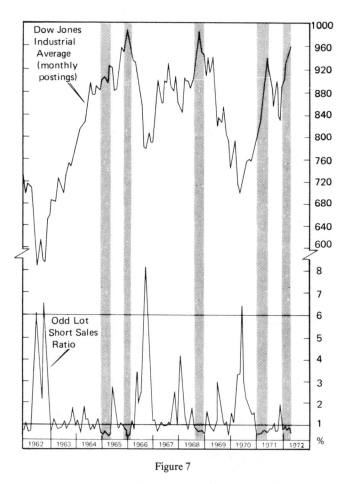

Figure 7

Source: Indicator Digest, *Palisades Park, N.J. 07650*

The odd-lotters are the least sophisticated of short sellers. They are generally late to short major declines, their short selling reaching peaks at bear market lows. The ratio is computed by dividing odd-lot short sales by the number of odd-lot sales, and smoothing the data with a ten day moving average. Data available in *Barron's*. Several chartbooks carry the plots. I prefer this method of measuring odd-lot psychology to any other, for instance, measuring odd-lot volume against total N.Y.S.E. volume or the measure of odd-lot sales vs. purchases. However, the method works effectively only at bottoms when sharp peaks in the area of 6% indicate an impending turn. At tops, readings of less than 1% are bearish, but with frequently a long lead time. The preference for this system lies with the fact that short selling is an active move. Withdrawal from the market or simply selling are much less active.

For those who prefer to study the relationship between odd-lot purchases and sales, the procedure is to study changes in direction. Odd-lotters generally sell into rising prices (wisely) but step up their buying at major market tops. They buy into declines (relatively) but panic at bear bottoms. A decline is likely to end when the odd-lotter reverses his usual behavior of buying into the decline, and begins to sell heavily. See Figure 8 for the relationship between odd-lot purchases and sales.

For many years, the amount of participation in the market by odd-lotters carried significance, but in recent years odd-lot involvement has had a sharp downward bias, and seems to have become less significant. Perhaps mutual fund sales and redemptions will come to reflect odd-lot psychology.

The Ratio Of Odd-Lot To Specialist Shorts

This measures the most unsophisticated against the most sophisticated short selling. Divide the total weekly specialist short sales by the total weekly odd-lot short sales (data in *Barron's*). A reading in the area of 70 or below indicates a high relative percentage of odd-lot short sales and is very bullish. In theory, readings above 125 are bearish but during strong intermediate bull moves, readings of 300 have been achieved without serious price erosion. This is probably a more significant buy than sell signal.

Dr. Martin E. Zweig's Sell Signal

Dr. Zweig, already mentioned for his option activity signals, published in *Barron's* (May 1, 1972), the results of his study of short selling as a market indicator. He found that important sell signals are generated when the following conditions are met:

1) The Odd-Lot Short Sale Ratio, computed on a 2 week moving average basis, (data plotted weekly) drops to below .60, about half its normal value.

2) This figure rises briefly to .70 or better from any given low below the .60 level, before relapsing back to below .60.

3) The percentage of "public shorts" (public shorts as against total other short sales which includes specialists, exchange members and off-the-floor traders) drops below 12.5% (normal value, 20-35%). This indicates high optimism among the unsophisticated public.

4) The above combination of extreme bullishness on the part of the odd-lotters and the uninformed public has rendered highly accurate sell signals of intermediate to major scope. The average decline following such signals was 17.7%, lasting an average of 34.8 weeks.

Relatively few sell signals have been flashed by this system, (only seven signals between 1945-1972), but each one has been profitable. Dr. Zweig's results are impressive. This appears to be an indicator worth following.

Miscellaneous System #3
Techniques Of Short Selling

RATIO OF ODD LOT PURCHASES TO SALES - PLOTTED INVERSELY

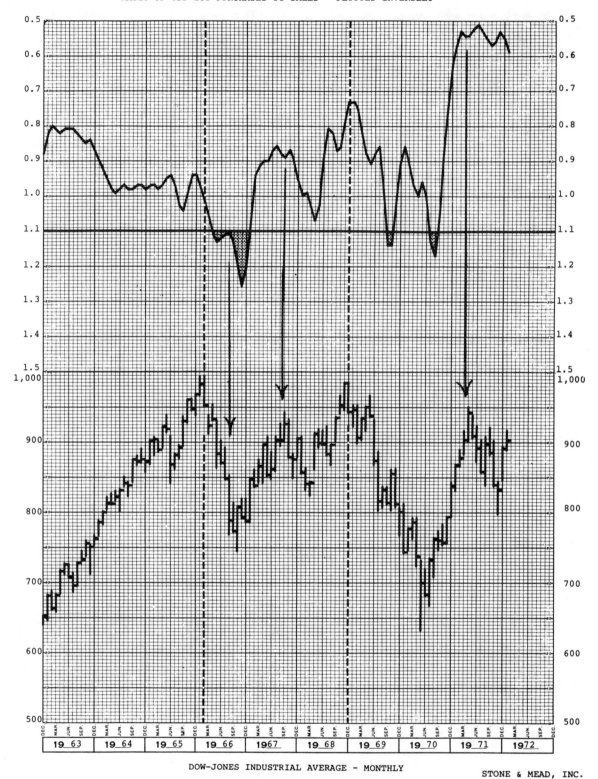

DOW-JONES INDUSTRIAL AVERAGE - MONTHLY

STONE & MEAD, INC.

Figure 8

Contrary to popular opinion, the odd-lotter usually exercises sound market judgment, buying into declines and selling into rallies. However, at market extremes, odd-lotters sometimes begin to buy into advances and to panic at market lows.

Source: Long Term Technical Trends, *15 Broad Street, Boston, Mass. 02109*

[*Arrows by author*]

We have observed that heavy public short selling is bearish. Nonetheless, there is a time to short, as well as to long and the complete trader swings either way. The following tactical tips should help you in your short selling operations:

1) Short only when the primary or major intermediate trend is down. Do not fight the market. Short near upper channel boundaries.

2) Select your short sale candidates from the weakest performing stocks in the weakest performing groups.

3) Try to short stocks with dubious fundamentals, high price earnings ratios, preferably after an emotional rise.

4) Try to short stocks revealing a risk-reward ratio of at least 4 to 1. These stocks should have developed top formations discussed in Chapter 3.

5) Do not short thin stocks. The float should be at least two to three million shares. You can really be hurt shorting scarce stocks. Also stay away from stocks with high short interest ratios, more than ½ to 1 per cent of their total capitalization.

6) Look to short stocks in longer term downtrends, preferably below significant downtrended moving averages.

7) Try to time your shorts to the top of at least minor rallies. Don't chase your shorts down anymore than you would chase a stock up.

8) Place stops no more than 10-15% above your shorting price. Follow your shorts down with stops.

9) Be patient. Shorts don't always work out instantly.

10) On a cover signal, cover instantly. If the market turns, run. A short is not usually a long term investment.

11) If you observe the above rules, you need be no more afraid to go short than long.

Tip

In strongly downtrended markets it can be difficult to get shorts off since short selling has to be done on an uptick. On a weak opening do not put in a market short order. You will be stuck with the first uptick which will very likely be near the lows for the day. Pick a price. Ask your broker to get a sizing from the floor—how many people want to short at that price ahead of you. Be careful if you can get your shorts off easily; sometimes the pros trap amateurs by letting them in.

If there are a lot of traders on line ahead of you, consider shorting an odd-lot. Odd-lot trades are matched to the last round lot trade. Any uptick will take all the odd-lot short orders along with it. You can also short on the Third Market (see Chapter 10), which requires no uptick since trading is done O-T-C. Finally, consider buying puts (Chapter 10).

For the suicidal only: If you are really bearish you can execute the following double play: (1) Short the stock you think will collapse. (2) Sell a naked call on the stock (Chapter 10). If the stock declines, you will pick up the profits from the short plus the premium from the call for which you have outlayed nothing. In the event of decline, the call will not be exercised. Of course, if you're wrong, you are out money on the short and you will have to buy in at higher prices to cover the call. As I said, this is for the suicidal only.

Miscellaneous System #4
The Consultant's Glamour Index

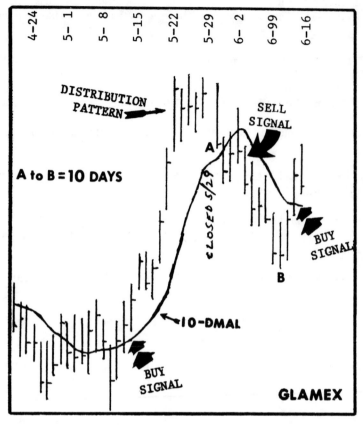

Figure 9

Source: The Consultant Publications, Inc., 3310 North 24th Street,
Phoenix, Arizona 85016

The glamour or high flyer group is frequently an excellent market indicator in itself. Professionals prefer to trade the volatile glamour stocks which tend to lead the market up and down, drawing the rest of the list with them. A rally in which the speculative stocks do not participate is suspect. Many advisories employ some form of glamour index as a key to the overall market, but the numbers of stocks so involved are usually too cumbersome for the do-it-yourself home technician. Ike Hasson, editor of the *Consultant*, does employ a "glamex", uncomplicated enough for maintenance by serious chart buffs, and, despite its size, an excellent representation of the entire glamour group. The components of this list include nine stocks: Burroughs x 1; Digital Equipment x 1; Disney x 2; IBM x 1; Memorex x 1; Polaroid x 1; Telex x 5; Teleprompter x 4; and Xerox x 1. Add the daily closings multiplied by each stock's multiplier (to adjust for past stock splits. For future splits after May 5, 1972, date of this writing, make the appropriate adjustments). Divide the total of closing prices by nine stocks for the daily average. A buy signal is generated when the glamour index rises above its ten day moving average; a sell when it closes below its ten day moving average. Note any disparities between the "glamex" and the Dow. The discrepancy will usually resolve in the direction of the "glamex".

Miscellaneous System #5
The Sentiment Index

SENTIMENT INDEX OF THE LEADING INVESTMENT SERVICES
(% of Total Services Surveyed)

Date	DJIA*	Bulls	Bears	Correction
12/10/71	859.59	55.4%	27.0%	17.6%
12/17/71	856.75	60.8	25.6	13.6
12/24/71	873.80	63.2	25.0	11.8
12/31/71	881.17	67.5	19.5	13.0
1/ 7/72	890.20	62.8	19.2	18.0

*Previous Friday Closing

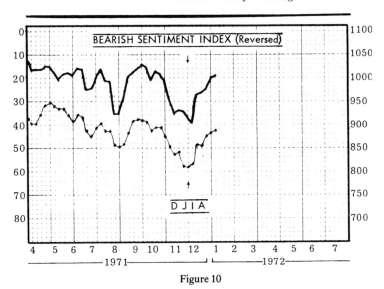

Figure 10

Source: Investors Intelligence Inc., Larchmont, N.Y.

Investors Intelligence, a fine advisory, has pioneered an indicator, *The Sentiment Index*, which has become widely followed and frequently quoted. *The Sentiment Index* measures the percentage of advisory services that are bearish. It is a contrary opinion indicator since the pundits generally follow the trend in harmony with the public. The more bullish the advisories as a group, the closer we are to a market top. Bearish readings, in recent years, have been indicated by a percentage of bearish advisories under 20%. Some years ago, low bearish readings were in the area of 10%. Significant advances do not usually end until the bulls clearly outnumber the bearish services. Major declines tend to end when the bears hold an edge over the bulls. For example, the following table shows the readings at recent important turning points:

Table I

Percentage of Advisory Services Bullish and Bearish at Major Turns

Date	DJIA	Bulls	Bears	Correction
October 5, 1966	774.22	25.4	52.5	22.1
April 3, 1968	840.67	25.4	64.7	25.0
December 25, 1968	966.99	49.3	22.4	26.3
May 29, 1970	662.17	28.3	55.0	16.7
April 30, 1971	947.79	67.7	14.7	17.6
September 24, 1971	908.22	60.3	15.1	24.6
November 26, 1971	810.67	37.0	37.0	26.0

Data based on reports by *Investors Intelligence*.

There is no automatic signal level, but as has been said, a low 20% bearish reading is clearly a caution sign whereas a high bearish reading (over 50%), indicates that a bottom is in sight. The Sentiment Index, charted, closely follows the Dow and may be trended. See Figure 10.

Miscellaneous System #6
Interpreting The New Highs, New Lows Indicator

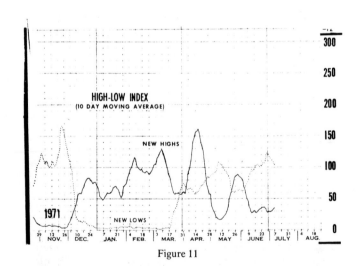

Figure 11

Source: Trendline Daily Basis Stock Charts, 345 Hudson Street, New York, N.Y. 10014

This data is available, both daily and weekly, in any newspaper with good financial coverage.

Strong bull markets involve the broad participation of the majority of stocks. We have seen how weakness in the Advance-Decline line indicates a weakness in the market, even if the Dow is being supported. Another indicator of broad as opposed to selective strength involves the number of issues making new yearly highs as opposed to the number of issues making new lows.

A solid rise takes many issues with it. If the averages are in new high ground, this should be accompanied by a new height in the amount of issues making new highs. Market reactions after a bull move will, of course, diminish the amount of daily new highs and increase the new lows. However, in a strong market the amount of new lows will not increase substantially. An expansion in the number of new lows is bearish. A contraction of new highs into an advance is bearish. The theory of their correlations is logical enough. An increasing number of new highs represents positive technical breadth, stocks breaking above congestion areas into areas of no recent resistance. Stocks plummeting to new lows represent technical weakness; there is heavy overhead. The inability of many stocks to break through resistance while the averages are advancing, indicates general churning at the top. Close study of a cross section of charts frequently reveals that many stocks are close to their lows even as the market is advancing, vulnerable to a violation of support upon the first market weakness. Conversely, should the averages drop to new lows while the number of stocks making new lows diminish, the evidence suggests that an increasing bulk of stocks are holding support and resisting further decline.

The New-Highs, New-Lows Indicator has called many significant turns in the past, by not confirming new market highs and lows in the averages, particularly the Dow. For example, the 1966 bear market bottom was reached in October 1966. However, the peak of new lows occurred in August 1966, two months previously. The 1968 bull market top developed in December 1968, but the peak point for new highs took place in June that year. The market advanced strongly, it appeared, into April 1971. We have already noted that the Advance-Decline line flattened after January 1971. The peak in new highs occurred also in January. Generally, bull phases last some several months or so after the new highs line peaks. The May-November 1971 drop developed four months after the peak of new highs in January. In 1967, the severe drop that began in October followed the new highs peak of May, that year. However, in 1970, the market averages and the amount of new lows bottomed simultaneously.

This data is plotted either on a weekly basis (my preference), daily or as a ten day moving average. I prefer to do my own weekly plot from data in *Barron's*. It is a simple procedure. I look for evidence that the new highs, new lows line is operating in tandem with the Dow. The plot employed is of the net of new highs minus new lows. Some charting services plot the new highs and the new lows as two separate lines on the same graph (Figure 11). Bear markets are usually close to completion when the weekly net of new highs minus new lows drops into the area of minus 750-1000. Tops take longer to form but should the ten day moving average of new highs exceed 200, a top is probably close. Recently, on a weekly basis, nets of 400-500 weekly new highs over new lows have represented climactic bullish readings.

Miscellaneous System #7
Interpreting The Most Actives List

This data is published daily for daily figures in most thorough financial newspapers or in the financial section of large daily newspapers. Weekly figures appear in *Barron's* and elsewhere.

The most actives list shows where the big money is going—into what stocks and what industries. The appearance of a stock on the ten or fifteen most actives list demonstrates trading interest in that stock (barring a one time institutional transaction). Repeated appearances indicate some unusual developments or a sudden explosiveness in the stock. Alaska Interstate appeared, after months of quiescence, on the most actives list, in the spring of 1972 because of developments regarding the trans-Alaska pipeline. The stock erupted within several weeks from the low twenties to over fifty. Needless to say, an advance in a "most active" stock is bullish. Repeated declines in a "most active" stock are very bearish. Some traders use as a buy signal for a stock, the following criteria: 1) the stock appears on the most actives list and 2) it makes a new high. There is some validity to this method providing that close trailing loss cut points are employed and that the volume burst in the stock is not at the top of its move.

The most actives list tells its own story regarding the market as a whole. The general rules for interpretation are:

1) It is bullish if on a daily or weekly basis, the majority of most active stocks are up. The proportion should be commensurate with the action of the averages. On a day that the Dow is up some ten points, at least nine or ten of the fifteen most active stocks should be up.

2) It is bearish if the majority of most actives are down. However, it is not bearish, for instance, if the Dow is down some ten points and only eight most actives are down and seven are up. The most actives list is showing greater relative strength than the rest of the list.

3) It is bullish if the majority of most actives are down following a market decline, but they are down only fractionally on heavy volume. This implies high volume support—stocks giving ground grudgingly.

4) It is bearish if the majority of most actives are up on very heavy volume, but up only fractionally. This indicates high volume churning (review Chapter 2).

It usually pays to examine the quality of representation on the most actives list both to see which groups are well represented and to determine the phase of the advance and/or decline. During the early phases of important bull moves, the most actives list will be dominated by the glamour, blue chip and speculative trading vehicles—perhaps a special group or two. During the last phase, low price stocks make an appearance, on both the New York and American exchanges. When the dogs begin running on high volume, it's time to go. Following a major decline, look for the stocks trading heavily on the most actives list while resisting decline. They are the wave of the future.

A Most Actives Indicator

Barron's publishes on a weekly basis the twenty most active stocks for the week. This list can be used as a lead market indicator. The technique is straightforward and requires little time.

1) Add the number of the twenty most actives up for the week. Add the number down for the week. Compute the net difference (plus if more are up, minus if more are down).

2) Create a three week moving total of these results and chart the three week moving total with a line graph.

Rules For Interpretation

1) It is bullish if this moving total keeps making new highs with gains in the market or if it resists making new lows with a declining market.

2) It is bearish if the moving total fails to make new highs with a rising market or makes new lows as the market declines.

3) A three week total of greater than plus 40 is probably climactic and implies a consolidation or correction to follow.

4) A three week total of below minus 40 is probably climactic and implies an upside reversal or consolidation.

5) The line graph is trendable and buy and sell signals can be generated on trendline breaks.

This is a good indicator, all the better since it tends to operate as a lead indicator—one that foretells market action rather than coincides with it. For example, this indicator peaked in February 1971, two months before the April top. It bottomed three weeks before the major November 1971 bottom. The early April 1972 rally was not confirmed by a new high in the most actives indicator, presaging the decline that followed later that month.

Another Most Actives Indicator

Indicator Digest has recently originated a new most active stocks (MAS) indicator which calls intermediate moves very well.

Compute, on a daily basis, the net difference between the amount of the fifteen most active stocks that day that are up and the amount that are down. If ten are up and five are down, that day's entry is plus five. If nine are up, two unchanged and three down, the significant total is plus six.

The MAS indicator is a 30-day moving total (divided by 3) of the net difference between gainers and losers among the N.Y.S.E. 15 most active stocks. This is like a moving average except that we divide by 3 instead of 30.

Intermediate buy signals are generated when the 30-day moving average crosses above plus three. Sell signals are generated when it crosses below minus three.

Figure 12 shows the relationship between the MAS and IDA, an unweighted market average.

Miscellaneous System #8
Composite Indicators

Many advisory services employ "composite indicators" of one sort or another to determine important market trends. These composite indicators consist of several technical and technical-fundamental indicators, sometimes individually weighted, the composite used for signalling. Bullish readings consist of the majority of indicators in a positive area; bearish significance is attached to the majority of indicators lying in negative readings.

In theory, the employment of a composite rather than a single indicator precludes the possibility of false conclusions from a single indicator going "haywire", which does occasionally happen. Composite indicators are not meant for short term action. They are designed to measure at least the intermediate trend. One of the best known of the composite indicators is the Composite Index (Figure 13) employed by *Indicator Digest*. You may note from Figure 13 that this index does not bring you in and out of the market near peaks and bottoms, but that on a long term basis, operations in accordance with its signals would have been quite profitable.

Among the components of this index are:

1. Weekly Advance/Decline line.

2. Dow Jones Industrials 30 week moving average.

3. 30-Day High/Low Differential

4. Odd-Lot Index (Sales vs. purchases)

5. Odd-Lot Short Sales Ratio

6. Confidence Index

7. Specialist Short Sales Ratio

8. Mutual Fund Cash Position

9. Amex Median P/E Ratio

There are other components, some particular to *Indicator Digest's* own indices which are available only through the service. For readers who prefer a composite system, I suggest experimentation with the above components, to which I would add the following:

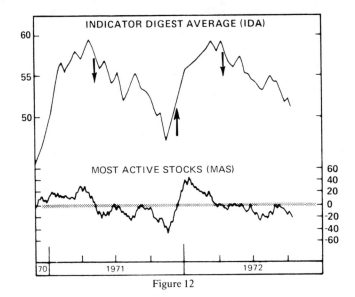

Figure 12

Source: Indicator Digest, Inc., Palisades Park, N.J. 07650

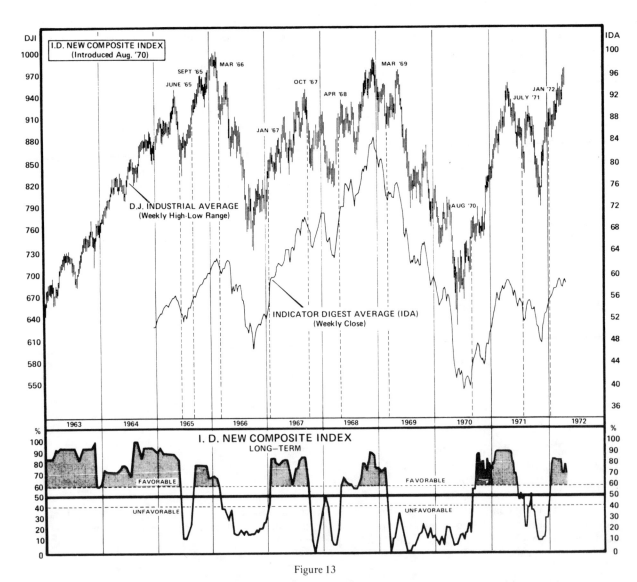

Figure 13

Source: Indicator Digest, Inc., Palisades Park, N.J. 07650

Fundamental Indicators

1. Free Credit Balances

2. Stock Margin Debt

3. Muncipal Bond Yields

Technical Indicators

1. Most Actives List (weekly readings)

2. Glamex Reading

3. New York Stock Exchange 28 Day Moving Average

4. Percentage of Industry Groups Advancing (*Barron's*).

I would delete the Confidence Index as having little value. Interpretation of these components has already been discussed.

Is It Worth The Time And Trouble?

Frankly, I think not. *Indicator Digest* is a fine, relatively inexpensive service and I would recommend letting I.D. or another service that you like (Chapter 10) carry this work so that you can devote your time to the study of individual stocks and market timing devices which are more sensitive. The Haller Method (Chapter 7), in and of itself, will provide broad timing signals as accurate as most composite indicators, and is very simply maintained. If, however, you have the time available and do not wish to subscribe to a service, I do recommend you study, in some form or other, the components mentioned above.

Miscellaneous System #9
Constructing A Momentum Oscillator

The concept underlying momentum study is relatively simple. The market moves in waves, larger and smaller. As the wave peaks, its upwards momentum decreases, until the turn comes. The wave starts downside, first with increasing and then with decreasing momentum as the bottom is reached. The process then once more reverses.

Market momentum may be computed by measuring the current rates of acceleration (rise) and deceleration (fall). This is accomplished by comparing the current prices to past prices at a given time interval in the past. For instance, if the market is higher now than it was one year ago, the long term momentum is up. For example, presume that the market is now 50 points higher than it was 12 months ago. We might scale this as +50. However, presume also that six months ago the market was 100 points higher than it had been 12 months previous to that reading. This differential would have resulted in a reading of +100. The market is losing momentum; its rate of acceleration is slowing, if not already reversed. At some point, the wave will decline sufficiently to produce a negative reading. That is, the current market levels will fall below the levels of those recorded a fixed interval back. The momentum oscillator will show negative readings. The process may be depicted graphically as shown in Figure 14.

Momentum readings begin to decrease as the top of the wave is reached, thereby alerting traders to the imminence of a market reversal. The oscillator will gradually lose its negative acceleration as bottoms are reached, thereby alerting traders to the imminence of a rally.

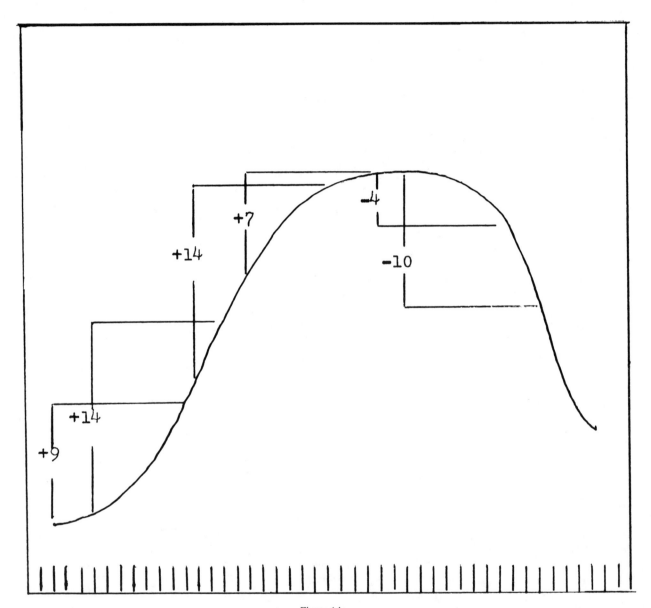

Figure 14

As the wave begins to peak, the momentum, measured by the difference between the last reading and the reading 10 units back, begins to diminish. It turns increasingly negative as the decline accelerates.

Ronald M. Maxwell, publisher of *Maxwell's Prognostications*, has devised a fine system of defining momentum and using the data for short term market timing signals. The method creates a momentum oscillator which may be used in conjunction with the 10 day moving average oscillator described in Chapter 5. Timing signals will be roughly similar in both systems. However, the momentum system does not render automatic signals. Trendline breaks (Figure 15) and changes in direction provide the most usable signals and require judgment for interpretation.

Definition

5 DDO means a five day differential oscillator. This is the "decision maker."

5 DDC means a five day differential, made cumulative.

15 DDO means a fifteen day differential oscillator and is a confirming curve to the above.

The methodology is simple.

Step 1

List the closing levels of the New York Stock Exchange Index for the past five days. Locate and plot the differential between the last day in the series and the first day. Continue the plotting in this manner. For example:

N.Y.S.E. Index	5 Day Differential Oscillator (5 DDO)
60.10	
60.25	
60.20	
60.40	
60.35	+ .25
60.40	+ .15
60.15	— .05

This system may be used with individual stocks as well, in which case translate the dollar change into eighths, e.g. a rise of one dollar equals eight eighths. The oscillator will call minor turns for stocks, but is too sensitive to be used for action signals on its own.

A decline in the 5 DDO as the market advances indicates the imminence of a market reversal. Sometimes, the oscillator turns down concurrently with the market; sometimes, it reverses direction a few days in advance. Conversely, an upturn in the oscillator indicates an upside market reversal.

Step 2

To construct a longer trend indicator:

Maintain a cumulative total of 5 DDO results, which total is the 5 DDC. When you have ten 5 DDC figures, compute and plot the differential between the tenth and the first, and continue to plot in this manner. The result (15 DDO) is the longer term trend confirming signal.

Below is the plot of the market from April-June, 1972.

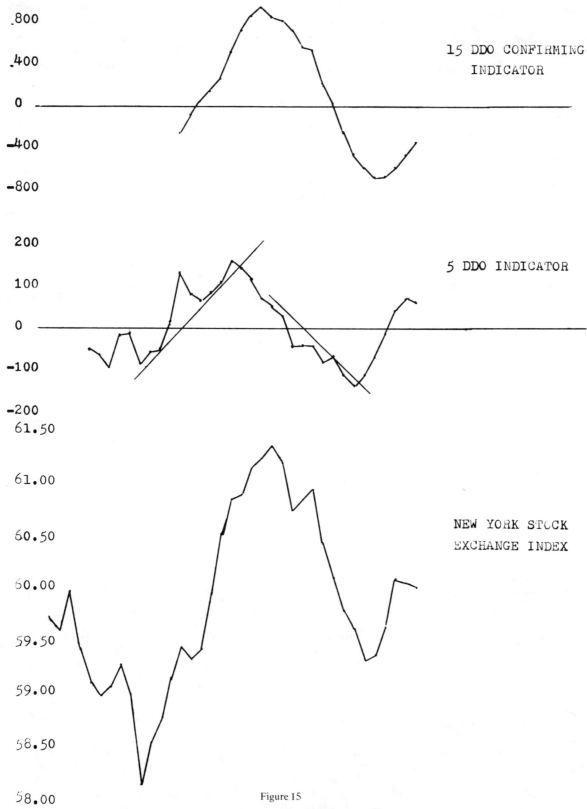

15 DDO CONFIRMING
INDICATOR

5 DDO INDICATOR

NEW YORK STOCK
EXCHANGE INDEX

Figure 15

Figure 15 shows the relationship between the differential oscillator and the
N.Y.S.E.Index. The period shown is from April-June, 1972.

N.Y.S.E. Index	5 DDO	5 DDC	15 DDO
59.62			
59.69			
60.00			
59.46			
59.12	— .50	— .50	
59.00	— .69	—1.19	
59.10	— .90	—2.09	
59.30	— .16	—2.25	
59.01	— .11 (1)	—2.36	
58.17	— .83	—3.19	
58.58	— .52	—3.71	
58.80	— .50	—4.21	
59.19	+ .18 (2)	—4.03	
59.47	+ 1.30	—2.73	—2.23
59.35	+ .77	—1.96	— .77 (3)
59.45	+ .65	—1.31	+ .78
59.98	+ .79	— .52	+ 1.73
60.54	+ 1.07	+ .55	+ 2.81
60.88	+ 1.53	+ 2.08	+ 5.27
60.92	+ 1.47	+ 3.55	+ 7.26
61.18	+ 1.20 (4)	+ 4.75	+ 8.96
61.28	+ .74	+ 5.49	+ 9.52
61.38	+ .50	+ 5.99	+ 8.72 (5)
61.21	+ .29	+ 6.28	+ 8.24
60.76	— .42	+ 5.86	+ 7.17
60.88	— .40	+ 5.46	+ 5.98
60.95	— .43	+ 5.03	+ 5.58
60.45	— .76	+ 4.27	+ 2.19

60.12	— .64	+ 3.63	+ .08
59.81	—1.07	+ 2.56	—2.19
59.63	—1.32	+ 1.24	—4.25
59.35	—1.10	+ .14	—5.84
59.40	— .72	— .58	—6.86
59.66	— .15 (6)	— .73	—6.59
60.11	+ .48	— .25	—5.71
60.09	+ .74	+ .49	—4.54
60.04	+ .64	+ 1.13	—3.14

1. The sharp rise in the 5 DDO line predicted the rally that followed. The drop two days later to .83 did not match the previous low at .90.

2. A buy signal was clearly given as the momentum indicator crossed over zero.

3. This buy signal was confirmed by the longer term indicator.

4. The sharp drop in the 5 DDO indicated the rally end two days before the actual top. A confirming sell signal followed four days later.

5. The 15 DDO indicator topped on the exact day of the high.

6. A rally was signalled by the 5 DDO indicator, confirmed by the 15 DDO on the same day.

This data is plotted on Figure 15. The relationship between the 5 DDO, the 15 DDO and the N.Y.S.E. Index is apparent. The 5 DDO is the more sensitive indicator. The action of the 15 DDO is smoother. Notice that the 15 DDO indicator, in particular, rendered excellent signals as it changed direction.

In order to ascertain whether this system had intermediate application, I plotted the 5 DDO and 15 DDO indicators, using weekly closings, therefore plotting the five week differential. The pattern formed revealed no automatic timing technique that outperformed the market. The oscillator did demonstrate the weakening of the market as tops were approached and did begin to turn up at major bottoms in advance of the market. It is suggested that readers experiment themselves to see if the configurations prove helpful. All told, the results were similar to plotting the differential between the last N.Y.S.E. Index weekly close and its 10 week moving average (Chapter 5).

Larry Williams suggests another approach to momentum study. He recommends that a 10 day moving average be computed and then that a plot be made of the difference between the 10 day moving average today, for instance, and the ten day moving average 10, 20 or 30 days ago, depending upon which period of time you want to study. The line produced resembles other oscillators we have examined, but is smoother and quite trendable.

Miscellaneous System #10
Two Day Runaways

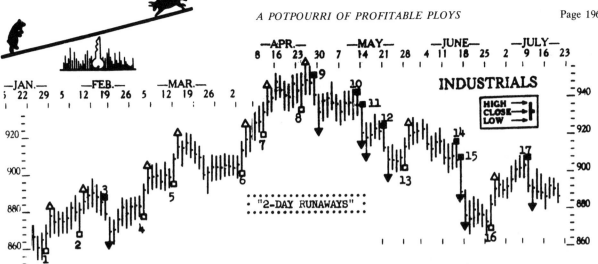

It is a fairly frequent occurrence that on two trading days in a row, the DJI covers a span of 22 or more points, between intraday high and intraday low. We chose to call this occurrence by the unglamorous but descriptive name of "2-Day Runaway". Thus far in 1971 there have been 17 "runaways", 9 on the upside and 8 on the downside. They are consecutively numbered 1 through 17 on the chart and in the statistical table. On the chart, the start of a runaway is marked by a box, the end by an arrowhead. WHITE box and arrowhead indicate an UP move, BLACK box and arrowhead indicate a DOWN move.

Figure 16

*Source: Key-Volume Strategies, Inc., P.O.Box 407,
White Plains, New York 10602*

From Key-Volume Strategies

A "Two-Day Runaway" is a period of two trading days in a row in which the Dow covers a span of 22 or more points, between intraday high and intraday low. Figure 16 shows seventeen runaways from January-July, 1971. Runaway starts are marked by boxes; runaway completions, by arrowheads. White boxes indicate the start of upmoves; black boxes, downmoves.

Operating Rules

Rule #1: The direction of a two-day runaway usually determines the short term direction of the market. See Rule #2 for exceptions.

Rule #2: The implications of Rule #1 are cancelled if within three trading days following the second day of the runaway, the Dow Jones Industrial Average touches or breaks the starting level of the runaway. (See Runaways 3 and 8, Figure 16.)

Rule #3: For an uptrend to remain intact, upside runaways must start at successively higher levels. For a downtrend to remain intact, downside runaways must start at successively lower levels.

Rule #4: White boxes (upside runaway starting points) act as support levels. Black boxes (downside runaway starting points) act as resistance levels.

Rule #5: Following each pair of runaways in the same direction, expect a correction or at least a consolidation (Note the periods between runaways 5 and 6, 12 and 14).

Rule #6: To measure the relative strength of an advance or a decline, proceed as follows: a) *Advance*. Total the Dow points between successive runaway starts. For runaways 1 through 8, entries are 8.89, 8.97, 17.32, 6.44, 19.74, 13.71 for a total of 75.07. Divide by the number of runaways during the advance, including downside ones (e.g. #3). Dividing 75.07 by 8 gives us an advance strength quotient of 9.38. b) *Decline*. Repeat the above procedure. Using entries 9 to 15, we add 9.28, 6.88, 11.46, 8.61 and 8.61. Total, 44.84. Divide by 7 runaways in series. Decline strength quotient is 6.41. A comparison shows a bullish bias in the magnitude of a 3-2 ratio (9.38-6.41) during this period.

Rule #7: *Using Two-Day Runaways to Predict Market Reversals.*

This is an added feature of this system, the ability to use two-day runaways to predict market reversals. Experience has shown that, generally, some market reversal, at the least short term, will occur following a series of four or five two-day runaways. A series includes a number of two-day runaways in the same direction, interrupted by not more than one two-day runaway in the opposite direction.

In the event that the series has been interrupted by a runaway in the reverse direction, an extra runaway will be needed to offset the reverse runaway. Thus, a "4 series" of up runaways will need 5 runaways in the up direction to trigger the signal if the series has been interrupted by a down runaway. A "5" up series would need six up runaways. While one reverse runaway may be offset, two break the series.

Signal

Following the completion of a series of four or five two-day runaways in the same direction, take positions *within two trading* days, in the opposite direction from the series just completed. If the runaway series has been up, go short and/or sell. If the runaway series has been down, go long and/or cover shorts. Hold the new position until the next short term reversal.

Results

Whether or not you wish to employ this system for short term trading, two-day runaways certainly call attention to impending market reversals and help you to initiate action early. The system does not catch every turn but is quite accurate when it does signal. Review Figure 16. Notice the reversals that occurred after the "4 series", runaways 4-7, and "5 series", runaways 4-8. Notice, also, the reversal that occurred after the "5 series", 9-15. Action signals between January 1971 and March 1972 produced total gains long and short of over 380 Dow points for the "4 series" signal and over 310 Dow points for the "5 series" signal. There were no losses. These results presume action taken at the best available level on the first or second trading day after the signal. Any clear daily chart can be employed for this system, the charts in the *Wall Street Journal* particularly recommended.

Miscellaneous System #11
Investing With The Long Term Trading Range

Many stocks, through major bull and bear cycles, oscillate within long term trading ranges. Each bull market carries them to certain historical peak areas and each bear cycle carries them to certain historical low areas. Surprisingly, peak areas often remain fairly constant throughout several cycles and low areas do also. It follows, therefore, that purchases made within the lower boundaries of the stock's trading range will show a high profit ratio to patient investors who are willing to sit through the long base building activity whilte the stock prepares for its bull thrust.

At least two books have appeared which discuss this concept. One, *How to Buy and Sell Low-Priced Stocks for Profit*, by John S. Villella, is available through Cen-Com, Inc., Advisory Dept., K, P.O. Box 295, Pinellas Park, Florida 33565. $2.00.

The author recommends the purchase of stocks $15 or under, highly volatile, listed on the Amex, at a price of 60% (or lower) of the issues lowest high for the previous five years.

A more recent book, *The Stock Digest Price Rate Test Method to Stock Market Success* by Robert L. Robertson (Windsor Books, Brightwaters, N.Y. 1972. $12.50), suggests the following technique:

1) Locate stocks that have recently made a new yearly low.

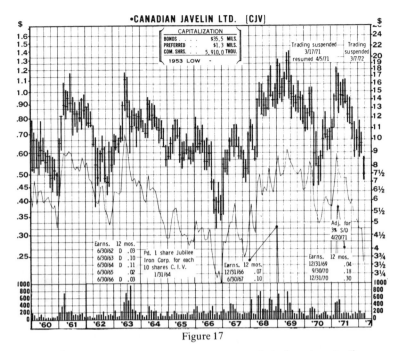

Figure 17

Canadian Javelin has been an ideal stock to trade by long term trading
range methods. Although the company reports no earnings, it has
fluctuated from between near 5 to near 20 for the past twelve years.
Source: Securities Research Co., 208 Newbury Street, Boston, Mass. 02116

2) Using a chart book, determine which of these are the most volatile.

3) For the period of the past five or more years, locate the high price achieved by the stock in each of those
years. Compute an average for these highs. Secure the average annual low price for the same period. Add the
average high to the average low and divide by two to secure the average medial price.

4) Stocks under $15 are buy rated if they are selling at no more than 15% above their average annual low for
the preceding five or six years. You can purchase stocks above $15 if they are no more than 10% above their
average annual low.

5) Sell off your holdings in increments as your stock passes its medial point.

Both authors suggest that investors concentrate on stocks showing rising earnings and having small float.
Either method should prove profitable to patient investors. Low price stocks are best suited to this technique.
Research has demonstrated that low priced stocks rise by greater percentages during bull markets than do
higher priced stocks. Since these investment techniques require patience, the investor should have some hope or
expectation of a sizeable return once the bull move begins. I would suggest that you avoid corporations showing
heavy deficits or erstwhile flyers come upon disastrous times (e.g. National Video). Confine yourself to low
priced cyclical stocks with at least flat earnings.

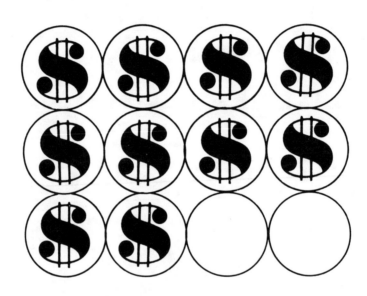

chapter ten

MISCELLANEOUS MONEY SAVERS

Money Saving System #1
Convert To Convertible Bonds

The following section is an expanded reprint of an article by the author which appeared in the January 1972 edition of *The Capitalist Reporter*.

How about a nice conservative investment that delivers more income than a bank, with interest each and every day, and an added kicker to boot that can bring in a real killing every so often? Risks? Sure. I'll get to them later. Right now, I want to give you the goodies. And what goodies am I talking about? Convertible bonds, that's what, where a lot of big smart money goes and what nine out of ten brokers won't mention. And I'll tell you the why about that too.

Understanding Convertibles

What is a convertible? It's a bond with an added sweetener that makes it stand out from the crowd—the right of its owner to swap it in for company stock. First, let's look at the bond feature. Where you and I, maybe, go to Beneficial Finance, companies issue bonds when they need money. A bond is a certificate representing a note owed by the company to the holder, with so much fixed interest each year and lump sum payment in full when the note falls due (due date).

Bonds, like stocks, are traded on the open market, and their prices fluctuate—rising generally as interest rates decline and dropping when money tightens. Regardless of these trading fluctuations, the issuing company keeps paying out the same amount of interest each year. However, the *rate* of interest to the purchaser varies with the price moves of the bond. For example: a bond carrying a 5% coupon (initial rate of interest) might drop in price from $1000 initial price to $750. Since the issuer continues to pay $50 interest (5% of $1000), a buyer at $750 would receive 6.7% interest ($50 per year for a $750 investment).

So long as the issuing company appears solvent and able to meet interest payments, its bond has a certain limited downside risk. It will not drop below the point where it yields the prevailing interest rate for the amount of risk involved in the loan. American Telephone does not have to pay as much interest to get a bond off as some fly-by-night, C-rated outfit. Whereas all bonds have a floor to their price, non-convertible bond prices cannot rise beyond a certain level. The more you pay for a bond, the lower your percentage of return. If you can do better in a bank, why bother with bonds?

A convertible bond has all the advantages of any bond. It draws regular interest computed to your account every day you hold it. It is a senior security, which means that your claim on the company's assets has to be satisfied before those of the stockholders. And its price is protected by the interest it pays. However, the price ceiling which limits the potential profitability of other bonds does not apply to convertibles. The conversion or swap feature gives convertibles the best of both worlds—safety plus the possibility of significant profit. Here's how it works.

Occidental Petroleum has a convertible bond listed on the New York Exchange as Occidental Petroleum 7-1/2s 1996. That means that the bond pays 7-1/2% interest based on the original price, in this case the usual $1000, and is due to be paid off in 1996. Because it is a convertible, bondholders, in lieu of taking payment, can redeem the bond until 1996 and receive 50 shares of Occidental Petroleum common.

The Upside Potential

At the time of this writing, Occidental Petroleum is selling at around 14, the bond at $940. This will be quoted in the newspaper at $94. For the usual $1000 bond, multiply by 10 for the total price. Multiply the stock price by 50. If you converted, you would receive $700 worth of stock. Better to keep the bond. But suppose the stock goes to $30. Then, if you convert, you will receive $1500 worth of stock (50 times $30 per share). You will not actually have to make the exchange—the price of the bond as traded will be rising to reflect its increasing value.

O.K. The upside looks interesting. Let's review the downside again. Suppose Occidental Petroleum drops to

7. There will be little immediate prospect for a profitable conversion, and the right to convert will be worth much less. The bond may then decline to its value as a straight loan (investment value)—say to $750—but probably no lower. At that price it draws interest at the rate of 10%. I have already pointed out the limited downside risk inherent in any bond. Upside potential? No firm limit; some convertibles have doubled and tripled over face value. Remember, Occidental once sold above $50. Downside risk? Much less than the common stock, particularly if you buy the bond at or below par (the issue price). In the example given, a 50% decline in Occidental Petroleum common resulted in only a 22% decline in the related bond. And if you held until 1996, you would stand to get all your money back plus nice steady interest checks each quarter. Besides, who knows what that stock might do in some twenty odd years?

You can't stand a 22% loss? Then consider limiting your investigation to bonds largely discounted from par. For instance, during early October 1971, TWA 4s 1992 was selling at around 50, yielding 8% currently with about a 9.3% yield to maturity. Purchasers at 50 who hold until 1992 stood to receive 8% interest ($40 per year on a cost of $500) plus $500, or 100% profit, when the bond falls due. If the airline stocks were to take off again, the bond stood to take off with them. If the airlines were to crash, the bond figured to gently glide to a soft landing, maybe down 15% to 43. And that's only if you sell before 1992. The big risk, of course, is that TWA will become too insolvent to pay off, in which case you'd better forget about that new Porsche. It has happened and can again. As for TWA—the government has kept Penn Central on the tracks and has prevented a lockout at Lockheed. Will it ground TWA? I doubt it. Nor is TWA the best yielding bond by any means. Collins Radio 4-7/8s 1987 provides a yield to maturity of nearly 12%. Some riskier bonds do even better. (Author's note: From October 1971. when the above was written, to mid-May 1972, the TWA convertibles rose to 78-1/2, a gain of 57%.)

Discounted Bonds

There have been some real gold mines in deeply discounted bonds. National General 4s 1993 was selling in mid-1970 at about $400, yielding 10%. National General common was then hanging around $10, following a long slide from $60. The bond was selling at roughly a 100% premium over conversion (20.62 shares per bond times $10 per share equals $206.20). The stock has since risen to over 31 and the bond to near $750. That's better than an 87% profit on the bond, plus the 10% interest. Sure, you would have done better in the stock, better yet in the warrants, but without the safety and yield—and do you have any way of knowing which stocks are going to triple? You could have bought the National General 4s 1993 at several points over the last year or so at around 60, yielding 6.7% currently and 7.8% to maturity, and selling at a modest 9 to 10% premium over conversion. The bonds move almost dollar-for-dollar with the stock, which pays less than 1%, and they offer more safety. Small wonder that the smart boys play the bond.

Other Advantages

You aren't too likely to hear your friendly stockbroker touting convertible bonds. And for a very good reason. Commissions are the name of his game, and commissions at most houses are still $5 per bond. That's right—five dollars. Your broker takes maybe $1.25 of that, and let's face it—there aren't many yachts for him on that kind of trade. Let's compare. To handle 100 shares of Occidental Petroleum, price $14, round-trip, you will have to pay roughly $60 in commission charges. You can handle 100 shares via the convertible route for round-trip costs of $20. (Two bonds at 50 shares per bond times $10 round-trip per bond.) Before they called the bond it was possible to swing in and out of Bannister Continental 6-1/2s 1989 for $10 round-trip. That covered 95 shares of stock. A trader could turn a profit on a quarter point rise in the common. Anyone who buys stock without first checking the convertible possibilities deserves anything his broker does to him.

One last extra: If you want to swing a little, you can play convertibles at 50% margin. Stocks require 65%. Not much difference but everything helps if you want to raise your ante. Not a bad package: higher yield than stocks, greater safety, lower commissions. All you have to do now is get to the bank.

Which Bonds To Buy

Although as a rule, convertible bonds provide better value than their related common, this rule does not always hold true. The relationship between the common and the convertible has to be evaluated in terms of your investment objectives. A convertible selling far below conversion offers the greatest yield and safety advantages, but will not advance proportionately to the common. Purchases of bonds so situated should be reserved for long term conservative holdings. The National General 4s 1993, selling at a 100% premium in mid-1970, is a case in point.

Bonds selling far above par, usually at little or no premium over conversion, offer usually a slight yield advantage and generally a definite commission savings. However, they provide little safety advantage in relationship to the common.

My recommendation is to seek out bonds selling near par and at no more than perhaps a 10% premium over conversion. These will drop more slowly than the common, will advance virtually dollar for dollar, provide both strong yield and commission advantages and can be employed for hedging (see System #3 below).

What To Avoid

It looks too good to be true? Well, nothing's perfect. Corporate bankruptcy has already been mentioned. That's nightmare number one. Stick to sound companies. Nightmare number two: Corporations can call (pay off) bonds before maturity. That's no headache if your bond is trading under par (face value, usually $1000)—you will get $1000 or a little more per bond. But if your bond is selling at more than par, you can get stuck. You'll get plenty of advance notice so you can sell or make your conversion. However, you do have to keep track of your bonds and what's happening. Third, as mentioned before, if the bond is selling at a large premium over the stock, the common is likely at first to move faster than the bond. In some situations, the common may be the better buy.

Brokerage houses don't make life easy for tinhorn players. Those fancy quote machines don't work as well for bonds as for stocks. You can get the last traded price quoted directly, but bids and offers often have to be sent for, from some mysterious room "downtown", and some houses take all day getting back to you. Shop around. Find a place that delivers fast quotes and good executions. Commission rates vary slightly, too. Some houses place a minimum commission, say $15 or $25, while others still charge $5 per bond, even if you just take one.

How To Sell

The convertible market is usually thinner and a little less fluid than the stock market. There are fewer transactions. That means that if you're panting to buy, you'll have to pay through the nose unless you're careful. And when you're dying to sell, there might not be a sucker on line. Solution: either stick to active issues or else put in firm limit orders. Before I knew better, I was once stuck in Stokely-Van Camp convertibles for two weeks in a crashing market, with no bid within ten points of my offer. I finally had to practically give them away. Positively, for trading purposes, stay with the active bonds. Daily trading volume is carried in those papers that provide good financial coverage. If you must buy a thin bond, decide what you want to pay and offer that—do not place a market order. You can always play the next hand if you miss out.

Before you hock the family jewels, one more suggestion. Many bonds have special conditions—expirations of conversion privileges and so forth. You might also be interested in convertible preferred stocks—stocks that enjoy a high yield and are convertible, like the bonds, into shares of common. The data you will need is available from several sources. In particular, within some of the advisories specializing in this area. These are noted later in this chapter.

Money Saving System #2
Speculating With Warrants

The following is abstracted from an article by the author which appeared in the February 1972 edition of *The Capitalist Reporter*.

From December 1970 to April 1971, Ling-Temco-Vaught common moved from 8-5/8 to 27-1/4, a gain of nearly 220%. Not bad. Not bad at all. However, if instead of rolling the common, you played the warrants, which moved from 2-1/4 to 12-1/4, you would have profited to the tune of 444%—in less than five months! How's that for a joyride? In terms of dollars, not including commissions, your happy buy of LTV common would have netted $2200 profit for every thousand you put in. The LTV warrants would have netted $4440. Better than two to one.

Intriguing? Yes. Risky? Often, but sometimes much safer than the common. Rare? Not at all. Look up the Loews Theatre warrants for another example. Interested? Fine, let's define our terms. A warrant is an option to purchase from the issuing corporation a stipulated number of shares of common at a specific price, usually for a limited period of time. For example, holders of National General Corporation New Warrants are entitled to purchase one share of NGC common at $40.00 for each warrant held until the expiration date of the warrants, September 30, 1978. Currently, the common is selling near $23; the warrant at about $6. Obviously, at this time, the warrant has no tangible value, since its exercise would result in a loss. Why pay $40 plus the cost of a warrant if you can buy the stock for $23 on the open market? In fact, why bother with the warrant at all? here's why. 1978 is a long way off. For your $6 you are getting a six year play on a $23 stock, a risk limited to $6, and the ability to use the extra $17 somewhere else.

Suppose that, between now and September 1978, NGC rises to $80 per share. The warrant then has to be worth at least $40. (Warrant plus $40 equals $80.) The warrant, in that case, will have appreciated nearly 570%; the common less than half, about 250%. The warrant clearly offers more upside leverage than the common— that is, your money carries more wallop and greater profit potential. Actually, the NGC warrants are likely to sell at more than $40 should the common reach 80. Investors will be willing to shell out something extra for the ability to play an $80 stock for a $40 investment. Probably, with the common at 80, the warrants will sell between $45 and $50. They could not sell below $40, because if they did, some quick smart traders would snap them up, exercise, and make a quick profit. (For instance, if warrants sold at $35, total exercise cost for $80 NGC common would be only $75—$35 for warrant plus $40.)

Upside Potential, Downside Risk

The National General Corp. New Warrants are very well situated. They have a long remaining life (approximately six years), and are selling only four points above their bear market low of 2-3/8. Let's presume a drop in the stock to 9, its 1970 bear market low, and a related drop in the warrants to 2-3/8. The stock will have lost 61%, the warrants 60%. So the NGCN warrants offer more potential than the common on the upside, similar downside risk. You could match the appreciation potential of the common with only half your funds invested, leaving the other half either in reserve or in income producing securities such as convertible bonds.

Many warrants offer this fine upside leverage, but many are far riskier than the NGCN warrants, and for them the leverage works both ways. For instance, let's consider the NGC Old warrants, now selling at $12, and exercisable until May 1974. They have a current tangible value of $8. That is, the warrant is actually worth $8 towards the purchase of a common share ($8 + $15 equals $23). They are selling at a $4 premium over tangible value because of the value of the leverage factor. A rise in the common to $80 (250%) will result in a percentage increase in the warrant of 440% (the warrant will be worth at least $65.). However, a drop in the common to $9 (61%) is likely to reduce the warrant in price to about $3, a 75% loss. So, these warrants have, potentially, greater downside risk or leverage than the common. Also, they expire in 1974, only slightly less than two years away. Should the common be selling at below $15 at that time, the warrants will be worthless.

By and large, leverage relationships are most favorable for warrants that have little or no tangible value, particularly if the warrant has a long remaining life. A high common to warrant price ratio is also favorable. There are usually excellent warrant values available during periods of market depression. Warrants become riskier as common and warrant prices advance and downside leverage builds up, particularly as expiration approaches. Remember, if NGC common is selling at 14 in May 1974, a loss of 39%, the NGC Old warrants will have lost 100%, a complete wipe-out.

In considering the purchase of any warrant: (1) make sure the warrant has good upside leverage; (2) check out the downside leverage; (3) check out the remaining life of the warrant; and (4) make sure you like the company. Do not ignore any of the above. Keep in mind that warrant holders receive no dividends and have no voting powers. Warrants are often excellent investments but should be evaluated against the related common and the possible availability of convertible bonds. Warrants are traded in a manner similar to common stocks, on the major exchanges and over-the-counter. Commissions, quotes, and executions are handled as though you were trading the common.

As usual, nothing's simple. The terms of exercise for warrants sometimes change, leverage factors are variable, and in some cases related corporate bonds are usable at face value instead of cash in exercising. This can add to the value of the warrant, if the bonds are priced at a discount, since a warrant holder could purchase the bond, say at $800, and use it at its $1000 face value for exercise purposes. A synthetic convertible bond could be created by a simultaneous purchase of warrant plus bond that is usable in this way. As opposed to purchase of the common such a combination would offer the conversion feature via the warrant, plus yield and safety in the total investment.

Money Saving System #3
Hedging Warrants And Convertibles

Tired of playing market games? Can't find a system to excite you? Going on vacation for a year? Consider hedging as a technique. Sure, the profit potential is limited but risk is almost nil. You'll make money on any major swing in the market, regardless of direction. Profitable hedges can be set up with both convertible bonds and warrants. Here's how it works.

The basic convertible bond hedge involves going long a convertible bond while shorting the related common. The presumption is that the bond selected is so situated that it will advance as rapidly as the common should the common rise, the profit on the convertible offsetting the loss on the short. Should the stock drop, you will profit to the extent that the convertible drops less rapidly than its related common. Review System #1 for an explanation of how this takes place. The hedge play for warrants is similar. You short an amount of stock such that a balance is created between the leverage possibilities of the warrant if the common moves upside and the loss on the short of the stock.

The *Value Line Convertible Survey*, among other services, carries data required to establish hedge projections, or else you can attempt your own computations by estimating a rise and fall projection for bonds and warrants in relation to a move on the part of the common. *Value Line* suggests the following procedure for determining the ratio between common (shorted) and convertible (long). Let us, first, refer to the below hypothetical table:

In this table we will presume that the convertible (including warrants) will move in proportion to a related move in the common as listed.

Table I

Common	+50%	+25%	—25%	—50%
Convertible	+45%	+20%	—15%	—25%

To determine the proportion of common to short for a ±25% play, add the percentage of the convertible's projected move in the case of a 25% rise in the price of the common to the convertible loss should the common drop by 25%. Multiply the result by two. The total (20% plus 15% times 2) is 70%, the percentage of convertible value in common to be shorted.

Example:

We long $1,000 worth of convertible

We short $700 worth of common

Result if common advances 25% to $875.   *Result if common drops 25% to $525.*

Profit on convertible, $200.00 (20% of $1000)	Profit on short, $175.00
Loss on short, $175.00 (25% of $700)	Loss on convertible, $150.00
Net profit, $25.00	Net profit, $25.00

For a hedge with a 50% move in mind, we add the amount the convertible is expected to rise on a 50% upmove in the common to the amount it is expected to decline should the common decline 50%. Do not multiply by two.

Example:

We will again use Table I.

Add 45% + 25%, total 70%. We will again short 70% of the value of the convertible security.

We long $1000 worth of convertible.

We short $700 worth of common.

Result if common advances 50% to $1050	*Result if common drops 50% to $350*
Profit on convertible, $450 (45% of $1000)	Profit on short, $350
Loss on short, $350 (50% of $700)	Loss on convertible, $250
Net profit, $100	Net profit, $100

Exciting? Not really. Safe? You bet. More profitable results can be achieved by judicious selection of hedge candidates. *Value Line*, again, suggests the following formulae to determine which hedge candidates offer the greatest profit potential:

For a ± 25% move in the common

Subtract the expected loss in the convertible should the stock drop from the expected gain should the stock rise. Multiply the result by 4. The higher the result, the greater the profit potential in the hedge.

For a ± 50% move in the common

Subtract the expected loss in the convertible should the stock drop from the expected gain should the stock rise. Multiply the result by 2. The higher result is the superior hedge candidate.

We will illustrate one case only. First, review Table I, and its results. Apply the formula to the +25% situation. We subtract 15% (for a 25% decline in common) from 20% (convertible advance if common rises 25%). Result 5%. Multiply by four. Hedge factor is 20. We have seen that for each $1000 worth of convertible, the hedge will show a profit of $25, should the common fluctuate by 25%.

Let us now construct Table II, slightly altering the figures.

Table II

Common	+50%	+25%	—25%	—50%
Convertible	+46%	+23%	—10%	—15%

The hedge factor in this case is 52 (23% minus 10% times 4). Theoretically, this should provide greater profits than in the first situation. We will short $660 or 66% the value of our $1000 convertible holdings in common stock (23 plus 10 times 2).

Result if common advances 25% to $825

Profit on convertible, $230.00 (23% of $1000)

Loss on short, $165.00 (25% of $660)

Net profit, $65.00

Result if common declines 25% to $495

Profit on short, $165.00

Loss on convertible, $100.00

Net profit, $65.00

Balanced hedges provide small but sure profits regardless of the direction in which the stock moves. An unbalanced hedge, to emphasize one side or the other, can be created by shorting (in the case of a long hedge) just enough common to protect against a downside drop or (in the case of a short hedge) by shorting sufficient common against the convertible to offset a rise.

For an example, refer again to Table I.

To profit on the short side, while incurring no risk should the common advance 25%, we short $800 (20% times 4) common for each $1000 convertible owned. Should the common advance 25%, the $200 loss on the short is offset by the $200 gained from the rise in the convertible. Should the common drop 25% we profit $200 on the short while losing $150 on the convertible, for a net profit of $50. This is twice the profit of the balanced hedge, but on one side only.

To profit on the long side, we short just enough common to offset a 25% decline, in this case $600 (15% drop in the convertible times 4). Should the common decline 25%, we will profit by $150 on the short while losing $150 on the convertible, neither profit nor loss. Should the common rise 25%, we will lose $150 on the short, but gain $200 on the long, again a $50 profit, but on one side only.

For constructing an unbalanced hedge for a 50% move, multiply the projected rises and falls in the convertible by 2 instead of 4.

The following data is taken from the January 3, 1972 edition of *The Value Line Convertible Survey*. Apply the formulae to these high ranking hedge situations and evaluate the results yourself.

Projected Move of Warrant if Common Advances or Declines

Warrant	+50%	+ 25%	—25%	—50%
Guardian Mtg. Invs. Wt.	+ 90	+ 40	—35	—60
Hoerner Waldorff Corp. Wt.	+250	+105	—24	—55
National General New Wt.	+115	+ 50	—23	—50
United Brands (AMK) 78 Wt.	+120	+ 55	—20	—50
Wilson & Co. Wt.	+130	+ 60	—35	—65

In each of these cases, incidentally, we can see that the warrant offers far greater upside potential than the common against, in the worst cases, only slightly greater risk. Long hedges are readily established to prevent loss should the stock decline while ensuring profits should the stock rise.

Convertible bonds selling near par and at only slight premium are usually excellent hedge vehicles. The related common can be shorted for bear profits against a convertible long. This maneuver is made possible by the floor to the bond's decline.

There are situations in which it pays to short the warrant and to long the stock. Earlier in this chapter I mentioned the risks involved in holding the National General Old Warrants, selling at a four point premium and due to expire in 1974, less than two years away. Suppose we short those warrants at $12 and long the common at $23. Should the common advance, the warrants will also, but as expiration nears, the premium will vanish, providing a four point profit. Should the stock decline, the premium will still vanish as the warrant drops. The four point profit will be retained except if the stock drops below 15. No loss is possible unless the common drops below 11. Look into warrants approaching expiration for this play to see if sufficient premium remains to justify a long term short for the profit potential of the premium itself.

Data for any of these ploys is available from a number of sources, in particular from among the advisory services specializing in warrants and convertible bonds. Several fine services are cited later in this chapter.

Caution

The above computations do not include commission costs. In considering potential hedge situations, make certain to include costs of commissions.

Money Saving System #4
Saving On Stock Commissions

Let's face it. The Street isn't making life easy for the little guy. The rise in commission rates, effective during the Spring of 1972, didn't help the cause any either. A round-trip now costs $50.00 per 100 shares of a $10 stock, $89.00 per 100 shares of a $25 stock and $130.00 for a round-trip of a $50.00 stock. That means that in the last case, you're giving away almost 1-3/8 points of every stock move each trade.

Two avenues of relief have already been suggested. The convertible bond route is one, of course. A round-trip trade of 100 shares of Sante Fe Industries would cost, via the common, $103.40. The purchase of 4 convertible bonds, the Sante Fe 6-1/4s 1998, each convertible into 31.25 shares of common, or 125 shares in all, would involve $40.00 in round-trip commission costs. To repeat, don't buy the common without first checking the convertible.

Warrants also offer commission savings, although the principle is a bit more subtle. Since warrants usually offer greater leverage than the related common, smaller amounts have to be purchased for similar profit expectations. Therefore, smaller dollar amounts have to be invested, hence lower commissions.

There is a third avenue of relief—if you're willing to deal outside the private membership fraternity and don't need your broker's sales pitch, hand holding and advice and are willing to put up with certain Spartan conditions to your manipulations.

The Third Market

Consider trading on the Third Market, where you can get wholesale commission rates on retail orders. The Third Market is where over-the-counter trading of listed securities takes places, often big blocks that the large operators don't want showing on the tape. Almost all the popular listed stocks can be taken on the Third Market, and most others too. Some stocks have several market makers offering competitive quotes. Others just one or two. Stock is usually offered at quotes competitive to the "asked" on the floor, perhaps one eighth of a point higher. You can sell usually at the floor bid price or for one eighth of a point less.

Several Third Market houses have sprung up, actively seeking the kind of retail business which the fat cat operations discourage in one form or another. These houses offer discounts on exchange commission rates which can be considerable. However, nothing's for nothing. None of these offer a full range of brokerage services. Research reports are virtually non-existent. You receive no recommendations. The operation is strictly business. I've begun to do some trading myself with one of these houses. I find the people friendly, the service good and have just completed a trade on Loews, on which I saved some fifty dollars on commissions, even considering that I paid one-eighth more than the floor asked, and sold for one-eighth less than the floor bid. That adds up to good money over the year. The following houses offer discount commission rates. There may be many others. Write for their brochures for more details or call. I have found them very ready to answer any and all questions. The information below was accurate at the time of this writing, but house policies do change, so investigate further yourself.

Marquette deBary Co., 30 Broad Street, New York, N.Y. 10004. (212-944-4005).

Offers a range of commission savings, the rate of savings rising as the total order increases. You save 27% on a $25.00 stock (100 shares), about 40% on a $50.00 stock, No savings where the N.Y.S.E. member commissions would amount to under $26.00. You can trade through Marquette on the exchanges, but will receive no commission discount (standard policy for these houses). No margin accounts. Prefers to ship out certificates, but will hold them in customer's name upon request.

Odd Lot Securities Ltd., 60 East 42nd Street, New York, N.Y. 10017. (212-661-6755).

Also offers a range of commission savings, with about a 20% savings on transactions up to $10,000, and increasing thereafter. Maximum commission per trade, $40.00 per 100 shares. For high priced stocks, this means savings greater than 20%. Welcomes odd-lot transactions, one of the few places left, it seems, which really wants the little guy. Will supply some basic research reports, and perhaps an idea or two regarding stocks. No margin accounts. Prefers also to ship securities.

Source Equities Inc., 70 Pine Street, New York, N.Y. 10005 (212-425-3420).

The first investment firm to provide transaction service on a flat fee basis. You sign up for a contract, paying commissions in advance on a semi-annual basis. Fee scale is as follows:

Total Shares Traded	Annual Fee
2,000 (20 transactions)	$ 440
5,000 (must average 200 share lots)	900
10,000	1,600
25,000	3,300
50,000	6,900
100,000	12,300

They will guarantee a 1/3 savings on any commission if the trade can be executed in the Third Market. For cheaper stocks, this will mean a trade outside the contract, the charge made by the trade. Consult *Source* for further details. Savings are high, ranging upwards from over 50% on a 100 share transaction, $40.00 stock. Handles margin accounts. Fast executions. Accepts limit orders on only a few hundred different stocks. For the rest, you have to transact "at the market" or else call back. A definite disadvantage. Before signing, make sure that you trade enough to fill the contract.

Stock Cross, 141 Milk Street, Boston, Mass. 02109. (617-482-8200).

A real cheapie, charges a flat $28.00 commission for each transaction up to 1,000 shares. That amounts to $2.80 per hundred! On a 400 share order of a $40.00 stock the savings amounts to 85% of member rates. Certificates kept in custodial account, not mailed to customer. Additional charges if customer wants certificates, and for limit and stop orders. No recommendations. No margin accounts. Procedures are somewhat unusual but not impossible. Suggest you write or call *Stock Cross* for further details.

Recommendations

I cannot recommend one house over the other. Secure further details from the houses themselves to see which best meets your needs. *Tip*: If you're a large, active account, try some horsetrading. You just might get yourself a negotiated break on commissions over and above the stated rates.

Money Saving System #5
Consider Puts, Calls And Straddles

Properly played, options can be both speculative and conservative, used as insurance or for going broke, used to play the long or the short side of the market. How is all this possible? Read on. First the definitions, for those unfamiliar with option games.

A *call* is an option to buy 100 shares of stock at a previously agreed on (striking) price. It may be at or near the market, a few points above or below. The premium or cost of the option varies with the life of the option—usually about 12-1/2% for a 90 day call, higher as the length of time increases. Volatile stocks command a higher option price than quieter stocks. The mechanics are simple. Presume you pay $300 for a ninety day call on a $25.00 stock, striking price, $25. Should the stock rise to $35 within 90 days, you exercise. Your costs will be $300 for the option plus approximately one point round-trip commissions. Since you can sell the stock the same day you purchased it, without putting up any money, we figure no costs there. You have profitted by $600 for a 200% return on your $300 investment. Should the stock rise only to $27, you will still exercise, the two point gain more than offsetting commission costs but you will lose approximately $200 or 67% of your investment. Should the stock drip to $10? You simply do not exercise. Your maximum risk is $300.

Calls, therefore, can be a quite conservative vehicle for playing your favorites. Instead of risking $2500 (remember Case 3; the stock dropped to $10), you risk only $300. The rub? You've given away three points for the insurance. If you want to go wild, say you've heard that the company has a high potency pill or something which will shoot it to fifty, you can buy eight calls. If the stock goes nowhere, you've had it. But if it reaches fifty, you've made yourself $16,800 on a $2400 investment.

Calls can also be used to keep a position in a stock you're in, but about which you are feeling a little leery. Say you've bought the stock itself at $25 and it's moved to $35. You're itching to take profits, but think the stock may have more to go. Sell and buy a call. If the stock goes higher, you will participate. If it drops, you can chalk off the cost of the call against the 10 points you've made already, figuring that if you had held, the stock might have dropped that much anyway.

Puts

A put is a call in reverse, *the right to sell a stock at the striking price*. Puts can be used as insurance against a fall in stocks you already own, perhaps to enable you to hold for capital gains. Puts can also be used as a means of going short without the nightmare of the short skyrocketing in your face. Your maximum risk is the cost of the put, but again, you've given away a piece of the downmove in advance.

Straddles

A straddle is an option to both buy and sell a stock at the striking price. In the best of all possible worlds, you buy a straddle on our favorite $25 stock. It drops instantaneously to $15. You sell it at $25, as per your option, buying stock that day at $15 to deliver. The stock then rises to $40. Happy day! You now exercise the call portion of your straddle, so you profit both ways. In the real world, you are likely to profit on one side only, hopefully by enough to offset the added costs of purchasing the straddle.

Dividends

If you buy a call in a dividend paying stock, your striking price is reduced by the amount of dividends received by the seller of the call during the life of the option.

Capital Gains

You can achieve capital gains on options in the following manner: Buy calls for longer than six months. They are offered for six month, ten day periods and longer. Should the stock you are optioned for rise, do not purchase and sell the stock. Such action, on the same day, is a short term day trade (of course, you can buy and hold the stock but that involves putting up the purchase price). Instead, if possible, hold the call option for six months and then *sell the option*. Option houses will purchase the option for a slight premium and exercise it themselves. You will receive a capital gain on the profit between what the option cost you and what it is worth considering the increase in value in the underlying stock.

Buying Calls Against Short Sales

This is a variation of buying puts instead of shorting. The call protects you against calamity if you are short. Should the stock rise, you will profit from your call almost to the extent that you lose on your short.

Results

Most options are not exercised, so the purchaser of the option, more often than not, loses his complete investment. This does not necessarily argue against option purchases. As a point of fact, option activity is heaviest at market tops at which point purchase of stocks is contra-indicated in any event. The time to purchase options is when no one else wants them. Option purchases can be a great way to play stock market games on a limited budget. Use some of the systems in this book to tell you when to deal your cards.

A More Conservative Ploy: Selling Options

For every option buyer there has to be an option seller, and for the most part it's the sellers who make the money. How much? With a fairly conservative approach, 15%-20% per year should be an approximate target. Is it worth it? You have to decide that.

The mechanics are simple. If you own stock and are looking for an option buyer, contact an option house and inquire as to whether there is any option interest in your stock. If so, you may open an account at the option house or have your broker guarantee your holding of your shares. Some brokerage houses have option departments of their own. You will receive, perhaps, from 10%-15% of your stock's price for a 90 day call, somewhat more for a six month call. You promise to deliver at the striking price, if called within that period.

Selling puts is the same process except that you agree to *buy* the shares at the striking price, which, in effect, lets you into the stock at a discount or puts free cash in your pocket. You receive the most money for selling straddles, but these are likely to be exercised on you in one direction or the other.

Paradoxically, in selling both puts and calls, you should be bullish on the stock. When you sell a put, there is always the chance that you may have to purchase the stock. It follows then, that you should sell puts only on stocks in which you might want to take a long position. When you sell a call on a stock, you are limiting your ability to liquidate your own position. True, if the stock gives a sell signal you can sell out and hope it does not rise again which could force you to buy in higher to honor the call. You can also sell the stock and buy for yourself a call to offset the call on your stock. If the stock rises and you have to deliver, you simply exercise the call you hold to secure the stock you owe.

Mainly, though, you want to have your shares called by the person to whom you sold the call—the sooner the better. Why? The sooner calls are exercised against you, the more turnover you can achieve, the better the return. Suppose you sell four 90 day calls during the course of a year, unexercised, on a stock at 10% per call. Total annual return, 40%. Suppose, instead, these are exercised at one month intervals so you can sell twelve per year at 10%. Total return, 120% plus whatever return you can secure by compounding the cash you received during the year. The seller of calls doesn't begrudge the buyer his profits. The buyer is in looking for a speculative gain. The seller is looking for a steady income from his holdings. Most professional sellers of calls do not sell a declining stock. They continue to sell calls on shares until they are exercised. The procedure reduces commission costs and provides the highest rate of return.

Premiums paid to sellers vary with the volatility, popularity and general risk associated with the stock in question. Remember, the buyer gets the dividends if the call is exercised.

Bears can sell calls too, as a cheap way of going short. In this case you sell a "naked" call, that is, a call on shares you do not own. The prayer here is that the stock does not rise. Usually, you have to deposit 30% or so in cash against the possibility that the move goes against you. If you're right, you've paid no commission to buy or to short the stock and you stand to make a pretty return on the money you've deposited with the endorsing broker. You can, of course, protect yourself at any time by buying either the shares or a call yourself. Super bears, of course, can both short the stock and sell naked calls.

Puts can be sold against current short positions as a sort of hedge. Suppose your stock declines. You will profit on your short and will have to take the stock "put" to you, which shares you will use to cover your short. Result: profit equal to put premium. Should your short go against you, your put will not be exercised, the premium you receive thus offsetting your loss on the short. The only loss possible—should your short rise beyond the premium you received for the put.

Selling Straddles

The greatest demand exists for straddles. The advantages to the seller are, (1) he receives a greater premium than for a put or a call alone, and (2) there is a greater probability that he will find some interest or potential purchaser for the option. The seller of the straddle must be prepared for its exercise in one direction or the other. Should the stock rise, he will deliver the shares, receiving the profit from the call plus a free premium on the put side. Should the stock decline, he will have to buy the stock, but will have, in probability, an extra call premium in pocket. The seller of the straddle should be bullish on the stock; he will probably have to maintain at least one long position and may end up with two.

There are many fine points to the rules regarding option trading, too many to cover here. *Barron's* and most newspapers with broad financial coverage carry ads from option houses. I suggest you contact these for further information, free brochures, instructions, and listings of options bid for and offered.

Hint

If you are buying and/or selling, try a little negotiation on the price. The option house picks up a profit on the spread between what the buyer pays and what the seller receives. Sometimes, you can negotiate a slightly better deal than the original offer.

Recommended Reading

How To Make Money Selling Stock Options by Robert Asen and R. Scott Asen, Parker Publishing Co. Inc., West Nyack, N.Y., 1970.

Money Saving System #6
Trading No-Load Mutual Funds

Almost all trading systems work more consistently for the market as a whole than for individual stocks. In other words, the market is easier to call than any one stock at a particular time. So why not play with an investment that's almost certain to move with your market calls, while saving on commissions at the same time? Volatile no-load funds do provide just that sort of vehicle. Their cross-section of portfolios tend much more than single stocks to follow bull moves. The stronger funds resist intermediate decline fairly well and some have racked up real gains in hot years. Nicholas Strong, for example, gained 85.5% during 1971. An added kicker is that on any major sell signal you can go—no commissions to worry about—if you stick to the no-loads. You do lose some of the fun of self-selection of course, and of the occasional super-trade, but consistent profit and relative safety are nothing to sneeze at either.

Where To Find The Strong Funds

Barron's carries mutual fund quarterly results. *Forbes* rates funds annually and *Fundscope* carries extensive data. Several mutual fund advisories rank and chart funds, monthly and/or quarterly, all reasonably priced. Some of these are listed further into this chapter.

Picking Your Own Fund

Let's suppose that you want to go the no-load route but want to select your own. What criteria should you evaluate? Somewhat similar approaches are suggested by Edward E. Duke (*Selecting Your Mutual Fund*: A professional program for producing perpetual profits, Exposition Press, 1972) and Alan S. Feinstein (*Making Your Money Grow*, Selby Publishing Co., 1972). The former suggests that investors confine their investments to load funds on the theory that their sales force ensures a fresh money flow into the funds. The latter suggests no-loads on the basis that with limited advertising, fund managers have to pay more attention to performance (Author's note: a dubious conclusion; I doubt that any fund is not interested in performance).

The record, however, clearly indicates the superior potential of no-loads to load funds. Yale Hirsch, editor of *Mutual Funds Scoreboard*, reported in April, 1972, that the average no-load showed a net gain of 38.1% more than the average load fund. His special report, *No-Loads Have A Helluva Head Start*, demonstrates that a load fund, appreciating at 20% per year compared to a no-load, appreciating at 10% per year, will require ten years to match an equivalent original investment in the no-load. This is the handicap created by the typical 8-1/2% commission. To boot, five out of six of the best performing funds in 1971 were no loads. My own opinion, of course, is that the no-load is by far the superior vehicle.

The argument of load vs. no-load aside, Duke and Feinstein do agree on the essential characteristics of successful funds. Some of these are listed below:

1) The fund should be small. Smaller funds have greater flexibility of operation and do not have to diversify to such an extent that you are, in effect, buying the averages. They clearly outperform the larger funds in up markets, though they perform slightly less well in down markets. How small is small? Certainly assets under $200 million, preferably under $50 million.

2) It should be a performance growth fund.

3) Management should be respected and have a proven track record. The fund should have ranked among the top 25 during up years with relatively low depreciation during down years.

4) It should be currently performing well. Check the above sources.

5) There should be no or very minimum redemption charges.

6) The big one! The faster the fund is growing through new money flow (cash coming in for investment minus cash going out because of redemptions), the better it will perform. Funds generating new inflow of money have cash to invest during periods of market weakness, attract fresh investment ideas from brokers (what broker contacts customers having no money?), are the most flexible, and do not have to liquidate good stocks to meet redemptions. A good money flow is a growth in new money of more than 50% of the fund's assets value per year. Obviously, the larger the fund, the more difficult to sustain this 50% figure. A $10 million dollar fund needs to attract only $5 million dollars to maintain the ratio; a $2 billion dollar fund needs $1 billion dollars. The cut-off for high performance seems to be $50 million dollars in assets. Only five of the top twenty-five funds during 1971 were larger.

To Sum Up

Look for high current growth, small size and high money flow.

chapter eleven

THE MASTER SYSTEM:
YOU SKIP A STEP AT YOUR OWN PERIL

It goes without saying that the best time to initiate positions is towards the beginning of   major or, at the least, intermediate turning points. Short term swings are not always sufficiently extensive for in and out trading, but obviously within the intermediate move, positions should be taken on short term reactions.

The investor should approach his trading decisions systematically. The total position of the market and any stocks under consideration should be evaluated and the risk-reward ratio calculated. It is not sufficient, for example, to be aware of the existence of a major bull move. Other questions should be answered. How far along has the move progressed? How much room is left in which to profit? When is the next intermediate downturn due? The public gets hurt, not only because the public trader buys into bear markets, but also because the public buys into the tail end of bull markets, becoming locked in as the market changes direction. Likewise, public shorts are heaviest at the bottoms of bear markets, despite mounting fundamental and technical evidence that the bear is ready for hibernation.

The "Master System" is a checklist for evaluating the current and anticipated state of the market and of individual stocks. The procedure, of course, is to first determine the overall direction of the market and then to act in harmony with that direction. Intermediate trading can be done in opposition to the major trend, but only with short term profits in mind and with awareness that you are opposing the major tide.

Each step of the master system should be followed before placing your bets. Neglect of any step increases your risk. Some of the trading systems which may be employed in each step are enumerated. These have been placed in order of my estimate of a combination of their rank importance and the readiness with which the home technician can carry out the necessary work. These rankings are by no means absolute; work with those systems that feel best to you.

The Master System

1. *Determine the direction of the major trend of the market.*

    The Basic Trendline System (Chapter 1)

    Speed Resistance Lines (Chapter 1)

    The Haller Theory for Determining Major Tops and Bottoms (Chapter 7)

    The Haurlan Index, Long Term (Chapter 7)

    The Chartcraft Method of Point and Figure Trading, Long Term Bullish Support Lines and Bearish Resistance Lines (Chapter 4)

    Long Term Moving Average Study (Chapter 5)

    The Option Activity Ratio (Chapter 2)

    Trendway's Negative Volume Index (Chapter 2)

    Don Worden's Tick Volume System (Chapter 2)

2. *Determine how far along the market is in the major trend.*

Technical Systems

    Evaluate the strength of the Advance-Decline Line relative to the market averages (Chapter 7)

    Interpreting the New Highs-New Lows Indicator (Chapter 9)

    Interpreting Market Volume, which usually peaks several months before major tops (Chapter 2)

Ratio of American Stock Exchange Volume to New York Stock Exchange Volume (Chapter 2)

The Elliott Wave Theory (Chapter 6)

Long Term Time Cycles (Chapter 6)

Predicting Trend Line Breaks in Advance (Chapter 1)

Fundamental Systems

Evaluating Price-Earnings Ratios of Market Averages (Chapter 8)

Mutual Fund Cash Position (Chapter 8)

Use Money and Credit Indicators to Forecast Market Action (Chapter 8)

How Dow Yields Can be Used to Forecast the Market (Chapter 8)

Free Credit Balances and Stock Margin Debt (Chapter 8)

3. *Determine the direction of the intermediate trend.*

Technical Systems

The Basic Trendline System (Chapter 1)

Speed Resistance Lines (Chapter 1)

The Haurlan Index, Intermediate Term (Chapter 7)

Fundamental Systems

How to Use Municipal Bond Yields to Forecast Market Action (Chapter 8)

Using Money Stock Data to Forecast the Market (Chapter 8)

Using the Dow Jones Utilities to Forecast Market Action (Chapter 8)

4. *Determine how far along the market is in the intermediate trend.*

Time Cycles, Intermediate Peak to Peak and Low to Low (Chapter 6)

Channel System (Chapter 1)

Using Trendline Breaks to Measure the Probable Extent of Moves (Chapter 1)

10 Day and 28 Day Moving Average Systems (Chapter 5)

Advance-Decline Line Overbought-Oversold System (Chapter 7)

Formation Objectives (Chapter 3)

Intermediate Point and Figure Counts (Chapter 4)

Specialist Short Sale Systems (Chapter 9)

Odd Lot Short Sale Systems (Chapter 9)

Two Day Runaways (Chapter 9)

Sentiment Index (Chapter 9)

Application of the Short Term Trading Index to Intermediate and Long Term Trading (Chapter 2)

Predicting Trendline Breaks in Advance (Chapter 1)

5. *Determine the short term trend of the market.*

Basic Trendline System (Chapter 1)

Haurlan Index, Short Term (Chapter 7)

Using Chart Segments to Predict Moves of at least 40 Dow Points (Chapter 1)

Constructing a Momentum Oscillator (Chapter 9)

6. *Determine how far along the market is in the short term trend.*

Channel System (Chapter 1)

Time Cycles, Short Term (Chapter 6)

Formation Objectives, Minor (Chapter 3)

An Early Warning System (Chapter 2)

7. *Determine the exact turning points of the market.*

Cycle and Trendline Method (Chapter 6)

Basic Trendline System, Shortest Term Trendlines (Chapter 1)

The Short Term Trading Index (Chapter 2)

Look for Climactic Volume (Chapter 2)

8. *Select Your Stocks.*

Technical Systems

Basic Trendline System (Chapter 1)

Formations (Chapter 3)

Volume Action (Chapter 2)

Point and Figure Objectives (Chapter 4)

Establish a Risk Reward Ratio (Chapter 4)

Measuring Relative Strength (Chapter 9)

Speed Resistance Lines (Chapter 1)

Volume-Price Trend Charting (Chapter 2)

Measuring Accumulation-Distribution (several methods, Chapter 2)

Long Term Trading Range Methods (Chapter 9)

Fundamental Systems

Computing Price-Earnings Ratios (Chapter 8)

Compute Payout Time (Chapter 8)

Compute Growth Rate (Chapter 8)

Evaluate Balance Sheet (Chapter 8)

9. *See if you can save some money in miscellaneous ways.*

Convertible Bonds (Chapter 10)

Warrants (Chapter 10)

Third Market Houses (Chapter 10)

No-Load Mutual Funds (Chapter 10)

GOOD LUCK!

chapter twelve

SOME NEW GOODIES THAT I HAVE DEVELOPED OVER THE YEARS

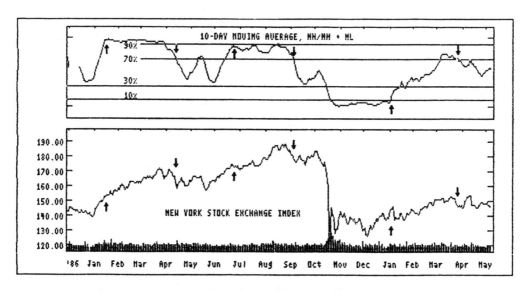

The 10-Day New Highs/New Highs + New Lows Oscillator:

Here is a truly excellent breadth mementum indicator.

The percentages of stocks making new highs (reaching new 52-week highs in price) tend to peak in advance of market peaks but tend to bottom along with market bottoms.

An oscillator created by dividing the number of issues making new highs each day by the total number making new highs and new lows can be very useful. I plot this indicator on a 10-day basis. First, we secure the number of issues making new highs. Then we secure the number making new lows. If there were 40 new highs and 40 new lows, our daily percentage oscillator would come to .50 (40/40 + 40). If we convert this to a percentage by multiplying by 100, then we have 50% of the issues involved making new highs. A 10-day average of the daily percentages is maintained.

The data is available in many newspapers such as the Wall Street Journal each day; many stockbrokers can provide this information during the day from their quotation machines.

Rules for Interpretation:

1) It is very bullish when the 10-day MA of NH/NH + NL rises to as high as 90%. This usually occurs only during the strongest of market periods, for example, early 1987 in the chart above.

Once the 90% level (or very close to it) is achieved, you can safely hold for the full intermediate term until the 10-day moving average falls to under 70%. I have tested the 90% - 70% parameters going way back to 1970. You can expect prices to be higher roughly 85% of the time if you hold between the time the indicator reaches 90% and the time it falls to below 70%.

2) You canusually buy for a trade when the oscillator falls to the 30% area (oversold) and then turns up. More significant low areas take place when the indicator falls to below 15%. Turn-ups in the stock market are sometimes delayed for a few weeks when this takes place, but the odds are that the stock market has fallen to a significant intermediate bottom at a minimum, often to a major bottom. The lows of the autumn of 1987 took place with the oscillator tracing out a double bottom formation in the area below 10%. Usually, readings of such low levels are not as protracted in time. Turns to the upside take less time to develop.

3) Fluctuations around the 50% - 70% region are not significant.

The most signficant signals generated by this indicator are generated when the oscillator reaches 90%. You know then that the stock market is very strong and that positions may be held until sell signals develop.

The 21-Day Advance-Decline Oscillator:

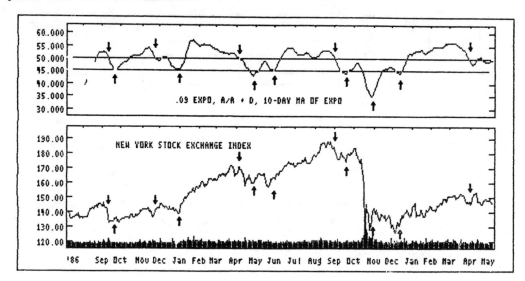

Here is another favorite of mine—the 21-day advance-decline oscillator.

To calculate the oscillator, you calculate a .09 exponential average of the daily ratio of advancing issues on the NYSE against the total advancing + declining.

For example, if there were 400 issues advancing on the NYSE today and 600 declining, the daily ratio would come to .400 (400/400 + 600). A 21-day exponential average is maintained of these daily ratios. This involves an exponential smoothing constant of .09. The formula is New Exponential = .09 (Today's ratio - previous exponential) + previous exponential. For a review of the calculations, refer back to Chapter 7. But remember, the A/D formulas in Chapter 7 are based upon the numeric differentials between advancing and declining issues. This indicator is based upon the ratio of advancing issues to advancing + declining issues.

Once you achieve the daily .09 exponential average (a 21-day period required for stabilization), you then maintain a 10-day moving average of the daily exponential averages. So we are working with a double smoothing —the .09 exponential and a 10-day moving average of this exponential.

Rules for Interpretation:

Good intermediate buy signals are *usually* generated when the 10-day MA of the 21-day exponential average first falls to below .45 and then turns up. If you prefer more rapid entry (recommended), you can employ a 5-day moving average for use as buy signals.

Usually—usually, again—the indicator will then rise to above the .50 region. You take as a sell signal a downside penetration of the .50 area (e.g. from .52 to .49). Do not use the 5-day moving average for selling; stick with the 10-day moving average. Advance-decline indicators usually peak in advance of the market averages and we do not want the lead time to become too great.

Intermediate traders can hold long positions for as long as the 10-day MA remains above .50. If the 10-day MA falls from above .50 to below .50 and then rises to above .50 once again, you consider a market re-entry signal to have been generated but such signals are not nearly as significant as signals which emanate from lower areas.

Do not employ this as your sole indicator. There are times (for example, September 1987) when the indicator will turn up and fail to reach the .50 level and there are times when it will fail, in a decline to reach the .45 area. In these cases, you will fail to receive sell and buy signals at important market junctures.

Nonetheless, the 5-day and 10-day moving averages of the .09 exponential average of the A/A + D ratio have had very fine records as intermediate timing models and belong in the technical arsenal of any investor.

The Key-Volume Strategies Breadth Climax Signal:

I am very pleased to include this signal system, courtesy of Bob Conrad, Key-Volume Strategies, PO Box 407, White Plains, NY 10602. Bob was one of the contributors to the original edition of Winning Market Systems. He has continued over the years to create new timing devices—rather different from the usual—and often surprisingly effective. The Breadth Climax Signal has proven its worth on many an occasion in real time. I have been personally using this device ever since Bob first published the method.

The System:

The Breadth Climax employs the differential on a daily basis between advancing and declining issues on the NYSE. You should also be aware of the level of the 30-week MA of the Dow Jones Industrial Average.

BUY SIGNALS AND EXCEPTIONS:

If declines on the NYSE outnumber advances by 900 or more on a single day, then a negative A/D climax is considered to have taken place. This is normally a BUY signal.

However, if the negative climax occurs on the day of, or no more than seven sessions past the HIGHEST INTRADAY DJI LEVEL SEEN IN FOUR WEEKS, then the signal is a SELL and not a buy.

If the negative climax occurs on the day of, or no more than seven sessions past a downside crossing of the Dow's 30-week moving average, and if there was at least one closing under the moving average, then the signal is a SELL and not a buy.

SELL SIGNALS AND EXCEPTIONS:

If advances outnumber declines on the NYSE by 900 or more on a single day, then we call this a positive A/D Climax. This is normally a SELL signal.

However, if the positive climax occurs on the day of, or no more than seven sessions past the LOWEST INTRADAY DJI LEVEL SEEN IN FOUR WEEKS, then the signal is a BUY and not a sell.

If the positive climax occurs on the day of, or no more than seven days past an upside crossing of the Dow Industrials' 30-week MA, and if there was at least one close above the moving average, then the signal is a BUY and not a sell.

LOGIC:

Breadth climaxes are similar to volume spikes in their action. If volume rises to a high level as a move starts in the one direction or the other, then the move is likely to continue. If volume spikes follow an extended move in the one direction or the other, then the odds favor a market reversal of at least a temporary nature. If breadth shows a very wide plurality at or near the start of a move, the odds favor a continuation of the move. If breadth poeaks after a move has been in effect for a while, then the odds favor a reversal of the trend in effect. The 30-week moving average is considered by many technicians to be a very significant moving average, reflecting the significant long term trend. Penetrations of this moving average in the one direction or another are often followed by continuations of market movement in the direction of the penetration. Hence, the exceptions.

EXITS AND ENTRIES:

Allow the Dow to rise by between 20 - 40 points following buy signals and to fall by 20 - 40 points following sell signals before taking action on signals. Take additional positions if repeat signals occur. From time to time, during volatile market periods, you may have positions running on both buy and sell signals. The average signal between 1982 - April 1988 produced gains of approximately 190 Dow points. Between 1986 and 1988, targets of roughly 210 points were achievable on sells, 275 on buys but this was a generally uptrended market period. If you have more than one entry, average your entries to set profit targets. *(Target levels are based upon research conducted by K-V Strategies which I have not verified. My own inclination would be to purchase puts or calls on signals—especially since you may have to average up or down—and employ trailing stops to protect profits.)*

Monetary Timing Systems:

The relationship between general monetary conditions—the trend of short and long term interest rates—and the direction of stock prices has been well established. Although correlations are not quite perfect—stocks can and often do rise during periods of rising interest rates—research has proven time and time again that it generally does not pay to "fight the Fed" (so sayeth Marty Zweig).

Here are two monetary based timing systems that I have learned over the years that did not appear in the original versions of WINNING MARKET SYSTEMS.

The first comes from WINNING WITH NEW IRAs by Dr. Martin E. Zweig, who has probably contributed more than anyone to the understanding of relationships between monetary conditions and the course of stock price movement. Marty's research has always been a model of what research should be; the ZWEIG FORECAST, his newsletter has earned an enviable and well deserved reputation for consistency and good sense. I thank Marty for his authorization to abstract from the book. (Also recommended, WINNING ON WALL STREET by Zweig).

The Prime Rate Timing Model:

The interest rate that banks charge to major corporations is known as the prime rate; rates fior lesser creditworthy borrowers usually are set at about prime. The prime rate usually receives a good deal of publicity when it changes; current levels are, in any event, reported in BARRON'S each week.

As a general rule, prime rate periods of above 8% indicate periods of relatively high interest rates. prime rates of below 8% represent relatively low interest rates. The prime usually changes direction a bit after more sensitive interest rates such as fed funds, CD's and short term commercial paper. However, the publicity surrounding the prime is usually greater.

Marty Zweig has developed the following major buy and sell rules based upon prime rate changes. Here they are.

Buy Signals:

If the prime rate stands below 8% ANY REDUCTION WHATSOEVER IN THE PRIME is sufficient to generate a buy signal. For example, if the prime moves in the following sequence—6%, 6½%, 7%, 6¾%—a buy signal is generated on the drop from 7% to 6¾% because A) the prime stood below 8% and B) there was a reduction in the prime.

If the prime stands above 8%, then you require for a buy EITHER A REDUCTION OF ONE FULL PERCENT IN THE PRIME (E.G. FROM 9% TO 8%) OR TWO SUCCESSIVE REDUCTIONS IN A ROW WITH NO INTERVENING INCREASE IN THE PRIME (E.G. 8%, 8½%, 9%, 9½%, 9¼%, 8¾%). The reduction from 9¼% to 8¾% was the second decline in the prime in a row so a buy signal would be generated.

Sell Signals:

If the prime rate stands at 8% or higher, then ANY INCREASE IN THE PRIME IS SUFFICIENT TO GENERATE A SELL SIGNAL. For example, let's presume that the prime has moved in the following manner—11%, 10½%, 10%, 9½%, 10%. The rise from 9½% to 10% is sufficient to generate a sell signal because the prime stands at over 8% at the time.

If the prime stands below 8%, then WE REQUIRE EITHER TWO RISES IN A ROW OR AN INCREASE OF 1% IN THE PRIME ON A SINGLE LIFT TO GENERATE A SELL SIGNAL.

There are no further rules to the prime rate battery of buy and sell signals.

Let's move along now to evaluate the past history of such signals.

The Track Record:

The track record presented by Zweig in WINNING WITH NEW IRAs spans the period from 1954 - 1986, a pretty good period over which to test a timing model.

There were 19 buy signals generated over the time frame—the prime rate indicator does not trade all that often.

Seventeen or 89% of buy signals were profitable. $10,000 invested on the first buy and kept in the stock market only during periods of buy signals grew to $389,421, an annualized rate of increase of +23%. During this period, the stock market (measured by the Zweig Unweighted Market Index) rose at a rate of 6.9% per year.

Twelve of eighteen sell signals produced profit on the short side. The annualized rate of return for the stock market while sell signals were in effect came to −10%. The stock market, for the entire period, advanced at the rate of 6.9% per year so sell signals have, indeed, separated the bears from the bulls.

Results are somewhat less dramatic if the Standard & Poor's 500 Index is employed as the reference instead of the unweighted market averages. 83% of buy signals were profitable between 1954 - 1986, producing an annualized rate of increase of +17.9% during the periods that capital was in stock. During this period, the Standard & Poor's 500 increased at a rate of 7.1% per year. Sell signals were 59% accurate, producing an annualized decline of −4.9% per year during periods that sells were in effect.

Had an investor purchased the S&P 500 on buy signals, moving into cash at an assumed 7% during negative periods, his capital would have appreciated at an annualized rate of +15.6% over the 32 years versus a 6.9% buy and hold return for the unweighted market averages.

It is quite clear that this timing model outperforms buy and hold strategies by far. For further details, I refer readers to the original source.

General Commentary:

Although many signals on both the buy and sell side have coincided very well with significant market peaks and valleys, this is not a pinpoint timing system.

Excellent buy signals were recorded in late January 1967 (late for the new bull market), October 1974, November 1975, early December 1979, late July 1982. Excellent sell signals were recorded in March 1974, late July 1975, mid-February 1980, and during August of 1983.

Poor buy signals were recorded during January of 1974 and in September 1968 but these were reversed by sells before too much damage was done.

Long term investors may employ prime rate timing signals as buy-sell triggers in and of themselves, or these signals may be employed as part of your "major mood" arsenal, against which to evaluate shorter term timing signals.

It goes without saying that short term timing signals are more likely to prove valid when they are taken in the direction of the primary market trend. In this case, the prime rate indicator does provide excellent reflections of the primary trend of stock price movement.

(A new sell signal was generated during May of 1988, shortly before these words were written. It will be interesting to see the outcome of this sell signal as it develops).

Summing Up:

The prime rate model is obviously not perfect. It does not provide rates of return to quicken the pulse or excite the heart. But, in its simplest form—no short selling—the model does outperform buy and hold strategies by ratios in the order of 2:1, and with minimal trading at that.

Hardly a fate worse than death and hardly an indicator to be taken lightly...

The Treasury Bill - Discount Rate Index:

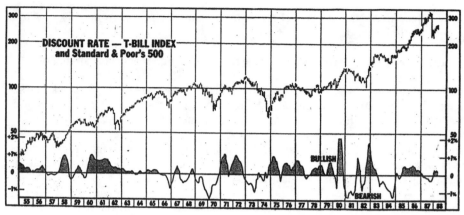

The chart, left is reproduced from MARKET LOGIC, 3471 No. Federal Hwy., Ft. Lauderdale, Florida, 33306.

MARKET LOGIC has become one of the most respected and influential of advisory services, with research contributions in their areas second to none in the industry.

The T-Bill - Discount Rate Index is of their origination.

The T-Bill - Discount Rate Index is a measure of the attitude of the Federal Reserve Board.

When the Fed is interested in tightening money, it allows the 3-month treasury bill interest rate to climb above the levels of the discount rate, the rate of interest charged to bankis by the Federal Reserve System. When the Fed is interested in easing credit conditions, then yields from 3-month treasury bills fall below the levels of the discount rate.

If, for example, yields on TBills stand at 5% and the discount rate is 6%, treasuries are yielding less than the discount rate—a bullish condition. If yields on treasuries stood at 6.5% and the discount rate stood at 6%, then a bearish condition would pertain. Market Logic recommends smoothing the weekly relationships with a 15-week moving average, though weekly readings do carry significance, even unsmoothed.

The yield relationships are available from many sources, but Barron's does carry the data each week, along with the prime rate data discussed above.

History:

The chart above, should provide a pretty good idea of the excellent track record of this indicator.

Essentially bullish conditions pertained between 1960 - 1966, a period of generally rising stock prices, the bear market of 1962 notwithstanding. The indicator was bearish for the most part between 1969 - 1970, turning bullish just in time to confirm the emerging bull market of 1970 - 1973. Conditions turned bearish at the end of 1972—a virtually perfect call, remaining bearish until the end of 1974, another perfect call.

The 1981 - 1982 bear market was predicted by the indicator which turned negative at the end of 1980.

A strongly bullish position existed between mid-1982 and mid-1983, the decline into bearish territory in mid-1983 coinciding with market weakness that developed at that time. The indicator turned positive at the outset of 1985, remaining in positive ground into early 1987. Stock prices advanced during most of 1987 despite weakness in the T-Bill - Discount Rate Index, but the crash in October that year vindicated the bearishness shown by the Index throughout most of the year.

You might wish to review the chart for yourself and to study the above periods and other periods that we have not cited.

I think that you will agree that this simple monetary model has had an excellent performance record, indeed.

Between this indicator, and the prime rate timing model, you will probably have to expend no more than 5 - 10 minuteseach week.

A 5 - 10 minutes very well spent...

Seasonal Tendencies In The Stock Market—How To Trade By The Calendar:

The following paragraphs summarize some of the recent research into seasonal tendencies in the stock market. The ideas are deceptively simple. Don't downgrade them for that reason. They do seem to work.

From Market Logic—

The strongest period of the month is the span that includes the last trading day and the first four trading days of the following month. Almost all market gains that take place, on balance, take place during this period.

Add to this span, the one or two days that precede market holidays. Sometimes, if the pre-holiday period precedes the five day month-end period, you secure 7 days or so of favorable market action. Market Logic has been maintaining a seasonal portfolio that hypothetically invests in Value Line contracts and in mutual funds on these seasonal bases. Their portfolio has been very profitable over more than eleven years of operation.

Interestingly, these patterns appear to persist in other world markets as well. For example, stock prices in the United States advanced at an annualized rate of 41% during pre-holiday periods (1980 - 1984) and at only a 7% annualized rate on the days that followed holidays. The London market showed the same rate of returns on a pre-holiday basis and showed an annualized rate of return of −46% on the days following holidays. The average for six countries showed an annualized rate of return of +37% for the days prior to holidays, a loss of 19% annualized on the days following holidays.

Mondays are the worst days to hold stocks in the US; Wednesdays are the best days.

From Yale Hirsch's SMART MONEY—

Yale, of course, has long been one of the world's leading authorities on seasonal tendencies.

The stock market records almost all of its gains during the period between November - April. Between 1950 and 1987, the Dow aggregated a gain of 2235. 18 points between November and April, losing an aggregate of roughly 405 points during the May - October periods. In short, buy during November, hold until April and then stay out of the stock market for six months.

These patterns do not hold as well during presidential election years, which tend to be strong between June and August if the incumbents lose office, and to be strong right into the ends of the year when the incumbents retain office. But, by and large, figure on trading between November and April. (Some of the finest stock market advances of recent decades have started during November or early December—for example, 1970, 1971, 1975, 1978, 1982 (during August, actually), 1985 and 1986 - 1987. The advance following the crash of 1987 started during November and December).

There seems to be a tendency for the stock market to rise during the weeks following expiration of the S&P 100 Index options, expiration taking place on the third Friday of each month. This tendency is more pronounced if the stock market has declined during the week of expiration.

Yale's January Market Barometer is not altogether accepted as gospel among market analysts but its record has, nonetheless, been excellent. If January is an up month for the stock market then the rest of the year is likely to show further gain. In fact, the first five days of January have excellent predictive value in their own right—in terms of calling the direction for the rest of the month and for the entire year at that.

The presidential election cycle did fail during 1985 - 1986, but, by and large, the stock market has had a strong tendency to advance during the two years preceding presidential elections and to decline during the year following presidential elections.

It remains to be seen at the time of this writing whether the pattern will re-establish itself during 1989.

So, to sum up, buy on Mondays during the month of November, double up on days prior to holidays and at the turns of months, and prepare to sell on. Fridays, especially between May and October—except during election years when you can hope for the re-election of the party in office. You should actually make money if you do.

The 10-Day Open TRIN—An Excellent Sentiment Oscillator:

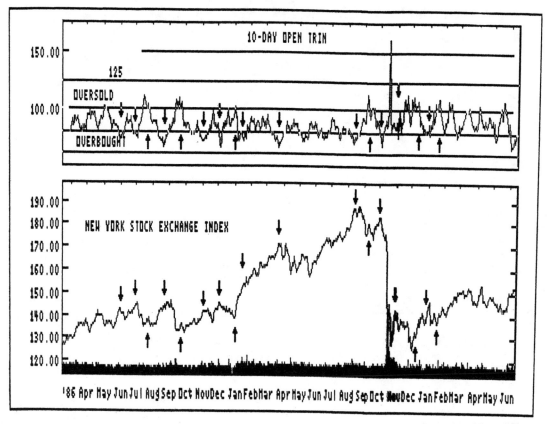

Open TRIN of the TRIN systems discussed in Chapter 2. The version that I will be describing is superior in that it provides, in its calculation, additional weighting to high volume market days and lesser weighting to lower volume market days.

The formula is the same as regular TRIN: (# of Issues Up/# of Issue Down) divided by (Up Volume/Down Volume).

Please review Chapter 2 for examples.

There is one major difference. 10-Day Open TRIN is calculated by first totalling the most recent 10 days worth of advances which is then divided by the total of the most recent 10 days worth of declines. For the second portion of the formula, you total the latest 10 days worth of advancing volume and then total the latest 10 days worth of declining volume. This is not the same as taking a 10-day moving average of the daily readings of TRIN. Results will often be similar, but at times there will be noticeable differences.

As a general rule, buy signals are generated when Open TRIN reaches 100 or more (95 during strong bull markets, 110 or higher during bear markets) and then turns down (e.g. from 125 to 120). Signals are more significant when a trendline of Open TRIN is broken and/or if buy signals occur roughtly 5 - 6 weeks from previous buy signals.

Sell signals occur when Open TRIN fails to below 80 and then turns up. Signals are more significant if a trendline is broken and/or if sell signals occur roughly 5 - 6 weeks past previous sell signals. During strong bull markets, look fior readings below 75 before sells are triggered.

The chart above shows some of the buy and sell signals generated between 1986 - 1988. Signals are not perfect. For example, there was a very premature signal during the winter of 1987. However, many signals have proven to be very accurate. Furthermore, Open TRIN buy and sell signals often provide one to three days of lead time to actual market reversals so you frequently have time to sell into strength following sell signals and to buy into weakness following buy signals. Low readings of TRIN indicate excess optimism (too much up volume); high readings indicate too much pessimism. All in all, an excellent sentiment oscillator to add to your collection.

The 30-Week Moving Average Trading Band System:

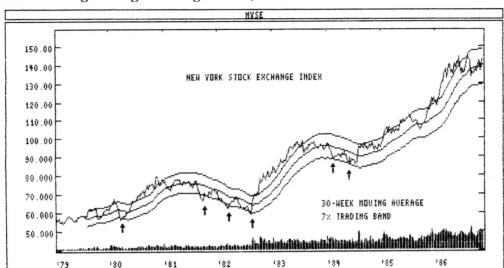

Here is a technique for entering into the stock market right at significant low points that has not had a failure in nearly 15r years (1974) and before that not since 1970 when my data begins.

The methodology is very simple.

First, you maintain a 30-week moving average of the weekly closes of the NYSE Index. You can use the S&P too, if you prefer.

Then, you calculate the levels that would be 7% above and 7% below the 30-week moving average.

The stock market is a good BUY whenever it falls on a weekly closing basis to a level more than 7% (or just at 7%) below the 30-week moving average and then turns up. If you want to be very safe, you can wait until the weekly close is less than 7% below the moving average (back within the band) but it is usually safe enough to buy on the turnup.

You can almost always count on a good trade lasting for at least 4 - 6 weeks. On most occasions, you will be buying right at or very close to a very major bottom in the stock market. The arrows on the above chart show the buying junctures between 1979 - 1986. The system caught the 1987 lows very accurately as well.

Hold Rules:

The stock market averages rise to above the trading band (more than 7% above the 30-week MA) only during the strongest of market periods. The ability to penetrate the band on the upside indicates very powerful upside momentum. Such strong momentum occurs only during dynamic market advances.

Upside penetrations are, therefore, no reason to sell. In fact, the rule is that you can hold stocks for as long as weekly market closings remain more than 7% above the 30-week moving average. You can see such periods during 1980, between 1982 - 1983, and during 1986, for example.

once the stock market rises to more than 7% above its 30-week moving average, the first downturn back to within the trading band is likely to end at the 30-week moving average. You can re-enter the stock market at that time for at least a trade good for several weeks. Such re-entries developed during 1981 and 1985, for example.

These rules will allow you to enter the stock market when pessimism is at its highest and to remain in the market when many investors are taking premature profits.

This has been a highly reliable use of the 30-week moving average for many years now. I do advise readers to make use of this technique.

For Further Study And Your Own Research:

The past several years have seen a revolution in the data and processing resources available to investors—notably the development of the mini, desktop computer, and the proliferation of computer programs for technical analysis, the latter accompanied by computer programs that provide access to historical, and even on-line on-time data for research and/or for intra-day trading.

These tools have been fostered, their development spurred on, by the initiation of trading in financial futures contracts—treasury bonds and particularly the stock index futures contracts based upon the Standard & Poor's 500 and other market indices. With so many traders now employing virtually the same tools at the same time—most technical programs have centered in on just a few timing oscillators (stochastics, RSI, MACDTM and the such)— the stock market has become very prone to rapid turns and accelerations at change of direction junctures. In many ways, the futures contracts have come to lead the stock market rather than the other way around.

I suspect that many investors now over-trade as positions in futures contracts held for just a few days have become for active traders "long term holdings," but, nonetheless, the tools have become available for each investor to accomplish ongoing research on his or her own, at minimum cost. When I first completed the first edition of Winning Market Systems, it required a number of days to secure and to work through with a hand calculator (revolutionary then in their own way) just a few years of testing basic moving average systems. With tools available today, I can process many years of data in just a few minutes. Today's programs provide charts, oscillator studies, research capabilities, profit/loss tables and more. I do recommend that you investigate the entire arena.

Recommended Literature And Computer Study Programs:

Compu Trac:

An initial pioneer in providing the facility for home research via a fine set of computer programs, Compu Trac has been seriously challenged over the years by less expensive competition. Compu Trac, nonetheless, remains in the forefront with an excellent and comprehensive computer program for the IBM and compatibles that can track, graph and evaluate the profitability of slews of technical indicators including but not limited to rates of change, RSI, moving averages, trading bands, stochastics and various charting patterns. The program also includes a feature that allows you to optimize the profitability of various parameter sets for indicators based upon your own input of trading rules.

This is a simple optimization procedure that does not readily allow for combinations of rule sets but can be useful nonetheless.

Compu Trac remains relatively expensive as technical analysis programs go, but also remains among the forefront of such programs. For more infcormation, you may contact the company at PO Box 15951, New Orleans, LA 70175-5951.

Also recommended—annual symposiums conducted by Compu Trac in various cities. Class affairs and informative.

EQUIS International:

Steve Achelis, its president, has developed, within just a few years, a set of computer programs that have become, in my opinion, the standard in value against which all other programs must be measured.

The Technician is a stock market indicator oriented program which provides not only the software for analyzing but the database for securing information regarding many technical indicators employed in the analysis of the stock market. These include market averages, advance-decline data, new highs and new lows, monetary data, short sale data and the like. The program is capable of a variety of mathematical manipulations of this data—moving averages, rates of change, trading bands, for example. Data collection is extremely rapid and painless. Graphing likewise.

MetaStock Professional is a program designed more for the tracking and analysis of individual stocks or futures contracts, though it works very well on market averages too. Super graphic capabilities, some optimization features, a full range of technical analysis capabilities—and compatible with many sources of data. The software for both MetaStock and The Technician is excellent, the manuals superb—the entire array as user friendly as you can get.

Highly recommended. Write or call EQUIS International, PO Box 26743, Salt Lake City, UT 84126, 800-882-3040.

There are a number of black box (or otherwise) computerized trading systems available to the public, ranging in price from a few hundred to several thousand dollars. A number seem to offer some promise, The Volatility Breakout System, the best in our testing and real time use—but for one reason or another I cannot wholeheartedly recommend any, especially for trading in the stock index futures contracts. Many do better in other contracts.

I do not necessarily discourage the investigation of such systems but would be very careful if the publisher does not provide some sort of return privilege. I do not at this time recommend any "black box" system, wherein the user is not provided the inherent rules and logic of the system.

There are even more trading systems offered through the mail, at prices ranging from a few hundred dollars to several thousand dollars. Most are totally worthless. Be careful before ordering, especially if the claims seem too good to be true. They are.

Book And Other Material:

Winning on Wall Street and Winning With New IRA's by Dr. Martin E. Zweig, Warner Books.

These books have also been available directly from The Zweig Forecast. See Barron's for advertisements.

Both are straightforward books whose heart lies in longer term monetary and price trend systems developed by Zweig over the years. The systems are very well documented, the research excellent. You will learn something about monetary matters and will pick up a number of rather efficient major trend models for the stock market along the way.

If I were looking for weekly based timing systems that provide the best return for the least effort, this would be the way I would go. Very readable. All told, a highly recommended pair of books from the person who I personally consider to be the leading advisor of the past two decades.

Secrets for Profiting in Bull and Bear Markets by Stan Weinstein, Dow Jones - Irwin.

Stan Weinstein is a highly regarded market technician, the publisher of the Professional Tape Reader. This book relates many of Stan's tools and techniques for the trading of individual stocks and for the timing of the stock market in general. Stan relies heavily upon moving average patterns; his approach is not revolutionary but is very sensible and organized. Reviewers have given the book high marks; I am among their number.

Don't Sell Stocks on Monday by Yale Hirsh, Facts on File Publications:

Yale is probably the foremost seasonal guru of our time—a student for many years of seasonal patterns in the stock market. The book covers just about everything from political stock market cycles to daily and weekly patterns in stock price movement. It is not always easy to trade on seasonal patterns alone but you should know them—they do provide an important edge at times. And Yale knows as much about the subject as anyone.

The Definitive Guide to Futures Trading by Larry Williams, Windsor Books.

Larry has written a number of fine books and many, many briefer publications relating to trading systems. I consider this his best. This is not a fefinitive guide—other books, for example by Jack Schwager are much more definitive, but the Guide does provide some very useful trading approaches and some very excellent research into pattern recognition approaches to the futures markets.

Very well written (as are all of Williams' books), The Guide provides a number of specific ideas, well documented for the most part, that may be employed immediately and with a minimum of fuss by traders in the futures markets. You should find it pragmatically useful, if a little short on theoretical underpinning. Given pragmatism or theory, we prefer pragmatics.

Technical Analysis of Stocks & Commodities, 9131 California Ave. SW, Seattle WA, 98136-2551.

A truly excellent publication that provides ideas for trading systems, reviews of new products, book reviews, research into market behavior and more. Started just a few years ago, the magazine has been enjoying a deserved success and increase in subscribership. Ideal for the serious student of technical analysis but do test yourself to verify claims made by certain authors in certain articles.

I hope that readers will forgive the conflict of interest involved, but I do want to acquaint you with the availability of research that I have conducted over the years which is beyond the scope of this work.

Scientific Investment Systems Research Group:

Members of SISRG receive 12 research reports at a price of $360 for all. Reports cover the use of timing oscillators such as RSI, stochastics, rates of change, chart patterns. Specific and well tested trading systems are provided using these tools with certain reports devoted to seasonal and day trading techniques, median line trading and the such.

Timing systems may be employed in trading the S&P contract and/or the stock market in general. Reports range between 20 - 30 pages in length and include full track records of all trading systems. Membership also includes consultation privileges with either myself or staff members.

Time-Trend II And Time-Trend III:

TIME-TREND II is a hard cover manual that describes an intermediate term trading system that my market letter, Systems and Forecasts, has been employing in real time for nearly 10 years. It is a system based upon rates of change and other data. The system has stood the test of real time trading for many years and has been highly rated by trackers of the performance of stock market letters. $70.00.

TIME-TREND III will be available during early 1989 and is a new timing system that has been back tested to 1970.

Its performance, hypothetically at least, has been outstanding, surpassing buy and hold strategies in the stock and futures contract markets by far.

Systems and Forecasts:

This is a stock market newsletter that I have been publishing since 1973.

S&F is a technically oriented stock market advisory that frequently includes reviews of new research, books, computer programs plus our own work as well. We usually offer some very interesting sign up bonuses to new subscribers including TIME-TREND II, mentioned above. Hulbert has rated the letter as among the five best performers in the industry since 1984.

For further information regarding all or any of the above, you may write or call Signalert Corporation, 150 Great Neck Road, Great Neck, NY 11021. 516-829-6444.

It goes without saying, of course, that the above list does not include all the worthwhile literature or research that has come down the pike over the years—as it goes without saying that Winning Market Systems does not include all of the timing models, approaches and systems that have proven profitable over the years.

But both will provide you with an excellent start.

And again, the rest is up to you.

NOTES

NOTES

NOTES

NOTES